FOREIGN CORRESPONDENT

A Memoir

H. D. S. GREENWAY

Simon & Schuster

New York   London   Toronto   Sydney   New Delhi

Simon & Schuster
1230 Avenue of the Americas
New York, NY 10020

First Simon & Schuster hardcover edition August 2014

SIMON & SCHUSTER and colophon are registered trademarks of Simon & Schuster, Inc.

For information about special discounts for bulk purchases, please contact Simon & Schuster Special Sales at 1-866-506-1949 or business@simonandschuster.com.

The Simon & Schuster Speakers Bureau can bring authors to your live event. For more information or to book an event, contact the Simon & Schuster Speakers Bureau at 1-866-248-3049 or visit our website at www.simonspeakers.com.

Interior design by Robert E. Ettlin
Jacket design by Archie Ferguson
Jacket photograph courtesy of the author

Manufactured in the United States of America

1   3   5   7   9   10   8   6   4   2

Library of Congress Cataloging-in-Publication Data
Greenway, H. D. S., date.
Foreign correspondent : a memoir / H.D.S. Greenway. — First Simon & Schuster hardcover edition.
pages   cm
Includes index.
1. Greenway, H. D. S., date. 2. Journalists—United States—Biography. I. Title.
PN4874.G6985A3 2014
070.92—dc23
[B]   2013051341
ISBN 978-1-4767-6132-9
ISBN 978-1-4767-6138-1 (ebook)

CONTENTS

Contents

For JB

FOREIGN
CORRESPONDENT

FOREWORD

In my cellar there are drawers full of notebooks, small notebooks, the kind you can put in your back pocket. Most are of uniform size with colored covers, yellow, blue, green, and red. Some were picked up abroad, from a Calcutta street stall or a Cairo market. Some are the kind you could buy cheaply in Saigon half a century ago, showing sentimental pictures of Vietnamese girls in flowing ao dais. Most have a place, month, and year written on the cover: Phnom Penh, 1967; Jerusalem, 1977; Peshawar, 1983; Berlin, 1989; Baghdad, 1991; Kabul, 2010.

They all have their stories to tell: quick descriptions and impressions of a time and a place in various countries, some of which no longer exist and some that were yet to be born. There are comments from soldiers, guerrilla fighters, despairing refugees, frightened civilians caught up in calamity. There are generals, prime ministers, presidents, kings and queens, and not a few knaves quoted in my notebooks, some truths and frequent lies from sources too numerous to count.

Some notebooks are relatively pristine. Others are dirt soiled, rain washed, and in one case, stained with blood. They would be an invaluable aid to writing about some of the trials and tribulations of the last half of the twentieth century—if only I could read them.

Too many notes were too quickly scrawled and are often illegible. They might have served in writing a story at the time but are all but indecipherable these many years later. In some you can see the handwriting deteriorate under stress and sometimes fear. "DG says LZ hot," says one in shaky handwriting taking up the whole page. It refers to the door gunner of a helicopter taking me into a firefight in Vietnam telling me that the place we were about to land was under fire. We were going in anyway because the helicopter's mission was to bring the wounded out.

Another, from Beirut in the eighties, says: "not till after 9." It was a time when Westerners were being kidnapped, and my source was telling me not to go out early in the morning for interviews, to wait until the traffic had built up. Kidnappers who would grab you and stuff you in the trunks of cars wanted to do it early so as not to get stuck in traffic.

Many notebooks list sources to be interviewed. In one, labeled "Saudi Arabia, 1979," I had written "Osama bin Laden." It was not anyone I had ever heard of, but someone had told me that he might be worth looking up. There is no indication that I ever did.

I regret now that I kept no diary or reliable notes over the years; there are just the notebooks and yellowing newspaper clippings of my stories to help jog my memory of more than half a century in the news trade.

If there is a thread that connects the following episodes of my reporting life, it is the great process of decolonization, the single most important phenomenon of the last half of the twentieth century. The turmoil that it brought is with us still, and the issues it created are unresolved. Overshadowed by the Cold War in the minds and memories of Americans, decolonization affected far more people around the world than our struggle with Communism. Indeed, it was so often the newly decolonized countries over which we and the Communist powers struggled for influence.

Too often, and in Vietnam in particular, America looked upon what was happening in the world through the lens of how it would affect its rivalry with Communist Russia and China. But more often than not it was nationalism, the desire to be free of colonialism, that drove the newborn countries that sprang up following World War II. And as so often happens when empires collapse, there was the inevitable struggle for power between competing groups.

Foreword

It was my fate to witness the last days of empires in some corners of the world, and to tramp through former colonies where the British, French, Germans, Spanish, Japanese, Portuguese, Dutch, Americans, and Russians had once ruled. It was also my fate to follow the sometimes tragic efforts of the United States to fill the vacuum of retreating empires, to back the French in its efforts to reassert rule over Indochina once the Japanese had been defeated, and when that failed, to take up the white man's burden with our own Indochina wars.

America would try to fill in where British influence had retreated, too, in the Middle East, the Persian Gulf. We would follow where Britain had previously failed in Iraq, a land that drove even the old imperialist Winston Churchill to question his country's wisdom.

America would follow in the footsteps of the British and then the Russians in Afghanistan, trying to bend that country to its will, hoping to create something in its image, where the British and Russians had failed before.

That is the overarching story of which my notebooks tell.

I

A Different World

I was born in 1935, into a world very different from today. The population of the United States had not yet reached 130 million, and unemployment stood at higher than 20 percent of the workforce. Two days before my birth, Franklin Roosevelt issued Executive Order 7034, creating the Works Progress Administration (WPA) to help dig the country out of the Great Depression. A gallon of gasoline cost ten cents, and the *New York Times* cost two cents on the newsstand. The average annual wage was $1,600. There was no Internet, there were no cell phones. Television had been invented but was not yet available. Newspapers, magazines, and the comparatively new medium of radio were how people got their news and entertainment. Parker Brothers' new game of Monopoly, introduced in 1935, was instantly popular with people still willing to dream of wealth.

Veterans of the Civil War, then considered the greatest generation, were still having their encampments and reunions. Benny Goodman's "swing" was the latest dance craze, and George Gershwin's *Porgy and Bess* opened on Broadway.

Travel was by train or ship, and only a privileged few got to go anywhere by air. There were as yet no commercial airplane flights across either the Pacific or the North Atlantic. Pan American would open up a seaplane route to Asia the following year, taking a week of island hopping to reach the Orient.

If you wanted to fly to Europe in 1935, your best bet was to make your way to Rio de Janeiro in Brazil and book passage on the 776-foot-long, lighter-than-air dirigible *Graf Zeppelin,* with a swastika on the tail, and fly to Friedrichshafen, Germany. The trip would take you and nineteen other passengers three days in comfortable, if tiny, staterooms. The *Graf Zeppelin* had flown to and from Lakehurst, New Jersey, where the zeppelin *Hindenburg* would meet her fiery end two years later, but regular transatlantic air service to and from the United States had not begun.

I used to think that my grandfather's generation had seen more technological changes than my father or I had. I might be flying in a more modern plane or driving a better car than my father's, but that is not the same as seeing both the birth of aviation and going from the horse-powered era to the internal combustion engine. I have better telephones, phonographs, and more technically advanced movies than my father did, but my grandfather saw them all come into use for the first time. The advent of the computer in the 1980s, however, changed my thinking. Computers are transforming the world as airplanes, automobiles, movies, and television once did.

In 1935 the United States was a world power but trending toward isolationism. Europe was still the cockpit of world affairs. The Nuremberg laws restricting German Jews were imposed the year I was born, and the same year saw Hitler's renouncing of the Treaty of Versailles and the beginning of German rearmament.

George V, king of England and emperor of India, was on his throne, and his imperial possessions occupied almost one-quarter of the world. My elementary school copybook, which somehow survived from the 1940s, contains an assigned essay on the British Empire. Much of the rest of Asia and Africa were part of other empires, French, Dutch, and Portuguese. Even the United States had its own mini-empire, the Philippines and scattered islands taken from Spain a little more than three decades earlier. The Soviet Union was absorbing the Muslim nations on its southern borders taken by the czars, and China was reeling from a new Japanese bid for empire. A month after I was born, China's Chiang Kai-shek had to concede control of North China to the invading Japanese.

Indeed 1935 might be seen as the high-water mark of imperialism. The British empire was swollen from territories taken from the German and Ottoman Empires after World War I. The French, too, had added Syria and would create Lebanon. The Italian colonies of Cyrenaica and Tripoli were joined to form Libya that year, and in October Mussolini invaded Ethiopia to snuff out the last remaining independent country in Africa.

Mussolini would be deprived of his African territories by the British and Americans in World War II, and, after the war, much to Winston Churchill's horror, the British would begin to divest themselves of empire beginning with India, always the "jewel in the crown." The letting go was hard, and we are still feeling the effects of the partition's creation of Pakistan, which split again with the birth of Bangladesh. The Palestine Mandate ended with Jews and Arabs at each other's throats, a situation little changed today. But then the Zionist dream of Israel became a reality. The French would fight against the end of empire in Indochina and Algeria. The Dutch tried at first to keep the East Indies but saw early on that it would be impossible. The Portuguese, who had begun the whole European expansion into Africa and Asia half a millennium earlier, were the last to hold out, leaving Macau on the South China coast only in the last year of the twentieth century.

Much good can be said about empires. At their best they brought modernization, the rule of law, and a bureaucratic impartiality and fairness that some former colonies have been lacking ever since. But there were also the downsides of exploitation, brutality, and subjugation. President Wilson had given false hope to colonial peoples everywhere after World War I; his ideas for self-determination seemed to apply more to European minorities, newly freed from Austrian and Russian rule, than they did to darker-skinned peoples in empires overseas.

Imperialism was acceptable, often abetted by colonized elites, until suddenly it wasn't. And when Europe emerged weakened from World War II, it became increasingly clear that peoples under foreign domination wanted their freedom.

An early memory of my childhood is of an aunt running down the hill from the house where I now live outside Boston on the banks of the Charles

River. She hurried to tell my father that the Japanese had attacked Pearl Harbor. I was six, but I already knew about the Japanese because my father had maps on the walls of our house showing the advances of Japan in China and the sway of war in Europe and Africa.

Another childhood memory is of an airplane, engine sputtering and losing altitude fast, coming straight at me. It was a two-seater training plane with an open cockpit. Clearly the pilot was trying to land in an open field in front of my house. Equally clearly he was going to overshoot the field. One of the airmen, in the forward cockpit, was waving frantically at the small boy to get out of harm's way, but I stood frozen. At the very last minute the dying engine caught for a moment and the plane rose up over me and over the house, straight up in the sky, only to fall into a copse of trees across the road in an explosion of fire and smoke.

They were two British naval airmen who were killed instantly while training for war in the Pacific. The newspapers didn't make much of it the next day. There were too many other deaths to be told. It was June 6, 1944. The invasion of Normandy had begun.

War was very much a part of my generation's childhood. Fathers were away in those years, and we lived with worried mothers. My father was in the Pacific. I remember vividly my mother in tears, and my grandparents in shock, when the news came through that my uncle had been killed in North Africa. It was December 7, 1942, the first anniversary of Pearl Harbor.

We all had little ration books for food, and my mother served as an air raid warden, lest the Germans should ever bomb the East Coast of the United States. It may seem far-fetched now, but we all took it seriously in the early forties.

My forebears came mostly from the British Isles, with a smattering of New Amsterdam Dutch. Many had come in the seventeenth century and had fought in all the wars on American soil. Some fought for the North in the Civil War, some for the South. Others were part of expeditionary forces in Mexico and Cuba. One was killed by hostile Indians. Another died a captive in Veracruz, Mexico, shot by General Santa Anna's men in a massacre of prisoners who had been fighting for Texas. A cousin died a prisoner of the Japanese.

There were a couple who signed the Declaration of Independence and one who was ambassador to the czar of all the Russians. Some were farmers, doctors, and engineers. Some were industrious and others too fond of drink.

My grandmother, in whose house I now live, was a Philadelphian whose mother and army-officer father died of diphtheria at an army post in the Dakota Territory before statehood.

I grew up in comfortable circumstances in the western suburbs of Boston. My mother's great-grandfather, Thomas Scott, had been president of the Pennsylvania Railroad. My father's grandfather, George Lauder, was a first cousin to Andrew Carnegie and a partner in his steel business. Ironically, Scott gave Carnegie his first important job on the railroad and helped him get started on his own. These two beneficiaries of the great nineteenth century industrial boom that followed the Civil War provided the resources that have sheltered the two families from the worst of financial vicissitudes ever since.

For my parents' generation, and mine in the 1950s, certain assumptions could be taken for granted. I have a studio photograph of my paternal grandfather, Andover, Yale class of 1900, standing ramrod stiff along with fourteen others in front of a skull and femur representing his Yale secret society, Skull and Bones. Next to it is my other grandfather, Groton, Harvard class of 1898, seated in front of a bronze boar's head symbolizing the jollier and older Porcellian Club.

My father was an ornithologist connected to Harvard's Museum of Comparative Zoology, which even today, with its stuffed specimens in dark display cases, looks like a place where Darwin might have just stepped out for lunch. My father worked in the vanished age of the gentleman amateurs who went around the world collecting animals and birds for museums. If they could afford it, they often mounted expeditions at their own expense. I have a photograph of some French forerunner of a Land Rover being transported on a raft in the Mekong River in what was then French Indochina during one of my father's expeditions.

He received two very grand-sounding and beautiful medals during his Indochina days: the Order of the Million Elephants and the White Parasol from the Kingdom of Luang Prabang, now Laos, and L'Ordre Impérial du Dragon d'Annam, Annam being what the French called central Vietnam, with the royal capital at Hue. I once asked him what he had done to deserve such decorations, and he replied that any outsider who even got to those places got a medal in those days. I never did get a straight answer, but I assume it was for his collecting work. Years later, during the Vietnam War, I, too, would come to Hue and receive a medal for it, a lot less beautiful than my father's, but that is a story for later.

Nor did my father ever tell me that, as a navy lieutenant, he had gone behind Japanese lines with a radio and a Solomon Islander during the Battle of Guadalcanal to report on enemy troop movements. In fact he told me very little about the war, which was typical of many fathers in those days.

We did get letters and odd souvenirs from the Pacific War, a couple of Japanese helmets and a bayonet. I found out years later that my father got in trouble for trying to send a Japanese skull back to Harvard. God only knows what Harvard would have done with it. The package was opened by military authorities before it got to Cambridge, Massachusetts, and the navy had a fit. Washington wanted an example made of him, but his punishment got less and less severe as the orders came down the line and closer to the war, first to headquarters in Hawaii and finally to Guadalcanal. His boss called him in and said: "Jim, just leave the old skulls alone, okay?" and that was the end of it.

He was never the same person after the war. When I would meet people who knew him before the war, I couldn't recognize the gay and amusing man of their stories. I knew him as ever more morose and remote, descending farther and farther into alcohol in my teenage years. He was often rude to his few remaining friends.

Was it what we now call post-traumatic stress disorder? Or was it because the war had been the most exciting and interesting time of his life, and civilian life was ever after boring? He would divorce my mother and marry his neighbor's wife, but that turned out to be a stormy marriage. After her death, when he was confined to a wheelchair with an amputated leg and more and more worn down by the indignities of old age, he took his shotgun and killed himself when he was alone in his house. He chose a narrow hallway, and years later when I visited Ernest Hemingway's house in Idaho, I noticed that he, too, had chosen a confined space in which to end his life.

But divorce and death happened long after I had grown up and was long gone from home. Childhood for me was an extremely happy time. I went to a small private school that my grandmother had helped found in her own house, where I now live. The school had moved to another town when I was a student there.

I and many others from the school went on to Milton Academy, founded in the late eighteenth century south of Boston. I wasn't much of an athlete, but I could run faster than most. That served me well in football and track, and I always got good parts in the school plays.

I was having my tonsils out in the summer of 1950 when the Korean War began. The Communist North Koreans, egged on by Stalin, invaded the south and took the world by surprise. Their armies took Seoul, the South Korean capital, and swept down the peninsula, only to be halted at last by some desperate American forces at the very tip. General Douglas MacArthur, in one of the most brilliant tactical maneuvers in twentieth-century warfare, put an amphibious force ashore halfway up the peninsula and sent the North Koreans reeling back. MacArthur did not stop at the former border but went right on chasing the North Koreans up to the Chinese frontier, when China intervened. The Americans were pushed back almost to where the war between the two Koreas began, and there it stalemated.

I was barely fifteen at the time, but many older brothers of my friends went off to fight and some never came back. I am convinced, however, that President Truman did the right thing to intervene in Korea and not let the Soviets alter the status quo. Unfortunately, the United States took the lesson of Korea with them when they went to war in Vietnam, and it turned out to be the wrong lesson.

In the summer of 1953, my older brother, my younger sister, my mother, and I sailed for Europe on an old Greek steamer from Hoboken, New Jersey, bound for Lisbon, Naples, and Piraeus. We would be getting off in Naples, bound for the grand tour of Europe that my mother had enjoyed between the two wars. We were in Rome when church bells told us that the Korean War was over.

A fellow passenger on the ship over was a young Portuguese singer who had just made her American debut in New York. When the mood struck her she would sing for the passengers, accompanied by her two guitar players. It was my first introduction to fado, the mournful folk music of Portugal, and it was unforgettable during that long passage in a slow steamer to Lisbon. Amalia Rodrigues would, in time, become the most famous person in the Portuguese-speaking world; her records, and later tapes, could be found on sale from Macau, on the Chinese coast, to Mozambique and Angola. When she died she received a state funeral.

My mother had been at a finishing school in Florence when Mussolini came to power, and she told us that for a while under fascism sidewalks were one-way. It meant that if you saw something you wanted to buy in a shop window you couldn't just stop and double back to the entrance. You might have to walk all the way around the block and come back to the store rather than violate the one-way-walking rules. I never believed this story until years later when I found out it was true.

Milton Academy in the fifties sent many of its graduates on to Harvard. I applied, and was accepted, but decided to follow my father's family to New Haven. Yale in those days had no women and resembled my father's college, or even my grandfather's, more than it did the Yale of my daughter in 1985. The days when someone like myself, a legacy and having gone to a private school, would automatically be accepted to Harvard and Yale are long over. Neither would take me today.

Sophomore year I returned to Europe with two roommates—not an unusual college experience. We included Morocco, which was just gaining its independence that year from France. The sultan had returned from his enforced exile and happy rebel soldiers were to be seen on the roads as French soldiers passed by the other way, bound for ships home. France was beginning to leave its North African empire.

There was trouble in Egypt in that summer of 1956 due to Egypt's strongman, Gamal Abdel Nasser, nationalizing the Suez Canal. I parted company from my roommates and headed for Cairo. The streets were full of demonstrators, encouraged by Nasser, denouncing the British. That summer gave me a taste of what would become my trade.

There were blackouts every night, just in case the vengeful British should retaliate against Egypt for seizing the canal. I fell in with some Egyptian students who asked me to come to some of their meetings in dingy cafés in old Cairo. They asked me if I thought war was coming and what America would do. I said it was inconceivable that the British would try to take back the canal. After all, this was the 1950s, not the nineteenth century. What about Israel? Israel was much too busy consolidating its newborn country, then only eight years old, and wouldn't dream of going back to war with the Arabs if it could be avoided, I said. As for America, it would not favor either a British or an Israeli attack, I said, as if I had just gotten the word straight from John Foster Dulles himself.

Of my predictions, only America's reaction turned out to be correct. That autumn the British and French, in a last gasp of imperial overreach, joined the Israelis in attacking Egypt to take back the canal. But when President Eisenhower said no, all three sheepishly withdrew their armies and went home. I have often thought of this in recent years when countries no longer jump when an American president barks.

Back at Yale I decided to major in English literature. My favorite course was "Daily Themes," in which you had to write a short piece of fiction for every class, to be critiqued by your fellow students and graded by the professor. I still have a couple of them, and reading them now, they are even worse than I remembered. But the greatest influences on my life at Yale were the history of art and architecture courses taught by the great Vincent Scully. Scully's lectures would forever change how I viewed the world around me.

I joined the Fence Club, a jolly establishment that no longer exists in the more serious Yale of today, and followed my father into Scroll and Key, a slightly younger and more lighthearted secret society than my grandfather's Bones. We boasted Cole Porter among our alumni, while Skull and Bones back then had President William Howard Taft as their most distinguished alumnus.

It was on a Yale ski trip in Vermont that I met a Barnard College student named Joy Brooks. She and her roommate, Polly, weren't planning anything that evening so we asked them to join us at a dinner party at our classmate Harold Janeway's house not far from Bromley Mountain, where we were skiing. My friend Bill Becklean and I drove over to pick the two girls up at their ski lodge. Bill was determined that "JB," as Joy was called, was to be his date. She was tall and blond, while Polly was quite a bit shorter. I tried to argue with Bill, who was the coxswain of the Yale crew, that JB was more my height while Polly was closer to him in size. I should have known that you don't get to be cox of an Olympic-winning crew by being wimpy in these matters, and Bill would have none of it. JB was his "date" for the evening, he said. There was no arguing. It was time for desperate measures.

In those days winter clothes were bulkier and heavier than they are today, and it was routine to store your overcoat and ski parkas in the trunk while you drove, to be retrieved when you got out. We were performing this maneuver after we reached the girls' ski lodge when opportunity knocked. As Bill leaned into the trunk to get his coat I took him by the ankles, upended him into the trunk, and slammed the lid.

I was freezing cold when I reached the door of the lodge, and the girls asked innocently, "Where's Bill?"

"Oh, he's waiting for us in the car," I said, and that was that. Bill, being a generous fellow, has long since forgiven me, and JB and I have been together now for more than half a century.

2

Going to Work for Uncle Sam and Henry Luce

When I entered Yale in the fall of 1954 the Korean War had been over for little more than a year, and many of my generation thought there would likely be more hot conflicts in what was shaping up to be the long struggle with Communism that we now call the Cold War. It meant that although the Soviet Union and the United States intervened in places militarily, they didn't confront each other directly.

I joined the Naval Reserve Officers Training Corps. Years later Yale, along with Harvard and several other schools, discontinued NROTC programs in the antimilitarism that swept Ivy League schools in the wake of Vietnam, only to reinstate them again in the new century. I always felt banning ROTC was a mistake. It was good for the military to have officers who had not gone to military academies in the mix, and the service was an invaluable experience for me and many in my generation. The all-volunteer military of today has its advantages, but creating a military class to defend the country while the general population stays at home seems to me another mistake.

NROTC obligated me to serve two years at sea following college. So, upon graduation I reported to Norfolk, Virginia, where I was assigned to the aircraft carrier *Valley Forge*. The ship, which had seen service in the Korean War, was the centerpiece of Task Group Alpha under the command of Admiral John Thach. The admiral had invented a fighter aircraft maneuver to overcome the superior agility of the Japanese Zero during World War II. It was called the "Thach Weave."

Time magazine put out a cover story on "Jimmy" Thach, as he was always called, while I was aboard. In the somewhat breathless fashion that was *Time's* style in those days, Thach's job was described as "no less than that of rewriting the Navy's antisubmarine book, of finding defenses against a new submarine revolution . . . The USSR has the biggest submarine force ever known—500 boats, almost ten times the number Hitler had at the start of World War II. At least half the Soviet subs are new and big enough to have missile-launch patrols into the western Atlantic waters," *Time* said.

"Hidden from the sun, the black bottom is an unimaginably terrifying land of ancient mountain ranges and valleys," *Time* reported, with "somnolent volcanoes, gargantuan canyons, bottomless chasms—a land filled with hiding places for a future generation of deeper-diving submarines."

Time quoted Russia's Nikita Khrushchev as having said: "Submarines can block American ports and shoot into the American interior, while our rockets can reach any target."

Needless to say, we junior officers had little appreciation for the apparently awe-inspiring role we were playing in the nation's defenses, nor had we focused on the "unimaginably terrifying land" beneath our keel. We just went about the often-boring task of running the ship, thinking only of our next shore leave.

I chose to become a communications officer, one of several entrusted with coding and decoding confidential and secret messages. We had special code machines and code books with leaded covers, just in case you needed to throw them overboard should the ship be taken and boarded. Our job was to track Russian submarines that were coming provocatively close to the East Coast. Our task force, made up of two submarines, eight destroyers, and our aircraft carrier, would roam the Atlantic sending out sonar signals into the depths, which would occasionally bounce off the hulls of submarines hidden below. We had propeller planes and helicopters that would fly off our deck and drop patterns of sonar buoys. The object of this cat-and-mouse game was to track Russian submarines just as long as we could, hopefully to force one to the surface. We never did, even though we had one top secret advantage. It was one of the deepest and darkest secrets of the Cold War, and we were told it could never be revealed to anyone. It was called SOSUS, for Sound Surveillance System, and it consisted of a string of microphones on the ocean floor that would alert us when a submarine had passed over them. The secret became common knowledge after the Cold War, and I believe traitors working for the Soviets had tipped Moscow off long ago, but in 1958 we took it very seriously indeed.

I asked our captain what he would do if we ever did force a Russian submarine to the surface, and his answer was: "Ask the Russian captain aboard for a drink." Alas, unlike other navies, there had been no alcohol allowed aboard US Navy ships since 1917, but it was not unknown for a bottle or two to be smuggled aboard. I once had to deliver an important incoming message to my captain while we were in port. It was late at night, and after knocking on his stateroom door, I was admitted to find him sitting with a good-looking woman in a glamorous dress. There was a very good bottle of brandy on the table between them.

I stood at ramrod attention with my eyes looking one inch above his head and not at all to the side. Cool as vodka, he politely introduced me to his lady and, gesturing toward the bottle, asked me if I had time for a glass of orange juice. "No, sir, thank you, *sir!*" I quickly said, and, performing a parade turn, I saluted and left with my glazed eyes staring straight ahead.

My tour of duty consisted of stretches of sea duty out of Norfolk into the Atlantic and back to Norfolk again with none of the exotic foreign ports that I had hoped for. My long-distance romance with JB, in those pre-Facebook, or even e-mail, days, was maintained by letters, much as romances had been in the days of Admiral Nelson. She was still at Barnard in New York, and I could tell from the tone of her letters that absence was not making her heart grow fonder. But there I was stuck at sea.

Fate intervened in the form of a kamikaze, which means "divine wind" in Japanese. It was not a World War II–style suicide attack but a fortunate wind for me. The *Valley Forge* ran into a particularly vicious storm at sea that rolled up the corner of our flight deck as if it were a can of sardines. The *Valley Forge* had to turn tail and run downwind to keep her stern to the wind and waves.

It was a wild ride, and I was glad not to be aboard a smaller destroyer in those enormous seas.

When the storm was over the captain got on the loudspeaker and said: "Now hear this." The Norfolk shipyard was too busy to take us, so we would be putting into the Brooklyn Navy Yard for repairs. In port there was no need to encode or decode messages, so my evenings were free to go uptown to pick up JB at the Barnard campus. We would go out to dinner in restaurants in Greenwich Village, listen to Mabel Mercer and Edith Piaf in what turned out to be her last engagement in America. The romance was sealed, but to this day JB has a recurring nightmare that she is flunking her Chinese exam.

My career in journalism began on the *Valley Forge* when I was assigned to the ship's newspaper. We put out a little fleet journal that was distributed to other ships in our task force. We stole news items from wire services, which we could intercept, and I was tasked with choosing the news items and editing them. France's war in Algeria was raging then, and I thought I would write a short essay of my own about what the French were up against and sneak it in the paper. Alas for me, it was noticed up on the bridge, and I still have the note that was sent down from on high.

COMMANDER J. T. STRAKER, USN
Executive Officer
USS Valley Forge (CVS-45)
Memorandum for: Comm Officer
Subject: Press News

Comment: The article in today's press on conditions in Algeria is, or was, well-written and informative, but it reads like part of a political science text book. It is analysis but not news.

Names, scandal, political dirt, murder, rape, love-nests make news. Articles on the economic potential, ethnic groupings and industrial problems of Algeria are not news.

The editor of the New York World Telegram told his reporters that to catch the public's eye news must involve (1) a name, preferably famous; (2) a situation which would let the reader's evil little mind finish the story in his own way; and (3) the common touch, slang, mild profanity, etc. Then he offered a raise to the reporter who could give him the best line in the fewest words. The winner: "Hell," said the duchess, "let go of my leg."

He was right, of course. Only the pretensions of youth could have induced me to write such an article for the fleet newspaper. Old Straker knew how to arrest a prig in his downward slide. I certainly never told him that my mother's grandfather Scott had once owned the New York *World*.

I look back upon my brief navy career as a valuable experience. Later on, when I was required to suffer the indignities of "consultants" whom the *Boston Globe* hired to teach its editors the fundamentals of leadership, I found they never went beyond what I had learned as an officer in the US Navy.

Having decided that I really should have majored in history at Yale, I decided to apply to Oxford when my tour was over. I was discharged and, despite my journalistic lapse, was pleased to be asked to remain in the navy. But I had other adventures in mind. One very cold winter afternoon, when the *Valley Forge* was in Bayonne, New Jersey, for some further repairs, I walked out on the signal bridge to see the *Queen Mary* in all her three-stacked glory, heading for the Verrazano-Narrows, picking up speed for a transatlantic crossing. In my imagination I heard an orchestra playing in the grand salon, and I thought when I was finished being at the beck and call of my senior officers, I would book passage on the *Mary* and sail to Europe with my beloved.

And so, as soon as I was released from active service, JB and I were married. The great transatlantic liners were in their final decline by 1960, but they didn't know it yet. The day we sailed there were photographs in both the *New York Times* and the *Herald Tribune* showing many of the great liners lined up alongside their Hudson River piers. My Greenwich grandmother's chauffeur drove us to the dock, and we departed with the ship's deep-throated horn echoing across Manhattan. E. B. White once wrote that when he heard the *Queen Mary* blow, "the sound captured with it the whole history of departure, longing and loss," but not for us. For us it was the fanfare of a new adventurous life together.

We had all our worldly goods in a steamer trunk and we would not see the United States again for three years. I had not been accepted at Oxford when we sailed, but in what JB would later call my hopeless optimism, I just assumed everything would turn out all right, and it did. I got an acceptance telegram in mid-Atlantic.

Oxford didn't start until October, and so we had a whole summer before us. Without telling JB, I had rented a small villa on the French Riviera, just off the Moyenne Corniche overlooking the village and bay of Villefranche. We drove down to the Côte d'Azur from England, and not sure of what her reaction would be, I told her we were going to visit a friend with a beautiful view when we reached that storied coast. We were let in, and, as I had rented the place sight unseen, I was happy to see that the view was even better than I had expected. On a terrace overlooking Cap Ferrat and a great expanse of the Mediterranean, JB said, "Gosh, I wish we were staying here all summer," and I told her there was no friend, and that the place would be ours.

When the summer was over we repaired to England and Oxford, which I found intellectually exhilarating and great fun. The friendships we made there have lasted all the rest of our lives, and our first daughter, Julia, was born in a chilly house on Museum Road the following year.

But before Julia was born we spent an Oxford summer in East Africa, which was then still under British rule and recovering from the Mau Mau rebellion, which had shaken the colonial establishment a few years before. Our friend Michael von Clemm and his wife, Lisa, were living in Northern Tanganyika. He, being an anthropologist, was writing a paper for an Oxford PhD. He knew Ernest Hemingway's son Patrick, who was then a white hunter who had said he would take us for a shoot. Who could resist? But unfortunately, Patrick's father had just killed himself that summer, and Patrick had to fly home. But the young Hemingway had allowed us to use his trackers and skinners, and so we mounted our own safari on the cheap, without a professional hunter and without even tents. We bought a secondhand Land Rover and slept on the ground in surplus army blankets. We built thorn fences to keep out hyenas, which can sneak in at night and bite off your hand or your cheek while you sleep.

Years later, when poaching had reduced the game and shooting African animals became politically incorrect, I had to pretend to my children's friends that the animal heads in the cellar had been shot by my grandfather in Teddy Roosevelt's time.

It turned out that the proprietor of *Time* and *Life* magazines, Henry Luce, had himself gone to Oxford after Yale and had always employed a campus "stringer." A stringer is a reporter who is not on staff and is paid for each story filed. As a lark, having no idea it would lead to a lifetime occupation, I took on the job. It turned out to be a wonderful opportunity to interview Oxford dons whom the Luce magazines thought interesting and to write articles about campus life from time to time. One of them, a short item for *Sports Illustrated*, caught Luce's eye and got me a job. It was about the price of wolf's urine. It seemed that Oxford students who rode to hounds often held drag hunts—a drag being a bag soaked with wolf's urine pulled by a horse over a predetermined course, which hounds would then follow instead of chasing a fox. The wolf's urine was important because its smell was stronger than that of a fox, so the hounds would not be distracted by a real fox along the way. The London zoo was putting up the price of wolf's urine, and the cries of woe and doom from the Oxford hunt led one to believe that Western civilization was coming to an end.

Luce noticed the story, and when he made his next trip to London I was summoned. I was offered a job as a trainee in the London bureau. Luce asked me in what class I had traveled on the train down from Oxford, and I told him second class. He instructed me never to do that again. *Time* always traveled first class, he said, and the *Time* bureau chief in London was the second most important American in Britain after the ambassador. Alas, that did not last very long, but *Time*'s presence in London was very impressive. The Time-Life Building on the corner of Bruton and New Bond was either the first or one of the first buildings to be built in London after the war, and it had Henry Moore friezes on top and rotund Henry Moore statues in the courtyard. The bureau hummed with reporters, photographers, darkroom technicians, librarians, and researchers. The bureau chief went about in a chauffeur-driven car, and correspondents were always flying off to dramatic assignments. A woman brought a tea trolley around to our offices at four in the afternoon.

Today the building is occupied mainly by Hermès, with not a single journalist in sight. The last time I inquired *Time*'s sole London correspondent worked from home on a laptop. As for *Life,* it is a pale and infrequent shadow of its former self.

It is hard to imagine now what a role *Time* and *Life* played in American journalism fifty years ago. Television had not taken over as the primary source of news in America. Newspapers and the magazines Luce created in the twenties and thirties were how people knew about the world around them. All across America, and beyond, people waited for their copies of *Time* and *Life*.

Time correspondents didn't get a byline in those days. Their material was rewritten back in New York. And because cable costs were expensive, one filed in a curious jargon designed to save money. "The" and "a" were eliminated and words were put together. So, if you were going to Cairo on the twelfth, you would cable "Cairowarding twelfth." There was a famous joke about the *Time* correspondent sending in his resignation: "Upstick job asswards."

Time style was open to being mocked in those days. "And backward ran the sentences until reeled the mind," wrote the *New Yorker* in a famous *Time* parody. Indeed, *Time*'s aforementioned cover story on Admiral Thach in 1958 had begun with the sentence "Ominous, black and still was the sea." It was not until I discovered an 1850 translation of Homer's *Iliad* in my library that I understood from where *Time*'s style came. "But wailing none was heard, for such command had Priam issued." I have no doubt that Henry Luce had been deeply influenced by early translations of Homer.

Although our files would all be rewritten in New York, we were encouraged to write as well as we could so that our files would be useful and attractive to the rewrite men. And sometimes, rarely, a bit of your prose would appear in the magazine. *Time* encouraged you to put in as much color and detail as you could, and one of the magazine's tricks was to put the reader right next to the person being interviewed to give the impression that you knew him or her much better than you actually did. So you wouldn't start out by saying:

"The prime minister said . . ." You would watch closely for the little details, so your interview might start out with: "Lighting up a Craven 'A' cigarette as he thoughtfully stirred his glass of Talisker whiskey, the prime minister leaned back in his thick leather chair, and staring at the ceiling, remarked that . . ." The idea was that the reader would be impressed that *Time* was so clubby with the PM, when actually you were just somebody the prime minister had agreed to see for a few minutes in the hopes of getting something across to *Time*'s vast readership.

Time magazine also pioneered what I called the moving-car lead. You wouldn't just say that the generalissimo had fired his cabinet that week. You would try to get enough detail to be able to write that "the gates of the presidential palace flew open as the black Bentley sped out to deliver the generalissimo to the ornate, turn-of-the-century government house where the cabinet sat frozen, waiting to be fired."

Sometimes this approach could be ridiculous, but at other times it could be effective. When I joined the *Washington Post* years later, some of the techniques I had learned at *Time* helped me to write graceful lead paragraphs. But I got my comeuppance on my first front-page story "above the fold," meaning it would start above where the newspaper would be folded over. My editor changed my lead to a simple declarative sentence. I said: "Whoa, I really gave some thought to that lead, and I thought it was pretty well written."

"Greenway," my editor replied, "when you work for a newspaper you gotta remember one thing. No good writing above the fold."

3

Assignments in London and Washington

My brief time in *Time*'s London bureau coincided with one of the great political sex scandals, at which the British excel. A young woman named Christine Keeler had been sleeping with both the British defense minister John Profumo and a Soviet military attaché. Profumo was less than forthcoming to Parliament about the affair and was later forced from office to spend a lifetime in charitable work seeking atonement.

My job, for a time, was to assist a formidable *Time* correspondent, Honor Balfour, who had been covering British politics since I was knee-high. I was assigned to do interviews with which she didn't want to be bothered. One time, however, she took me along on an interview with some ancient peer who warned Honor that he had not altogether forgiven *Time* magazine for some article or another. When we left, I questioned Honor as to which of the magazine's stories about the Keeler affair his lordship had objected to. "Oh, he was talking about our story on the abdication crisis," Honor said, when Edward VIII had given up his throne for an American divorcee in 1936. *Time* had been out ahead on that story too, Honor explained. The notorious Mrs. Simpson was described in the pages of *Time* as "King Edward's favorite dancing partner, his companion on numerous holiday excursions," at a time when the British press was staying mum about the royal affair.

England was on the verge of change when we lived there in the early sixties, but the "sixties," as a decade of disruption and social change, had not yet begun. The Beatles, long hair, the new fashions and bright-colored clothes of Carnaby Street—what *Time* called "Swinging London"—were just around the corner. The dark suits, tightly furled umbrellas, and bowler hats of that era still streamed into the city every working morning. Britain then, as America's statesman Dean Acheson said, had lost an empire but had not yet found a role.

I went to hear a speech by Conservative prime minister Harold Macmillan at the Oxford Union. The prime minister had begun to wax sentimental about his generation's losses in the trenches of World War I, when a heartless undergraduate rose in the back and said: "What about William the Conqueror, mate?" British youth was getting impatient with the old and longing for change.

After London, *Time* sent me to Washington, where our second daughter, Alice, was born. I arrived when America was still basking in the glamour and excitement of John F. Kennedy's presidency after the more staid Eisenhower years. I had the pleasure of meeting the president, and I could appreciate what a commanding physical presence he had. President Clinton had the same ability to dominate a room just by walking into it.

It was our first summer back in the United States after three years abroad, and the issue of civil rights had the country on the boil. JFK seemed uncertain about the issue, and it would take his southern successor, Lyndon Johnson, to meet the issue head-on.

The charismatic black preacher Martin Luther King Jr. was then rising on the wings of his rhetoric, the beautiful cadence of his speeches. In August of 1963 he organized a march on Washington. I still have the button: "March on Washington, for Jobs and Freedom," showing a white hand shaking a black hand.

What few remember now is the sense of alarm, almost panic for some, felt by white people in Washington. The fear was that thousands upon thousands of black folks descending on the capital might end up in rioting and looting. Some were making plans to leave town. Yet when the thousands and thousands of blacks, and some white people too, did descend on Washington, the demonstration was surprisingly orderly and peaceful.

I was part of a *Time* team covering the event, and I remember the great number of buses that had come from so many states. The sea of upturned faces on the Mall surprised me, for I hadn't seen such a large demonstration since Cairo. King was becoming a superstar and the rhythm of his speech, steeped in the traditions of the black church, was, in its way, as inspiring as Winston Churchill's had been twenty years before. My notebooks record that he repeated the iconic "I have a dream" nine times, his voice echoing out over the reflecting pool, out over the capital and America, and down through the decades to take its place as one of the most important and memorable speeches in American history. This was a call to action, but not to violence or sedition.

"There is something that I must say to my people who stand on the warm threshold which leads into the palace of justice," said King that summer day half a century ago. "In the process of gaining our rightful place we must not be guilty of wrongful deeds. Let us not seek to satisfy our thirst for freedom by drinking from the cup of bitterness and hatred."

With a nod to the statue of Lincoln, he said that Negroes—black people were still called Negroes then—had been given a check, but the check had come back marked "insufficient funds." Now it was time for America to make good on that promise. "With this faith we will be able to hew out of the mountain of despair a stone of hope. With this faith we will be able to transform the jangling discords of our nation into a beautiful symphony of brotherhood," said King. "With this faith we will be able to work together, to pray together, to struggle together, to go to jail together, to stand up for freedom together, knowing that we will be free one day."

It was a thrilling moment, the likes of which I would not see again until the Berlin Wall came down twenty-six years later, a moment of inspirational hope that the world could be a better place. King would be assassinated five years later, and today a statue of King, "hewn out of the mountain," stands near the Lincoln Memorial.

On the fiftieth anniversary of the speech King's face was on both the cover of *Time* magazine, which labeled him "Founding Father," and the *Economist*, which said "America had changed beyond recognition" as far as race was concerned. But King's dream still has a long way to go.

One day in the autumn of that year I was assigned to interview Averell Harriman at the State Department. Harriman had been an important figure in the Roosevelt administration and was happy that the Democrats were back in power. For reasons I cannot now remember, he began to talk about Henry Wallace, who had been FDR's vice president before Harry Truman. Harriman spoke about how he, and a group of like-minded people around FDR, had lobbied hard for Wallace's removal from the ticket. The old left-winger Wallace, Harriman said, would have been a disaster dealing with Stalin after FDR died. Harriman went on at length about how important it was to have a vice president who could take over immediately upon a president's death. Looking back it seemed almost as if Harriman had had a premonition of how that day would unfold, for it was the twenty-second of November, a day when people would forever remember where they were when President Kennedy was assassinated.

When I got back to the office the first bulletins that the president had been shot in Dallas were coming in. Those who regularly covered the president were, of course, in Dallas with the president, and I was told to go over to the White House to see what was going on. There I found staffers milling about desperate for news and not knowing quite what to do. The eyes of the world were on Texas now and the dying president. The White House had become, briefly, a backwater.

Soon after I arrived the television networks and wire services were saying that the president was dead. In Washington staffers were still arguing over whether it was appropriate now to lower the flag over the White House to half-mast. Some argued that nothing should be done until they had been officially informed, as if somehow lowering the flag might actually harm the president, though it was now clear that JFK was beyond harm.

I remember Fred Holborn, a White House aide whom I knew, wandering out to the Rose Garden and standing silently staring at the sky. I wanted to offer him some condolence. He had been with Kennedy since the early days of his campaign for the presidency, but I sensed that this was not the moment to interrupt his grief.

There was really nothing to report at the White House, so when we learned that Kennedy's body would be arriving in Washington soon, I went to the hospital, where I saw Mrs. Kennedy, still in her blood-spattered dress, climbing up the long steps with Bobby Kennedy. As the official party swept on into the hospital entrance, I looked back and saw that the vehicle carrying the president's body was left unguarded. For a moment even the driver had disappeared, and it looked as if anyone could have simply gotten in and driven away with the body of the dead president. Within moments, however, swarms of people had gathered to take the coffin inside.

The next few days were a bewildering haze of activity and preparation for the state funeral. I was upstairs in my house, trying for a few moments' sleep, when JB called to say I had better come down. There was something on TV that I needed to see. It was Jack Ruby's assassination of the assassin, Lee Harvey Oswald, in a bizarre twist to the tragedy.

When Kennedy's funeral commenced, my assigned station outside the church gave me a ringside view of little John-John, the president's son, giving his father's coffin a childish salute—an image that *Life* magazine captured so well.

The assassination was on a Friday, late for weekly magazine deadlines. Both *Time* and *Life* scrambled to change covers. *Time* had scheduled the musician Thelonious Monk, while *Life* had Navy football player Roger Staubach on its cover. *Life* ran a black-bordered picture of the slain president, while *Time* featured Lyndon Johnson, on the theory that *Time* never put dead people on the cover. Most of us thought *Life* had gotten it right.

The following year *Time* assigned me to their bureau in Boston, familiar territory indeed, but after the new president, Lyndon Johnson, decided to escalate the war in Vietnam, I sensed that this was to be a defining moment for my generation. So I requested to be sent to Saigon.

Kennedy had steadily increased the number of US "advisers" in Vietnam but had not committed large numbers of regular ground troops, as Lyndon Johnson later did. Some like to say that Kennedy, had he lived, would not have gone so far down the path of war as did his successor. But Kennedy's statements about Vietnam were contradictory. On the one hand Kennedy seemed to realize that going into a big war in Southeast Asia was not in America's interest. On the other he seemed to think that Vietnam was a time of testing in which he had to stand up to the Communist powers. The truth is no one will ever know, just as no one will ever know what kind of president Kennedy would have been had he lived and been reelected for another term. I suspect Kennedy would not have become so deeply involved in Vietnam as Johnson eventually did, but then it is likely that Kennedy would not have grasped the nettle of civil rights as firmly as did Lyndon Johnson.

The thousand days of the Kennedy presidency never were quite the "Camelot" of legend, but they live in memory as an optimistic moment trapped in amber before the great dissolutions, assassinations, and social changes at home and defeat abroad that roiled the later sixties and seventies.

4

Coming into Vietnam

My Indochina years began in the spring of 1967 when my plane from Hong Kong came in low over the Vietnamese coast. I could see fires burning on the ground below, and I assumed, naïvely, that I was witnessing the war with battles raging below me. I soon found out it was only brush being cleared and burned, as happened throughout Indochina in the dry season. That first night in my darkened hotel room I could hear the sound of artillery in the night. Was the city under attack? It was only outgoing "H & I"—"harassment and interdiction"—fire, meaning our side fired shells blindly into the woods across the river just to keep the Vietcong on their toes. Eight years later I would lie awake in the same hotel listening to artillery rounds from an approaching army landing in the city itself, but that was as yet undreamed of in 1967, when America still thought it could win where the French had failed. Vietnam was my first firsthand experience of America stepping into other people's empires.

I had left JB and the children in Hong Kong because *Time* did not allow families in Saigon, and I was about to become a war correspondent. One of my early friends in Vietnam was Michael Herr, whose classic book *Dispatches* is still the best piece of writing to come out of that war. Mike caught the madness of the entire American adventure in Vietnam better than anyone else, and he had this to say about the job I was about to take on: "I never knew a member of the Vietnam press corps who was insensible to what happened when the words 'war' and 'correspondent' got joined. The glamour of it was possibly empty and lunatic, but there were times when it was all you had, a benign infection that ravaged all but your worst fears and deepest depressions."

Mike was more reflective than most of us. He contrasted those for whom "Vietnam was more than enough" with incurable romantics who fantasized "about other, older wars, Wars I and II, air wars and desert wars and island wars, obscure colonial actions against countries whose names have since changed many times, punitive wars and holy wars and wars in places where the climate was so cool that you could wear a trench coat and look good." I have to confess I did see myself in the footsteps of intrepid war correspondents who wrote dispatches from the Anglo-Egyptian Sudan and World War I books with titles such as *With the Allies.*

Saigon in the spring of 1967 was a damp wartime capital, beggar ridden, flooded with refugees from the countryside, hot, noisy, obviously corrupt, and completely enchanting. I was given a comfortable room in the old French colonial hotel the Continental Palace, with a view overlooking Saigon's opera house on the corner of Tu Do Street, which the French had called rue Catinat. Saigon was still very much a French city back then, even though American trucks belching diesel smoke and traffic were polluting the town my parents had known three decades before as the "Paris of the East." Some correspondents preferred the newer Caravelle across the street, but I preferred the Continental.

The custom was that room boys, who would sleep in the corridors outside your room, expected a tip for any little service provided unless you tipped them on a monthly or weekly basis. I tried the former, until room boys started to bring one sock at a time back from the laundry. The gin would arrive separately from its tonic. I soon switched to a monthly tip arrangement. There was freshly baked French bread—never mind that I once found a cockroach baked into one baguette—and good "café filtre."

The famous "Continental Shelf," the hotel's terrace that was open to the street, had figured in Graham Greene's *The Quiet American,* which every Saigon correspondent worth his salt had read, along with *Scoop,* Evelyn Waugh's send-up of war correspondents. There was an inner, open-air courtyard at the Continental with palm trees where a pet peacock would strut, sometimes snatching your croissant from your plate if you weren't watching.

I had read about the Continental in a book called *East of Siam* written in the 1920s:

> With sunset comes the great French rite, l'aperitif. Men in fresh white and women in their best summer frocks gather on the terrace . . . of the Hotel Continental, a scene suggesting the Café de la Paix of Paris in a tropical setting. The awnings are trussed up, and the night life . . . grows with the evening. The very common-sense custom of the European men in going bareheaded after sunset is a delightful relief from the heavy sweat-begetting cork helmet. All the Frenchman's comforts of home, from creamy curacao of oil-like texture to rich green absinthe frappe are trotted forth by Annamese "boys" in white gowns, topped by their inevitable band-turban, jet black as the coarse hair most of them wear in a Psyche knot.[*]

Certainly the Continental was a lot less elegant when I got there in 1967. You could still get an aperitif at sundown, but the customers were scruffy American civilian contract workers and journalists from around the world. The odd Frenchman might wander by but feel somewhat out of place in America's wartime Saigon. But still, when the candles were lit for dinner on the balustrade, and the street outside quieted down as the sky darkened, there was a whiff of the romance of other generations. The waiters all wore white, but no longer topped with turbans, and were a good deal more scruffy than before the war.

The Continental Shelf that my parents remembered from the 1930s was filled with French businessmen and rubber planters in from the countryside for a night on the town. Here is a reminiscence that my father sent to me of those days.

---

[*] Harry A. Franck, *East of Siam* (New York and London: The Century Co., 1926), 11.

The Hotel Continental had after dinner, along around nine o'clock, a Concours de 'Orsey-'Orsey by which they meant a dance. If it is translated literally into English, which it cannot, it means a meeting of the horses (a horse show). The hotel guests and others came in two by two, following each other around a long room. It all began with a tune like "La Fille du Beduin." With lots of ta-ta-tas so that some hopping was accomplished by all the couples. All hands were dressed properly in long, dark skirts and dark suits just like Europeans on a Sunday. All the party was quite correct and well behaved. No one got fried as they would in America at the time.

In the following decade, after the Japanese surrender, the Continental was taken over briefly by the OSS, forerunner of the CIA. Frank White, an old *Time* magazine colleague, wrote to me describing those days.

Our group of less than 20 officers and men had been hastily recruited from various OSS, Office of Strategic Services, units operating in Burma and Thailand. Our original plan was to parachute into Saigon, but in noticing from the air that the Japanese below were drawn up in a reception formation, we landed at Than Son Nhut airport in the conventional way.

After many salutes and much bowing the Japanese provided transportation through Saigon's dusty suburbs and then through the tree-lined boulevards . . . to be deposited at the Continental Palace Hotel. The hotel now mirrored the signs of neglect and abuse that we'd noticed elsewhere in the once beautiful city.

The Japanese had their main command post at the Continental, White wrote, and "no one was having tea or aperitifs. Instead a full company of Jap Marines sat rigidly around the marble-topped tables staring grimly straight ahead."

Under the terms of the Yalta agreement, British troops were to take over from the Japanese in the south, while Chiang Kai-shek's Chinese were responsible for the north. According to White, the British troops, a contingent of

Indian Army Gurkhas with British officers, were garrisoned in Cholon, the Chinese part of the city, "miles from where they were to be most needed." This was so as not to humiliate the French, who were furious that their own troops were not taking the Japanese surrender. In fact the Vichy French had collaborated with the Japanese until almost the end of the war, when the Japanese turned on their former allies and incarcerated them. A small contingent of French, representing General de Gaulle's Free French provisional government back in France, had arrived, but according to White, they were little more than bystanders.

Annamese, Tonkinese, and Cochin Chinese[*] were all calling themselves Vietnamese by the time White arrived, a symbol of their nationalistic desire to be free of French colonialism. Roosevelt had not wanted the French to return, but President Truman backed France in its desire to reestablish a colonial administration.

> Our first American experience with the new spirit of Vietnam [White wrote] began mildly enough with parades and demonstrations in the evenings in front of the Continental. That the U.S. was part of their concern became clear from reading the signs and placards these Vietnamese groups carried. At first they read "Bienvenue aux Américains," which was fine with us. But the British and French were not happy with other signs which read "Vive L'indépendence du Vietnam Libre," and, in English, "Down with Anglo-French Colonialism." Even more unsettling was the way the demonstrations changed in mood and temperament. Where at first they were more in the nature of earnest entreaties, patriotic expressions of hope, they soon changed to being surly, threatening.
>
> We began hearing reports from the country and outlying suburbs that gangs of Viets had torched buildings, molested people and destroyed French administrative buildings and even one hospital.

---

[*] The French divided Vietnam up into three separate dependencies, Cochin China in the south, Annam in the center, and Tonkin in the north.

The situation took a dramatic turn for the worse when a group of Vietnamese, now wearing the conical-hats-and-khaki-shorts-type uniforms . . . had taken 200 French hostages and had threatened them with death.

Vietnam's long struggle for independence, the first of two Vietnam wars, had begun.

White and his OSS band had been instructed not to get involved with local politics, and it seemed to him that the Vietnamese had "legitimate aims of independence," as proclaimed by President Roosevelt. "On the other hand none of us were willing to sit by and take the chance of witnessing a potential massacre," White wrote. "Along with its already large French population, the city was already jammed with refugees pushing in from up country and the Mekong Delta. It was our belief that more than 50,000 Europeans were presently in the city, many of them without shelter or any physical protection."

The OSS went to Mathieu Franchini, a Corsican who owned the hotel, along with, according to White, the biggest bordello in Cholon, called Le Grand Monde. White offered to temporarily buy the Continental Palace in the name of the United States for $2, which were the only two greenbacks he had in his wallet. Franchini accepted, hoping for American protection in troubled times. The OSS put an American flag on the hotel's roof and another out of White's window. "With the hotel as US property we figured that even the Vietnamese extremists would hesitate before sacking US property and harming people inside," wrote White.

Official purchase and sale documents were drawn up, and "the response was fantastic," according to White. "The word having spread like wild fire that there was space and some possibility of safety at the Continental, people flocked to the hotel in droves. Mostly in family groups, they began by camping on the floors with their loyal Vietnamese servants preparing meals on charcoal braziers. They filled the corridors, then the restaurants, and finally the roof. Regular guests, ourselves included, opened their rooms so that new arrivals could use additional floor space and the bathrooms besides."

Demonstrations grew more aggressive. At one point a truck roared down the street "spewing machine gun fire in every direction." But no one tried to storm the hotel. The leader of White's OSS detachment, Peter Dewey, was ambushed and killed—perhaps the first American casualty of the long, thirty-year struggle to come.

Years later, White and Franchini met in Paris, where White was working for *Time.* They dined at Le Fouquet's, which Franchini said he owned. Neither had kept a copy of the fake bill of sale for the Continental, but, in Franchini's words, " 'on a fait du bien, là-bas,' roughly maybe we did some good."

Frank, and other OSS men, met Ho Chi Minh, and there was perhaps a moment when some understanding between the US and Ho might have been reached. Ho admired America and had been in Paris right after World War I, hoping that President Wilson's fourteen points might apply to Vietnam and colonized people everywhere. But it was not to be. Franklin Roosevelt did not want to see European colonialism restored, and he was dead set against the French returning to Indochina. But after Roosevelt's death the Cold War swept everything else aside, including the dead president's wishes, and the French re-established control. The Americans would end up bankrolling the French, supplying them with arms and ammunition, all in the name of anti-Communism. Even when the French wanted to throw in the towel, Washington insisted that the French keep on fighting, although the Americans had already sued for peace in Korea. Korea was not a "domino," the Eisenhower administration decided, but Indochina was. Should the French lose Indochina, British Malaya and Burma, Indonesia, perhaps even India would be next, or so it was said. Eisenhower's vice president, Richard Nixon, upon coming back from a visit to French Indochina, said: The French "cannot get out . . . We cannot let them get out because if we do the Communists—the Viet Minh—are the only ones capable of governing, the only ones capable of controlling the country."[*]

The French war against Vietnamese nationalism went on until 1954, when, after their defeat at Dien Bien Phu, the French left Indochina forever. Vietnam was divided at the seventeenth parallel between Ho Chi Minh's North Vietnam and non-Communist South Vietnam. There were supposed

---

[*] Fredrik Logevall, *Embers of War* (New York: Random House, 2012), 377.

to be elections to reunite the country. Although the US was not party to that agreement, John Foster Dulles, Eisenhower's powerful secretary of state, was having none of that, and South Vietnam became what amounted to an American protectorate.

But the old Continental was still there when I arrived. A French flag flew outside, and we thought Franchini's son, Philippe, who now ran the hotel, had some deal with the Vietcong not to attack French property. Whereas the American flag had once protected Frenchmen living in Saigon, now the French flag, we thought, might be protecting us Americans.

Time had an old French villa up Tu Do Street near the cathedral, number 7 Han Thuyen. A teletype machine would slowly tap out our stories from Saigon to Manila and on to New York. Power cuts were frequent. There were amusing restaurants. One of my favorites had a Basque theme with Vietnamese waiters dressed in white with red sashes and espadrilles as if in San-Jean-de-Luz. And from the roof of the old Majestic Hotel down by the waterfront a cool wind would come in off the river. You could sip your drink and watch the occasional flashes of gunfire in the distance across the river while a little dance band played fox-trots from the fifties.

Many in the press corps fell in love with Indochina in a way I have not seen since in other war zones. Younger colleagues covering Central America in the 1980s used to express envy at the way old Vietnam reporters would reminisce, for few of the new generation felt that way about El Salvador or Nicaragua. The Middle East was fascinating and compelling but had none of the soft, seductive charms of the Far East. I became enchanted with the beauty of the Annamite Cordillera, the chain of mountains running down the Vietnamese coast, and the rice paddies growing green as a parrot's wing.

My friend Tony Clifton, an Australian journalist for *Newsweek,* described our feelings on a Vietnam reporters' website many years later. "Of course we enjoyed Indochina. Many of us never had a better time in our working lives. We were appalled at times, too, and bored, and frightened. But more than three hundred old hacks wouldn't be waxing nostalgic today about the bars and the girls and the dope and the coffee and the quality of the bread . . . if they hadn't enjoyed or loved or were exhilarated by what they were doing in

Nam. I had a much more successful time as a reporter in Beirut immediately after Vietnam," Clifton wrote, "and even won the odd prize as against none in Vietnam, and made a lot of friends. But none of the snappers [photographers] and hacks [reporters] who covered a decade of the Lebanese civil war and the Israeli invasion . . . are today swapping tales and reminiscences about the quality of the hummus, the nights on Arak and Bekaa hash, and nobody is suggesting any kind of reunion on good old Hamra Street any time soon."

I quickly found out that I was not going to be spending much time in Saigon, however. My task would be to report the war in the provinces where I very soon was disabused of my preconceived opinions. I came to Vietnam thinking that the war was just and necessary, that Communism had to be stopped. But the complexities of the civil war in Vietnam, in which we were intervening on one side, were much more subtle than I had imagined, and the nationalist sentiments that colonized people were feeling everywhere were not on our side.

Reporters had more freedom to move around the war zone in Vietnam than they did later in Iraq and Afghanistan. You could hop on and off any American aircraft going anywhere, if there was room, showing only your MACV card, pronounced "mac vee," for "Military Assistance Command, Vietnam." We were given the honorary rank of major, and it meant you could take a flight from Saigon to Danang in the First Military Region up north near the North Vietnamese border, called "Eye Corps" in military speak.[*] From there you could catch a resupply helicopter or a medical evacuation "chopper" going into the thick of a firefight to pick up the wounded, and there you would be right in the thick of the war.

Vietnam was a helicopter war like none other before, and maybe since. Certainly reporters covering Iraq and Afghanistan never had the "lift" at their disposal to get around the country as we did in Vietnam. Indeed I was shocked in Baghdad to have a marine general tell me that I might have to wait several

---

[*] South Vietnam, during the American war, was divided up into four military regions. The first was called "Eye" Corps because the Roman numeral for 1 looked like a capital I. Two Corps incorporated the central highlands. Saigon and surrounds were in Three Corps, and Four Corps embraced the Mekong River delta.

days to catch a helicopter to a battle zone. In Vietnam there were helicopters going everywhere all the time, and the thrill of flying along at breakneck speed in a Huey with skids skimming the jungle treetops was intense. In the end, after being shot down in two helicopters, I began to fear them, and the *thwok, thwok, thwok* of helicopters today brings back a bad feeling.

My first recollection of combat was that it was not at all like the movies, in which the sound is synchronized with the motion. In real combat the sound travels well behind the sight. A shell lands with its geyser of dirt and smoke just before the noise. A machine gun, only a little distance away, starts to jump with recoil just a split second before the sound reaches you.

We would often spend a week or ten days with a particular unit, getting to know the soldiers or marines, marching with them on patrols that were often just a walk in the woods. Or you could end up in the middle of a serious firefight, pressed to the earth with bullets whizzing through the leaves above your head, and mortar rounds coming in, and people dying all around you. They called it being "embedded" in the Iraq and Afghan wars, but the term wasn't used in Vietnam. It was far easier in Vietnam to drop into, and out of, the war than in later conflicts where you might have to wait a week to catch a flight out.

I had feared at first that I might be undone by the dying and the people blown to pieces. No movie has ever really shown what high explosives can do to human beings. The television cameras, too, shied from the worst of it. Ironically, just when I thought I was going to be able to take anything I was exposed to on the battlefield, I went home to Hong Kong for a brief time with my family. My daughter Julia fell and cut her chin. It was just a small cut, a few stitches at the most, but I went to pieces as I have never done before or since. I wept uncontrollably and shook as if I had malaria.

One learned little tricks for survival in the field. You didn't walk too close to the guy carrying the radio because its bulky shape and long antenna were targets for Vietcong snipers hoping to black out communications. Also, officers tended to stick close to the guy with the radio, and snipers loved to pick off officers. We wore the same uniforms as the soldiers, with our names and affiliations sewn on the front of our tunics. Most of us didn't carry weapons, and I never did except on one occasion. We learned to say "*bao chi*," Vietnamese for "journalist," in case we were captured.

You found a hollow in the folds of the earth when you slept at night on operations to afford a little bit of protection should mortars start raining down. My most comfortable and safest night in the field was when our unit bedded down in a cemetery. I slept soundly at the bottom of an open grave.

You learned how to make yourself as comfortable as possible, digging a little depression for your hips when you slept on the ground, and you learned never to take your boots off just in case you needed to move quickly in the night. You learned how to boil water with C4 explosives, which would explode if compressed but just burned fiercely out in the open. C4 could boil water in seconds for your tea or coffee. And you learned which of the little tin cans in the combat rations were better than others. Everybody's least favorite was ham and lima beans, but everyone relished the cut-up fruit. You wore the little can openers that you found in your C rations around your neck with your dog tags so you wouldn't lose them. I was amused to see this invaluable bit of equipment featured in Tim O'Brien's classic *The Things They Carried*.

Many soldiers, and reporters, too, smoked marijuana, but not the hard drugs that came in later when more and more draftees started arriving and when morale was plummeting. As for me, my only drug was an occasional pipe of opium back in Saigon or Phnom Penh.

You tried to drink enough water so as not to get dehydrated in the appalling heat of the dry season. I once saw a marine drop from heat prostration. We all emptied our canteens on him to bring his temperature down, and when this didn't work the corpsman instructed us to pee on him. That didn't work either, and after a while he was dead before he could be "medevaced," meaning evacuated for medical reasons.

In the cool season, in the jungle-covered hills, it was the opposite. I have never been so cold as during those nights in the hill country near the Laotian border. You were issued a light plastic blanket and a poncho, but that often wasn't enough to keep you warm, especially in the rain.

5

Away to War, Home in Hong Kong

My parents were well acquainted with Indochina because they had been collecting birds on museum expeditions between the wars, and I wrote to my father about the rain.

"The northeast monsoon came early this year, and by September it was raining almost every day in the northern provinces. I cannot tell you how miserable conditions became up here, especially in the Marine outposts along the DMZ such as Gio Linh and Con Thien. It became impossible to stay dry. The mud got so thick that it would cake on your boots and clothes in heavy layers. And of course there was a lot of noise up here in September which made everybody very nervous."

The noise was the long-range artillery that would pour down fire on the marines from across the DMZ. The war of punji-stick booby traps and small-arms ambushes was giving way to a more conventional war in the north.

The North Vietnamese, who had really taken over the war from the local Vietcong in Eye Corps, were masters of terrain and concealment. You saw their dead bodies, turning the color of clay, but I rarely ever saw a live North Vietnamese or Vietcong. On rare occasions you would see a wounded prisoner or suspected guerrillas, their arms bound behind their backs, squatting on the earth awaiting interrogation. Prisoners were treated roughly. Once I saw some Americans set dogs on terrified suspects.

Often the first you knew that the enemy was even near would be the fireflylike muzzle bursts winking at you from a tree line across a paddy field. The bullets would snap when breaking the sound barrier in the air around you. The sound always reminded me of insects in the air, but the novelist Karl Marlantes, in his celebrated book *Matterhorn,* put it more dramatically when he described them as "cracking like the bullwhip of death."

The bullwhips of death could reach you before you heard anything, and reporters, like soldiers, had to get used to it. Some have said that the soldiers and marines held reporters in contempt, but I never encountered that. They were always amazed that you would be there when you didn't have to. But most of them wanted to tell you their stories, and when you spent time in the field sharing hardships and fears, and humping a pack, you tended to win their tolerance.

And we saw them die. Some would drop just like sacks from a clean bullet to the head. Others would die screaming in agony. So many were so young, still in or hardly out of their teens. I was in my early thirties then, but I seemed like a grandfather to them. From time to time we reporters would die, too. I lost half a dozen friends before the Indochina wars were over. I believe the total number of journalists killed was close to seventy-five.

On one truly horrible afternoon, after a firefight, I flew out in the back of a helicopter filled with dead men wrapped in their ponchos because there had been too few body bags. As the helicopter rose the wind caught the ponchos and blew them away, and I was left in the company of corpses. Soon the effluvia of their drained lives began to spatter me, and just for a moment I had an urge to fling myself out of the helicopter, to follow the fluttering ponchos down into the green jungle below.

We were a generation brought up on the movies, and we often talked about how such and such a situation would be portrayed in Hollywood and who might play the parts. I was cast as a doomed Confederate officer. Ours was also a generation heavily influenced by Ernest Hemingway. I might have thought F. Scott Fitzgerald the better writer, but that did not lessen Hemingway's grip on my imagination. Looking back, had I not gone to Pamplona to run the bulls during a college summer as in *The Sun Also Rises*? And why had I gone hunting in the green hills of Africa on summer breaks at Oxford? And, for that matter, what was I doing here covering a war as Hemingway had done in Spain?

"In the fall the Castillian plain is the color of a lion and as bare as a clipped dog," wrote Hemingway in a dispatch from the Spanish Civil War. "Looking across the flat yellowness from the hillcrest where the old front line had run you saw four villages and a distant town . . . the ultimate objective of the great government offensive of July." We all would have given a lot to have written those sentences.

From time to time I went out on operations with the US Army in the Mekong Delta, where you waded through water half the time. War in the Central Highlands could be physically demanding, with steep wooded hills, and in the rubber plantations along the Cambodian border the trees would bleed white latex when the bullets hit them. Sometimes I would go on operations with ARVN troops, "ARVN" being the acronym for "Army of the Republic of Vietnam." I always wondered if they would take care of me if I was badly wounded, not because I thought they wouldn't want to but just because their medical equipment was not as good as what the Americans carried.

But it was the marines that I stuck to the most, always with worse equipment than the army, older and fewer helicopters, and prone to take more casualties given their training in aggressive tactics. Marines were trained to rush in across beaches, not dig holes to hide in. The holes they did dig were dug reluctantly.

Sometimes television crews would ask you to carry big yellow bags filled with film for shipment back to Saigon. Everyone did this if asked because one day you might want a TV guy to carry out some hastily written story when there was no chance of getting to a telephone. I once saw an American soldier toss two rivals' film bags out of a helicopter door and keep the third. Was it that he preferred ABC to NBC and CBS? I never got a chance to ask in the roar of the engines. Besides, he had a funny look in his eye that made me wonder if I might be thrown out the door, too, if I brought it up.

• • •

The Marine Corps kept a press center at Danang, a major port city in Eye Corps. It was right on the banks of the Han River, and you could get a shower, a steak, and a beer. It was pretty spartan, but it was heaven itself after a week in the bush. The press center was where you could telephone your stories down the line to Saigon, and reporters today can only imagine the agonies of filing in those pre-computer days. You had to wait until it was your turn on the telephone. Then you had to build up a series of calls from one operator to another, patching the phone connections together, and if a circuit was broken the whole edifice of phone patches could come tumbling down and you would have to begin again. All the while you had to shout, "Working, working, working," so that operators downstream would not think your circuit was free and cut you off. Once the connection to Saigon was made it was often so bad you had to shout. My friend Jim Pringle of the Reuters news agency had a Scots accent so thick that Reuters in Saigon thought itself lucky if there was another Scot there to take down Jim's story. One time, after spending forty minutes to get a connection, I shouted: "It's David Greenway." But the person on the other end of the line said, "Greenway's not here," and hung up.

Here is another letter to my father, written in May of 1967.

I spent the better part of a week up near the Cambodian border during an Operation called Junction City. One day we camped near an old villa with a French planter still living there in the middle of the war. It is said that the French have their own arrangement with the Viet Cong and North Vietnamese. I had a drink with him, and a cigar, with the sound of tanks clanking on his driveway and 105 artillery barking amongst the trees. Soldiers shoot at any wild life they come across, you will be sad to hear. An elephant was shot with an anti-tank gun up near the Laotian border not long ago.

I have become very pessimistic about the chances of winning this war. Maybe with 600,000 troops and 20 years we might pull it off, but we will probably lose this one as the French did and go home.

In November I wrote to him again saying that General William Westmoreland, who was in charge of US forces, was telling people that "by next spring it will be clear to even the worst critics that we are winning the war. But it seems to me that he underestimates the ability and the determination of the Communists to hang in." My faith in the American enterprise was fading fast when I compared what I saw in the field with what was being said at headquarters in Saigon. And by the time spring came to Vietnam again, the war had come back to the cities, and the very opposite of what Westmoreland had predicted had come to pass.

I wrote my father,

> In the eight months I have been here we have managed to push most of the main force units back away from the population areas towards the borders. The big fights nowadays take place near the frontiers . . . But I can see no indication that the other side is willing to give up. Meanwhile the social fabric of South Vietnam continues to disintegrate. There is a dangerous apathy, a total mistrust of the Saigon government. Perhaps time and stability will bring them around, but what the villagers want is security and recourse, recourse meaning someone to turn to if their wives are raped and their crops stolen. Security meaning simply to keep the war away from their villages. Everything else, all the social services and other stuff we boast about giving them comes second. I hope I am wrong, but I don't see an end in sight.
>
> PS: Do you remember that rubber plantation I wrote to you about a few months ago? There was a big battle up there last week and, sadly, I went up to find the Frenchman dead and much of the place in ruins. He was caught in the crossfire and by the time I got there South Vietnamese soldiers were washing their clothes in the swimming pool. Others had broken into the wine cellar and were boozing it up. One soldier had smashed the strong box and had fistfuls of French francs. An American Special Forces lieutenant managed to con him into thinking it was all worthless, and the Special

Forces guy bought several thousands of francs for about 30 cents in South Vietnamese money.

I interviewed General Westmoreland often in those days, always a favorite with *Time* magazine, which put him on its cover. He had a quiet, controlled voice with not much inflection. He was always perfectly turned out. Even his fatigues had razor-sharp creases and an excess of starch. There was an amusing, and as it turned out prophetic, article written back then positing the thesis that the best-dressed generals usually lost to scruffier commanders. Think of sloppy Grant and the better-dressed Lee at Appomattox Court House. Think of MacArthur, open shirted and tieless on board the USS *Missouri,* compared to the immaculately dressed Japanese in formal clothes coming to surrender.

Creighton Abrams, who replaced Westmoreland, was an altogether different type. Gruff, down-to-earth, he soon ended the "sweep and destroy" tactics of Westmoreland's command, tactics that were forever leading Americans into well-prepared traps to be killed in large numbers. Abrams told me he was worried about morale, too, which had begun to flag as draftees poured into the ranks. He spoke of the French army mutinies of World War I, when soldiers began to feel they were cannon fodder in useless operations. "Fragging," soldiers murdering their officers, was on the uptick as the war dragged on.

Morale was flagging in the army of South Vietnam, too. I was witness to an execution when a young "aspirant," an officer in training, was sentenced to death for some infraction I have now forgotten. A crowd of people had gathered to see the young man die, and I was reminded about public executions in London a couple of centuries ago when they were occasions for a public holiday. He was dressed in white and brought in by two soldiers, one on either arm. He seemed on the verge of collapse as he was tied to a stake in front of a firing squad, which was standing around talking and laughing, perhaps out of nervousness. He was allowed his last words, which were: "I die for two sergeants," presumably meaning that two sergeants were the guilty ones.

If I had imagined a scene where the victim refuses the blindfold, flips away his last cigarette, and faces his end with some kind of dignity, I was quickly disabused. He died in a hail of bullets, having soiled his pants and slumping like an animal killed in a stockyard. I was sorry I had come.

———

It was *Time*'s policy to allow its Vietnam reporters some time off every few weeks or so. For me that meant a return to what was then the British crown colony of Hong Kong, where my family lived. The flight into the old Kai Tak Airport was a thrill in itself. Planes had to circle in from the sea; drop low over the apartment blocks of Kowloon, nearly taking the laundry off the lines; and bank hard right to touch down on a spit of land sticking out into the harbor.

We lived in a three-story house with a view looking west over the South China Sea and north to the purple hills of China in the distance. Today this view is often obscured by smog and smoke from the great industrial pollution that has overtaken China, but in the sixties the skies over Hong Kong were clear. There were flame-of-the-forest trees on our street, and between us and the sea you could see whitewashed cow barns in the near distance. The cows lived on land far too valuable to be used by dairy farmers for long, and indeed, today there is nothing but walls of high-rises where cows once chewed their cuds. Our old house, too, has long since gone to make room for even taller high-rises.

Our Chinese landlord lived on the ground floor. We lived on the middle floor, and on the top floor lived the four widows of our landlord's father, known to all as the upstairs "*tai tais*," Chinese for "wives." They were amiable ladies without a word of English. Once when one of my children was crying inconsolably on the balcony, a candy came down on a string from the floor above. Enchanted, my daughter stopped crying.

Hong Kong was an island of sanity in those days, with the agonies of the Cultural Revolution convulsing China and the whole restless rim of Southeast Asia brimming with insurrections and worry. Refugees from the mainland would bring lurid tales of Red Guard excesses throughout China, and from time to time bound corpses would float down the Pearl River into Hong Kong waters, testament to what was happening upstream in Canton. "Horror Bodies," the popular press called these unwanted intruders into British territory. We had a small Chinese junk to go out with friends and family on picnics, and we were always worried lest we encounter corpses in the clear waters off the coast.

In the colony itself there were demonstrations by leftist youths waving their little red books containing the sayings of Chairman Mao. Huge red banners with Communist slogans hung down the outside of the Bank of China building overlooking the cricket pitch where Englishmen in whites would play in between cups of tea. From time to time a bomb would go off— nothing too big compared to the bombs used today in Beirut, Pakistan, and Afghanistan, but disturbing nonetheless. In all about fifty citizens of Hong Kong lost their lives in those troubling times.

On one occasion, just back from Vietnam, I was walking on a Hong Kong street when the sound of a bomb several streets away sent me instinctively scrambling for cover. "For heaven's sake, Pop, it's only a bomb," said my small daughter with the insouciance of an old veteran of riot and insurrection.

My youngest daughter, Sadie, was born in Hong Kong, and alas, I did not make it back from Saigon for her birth. I did make it back sooner than I might have, however, because in the middle of the night in Saigon I was awakened by JB's voice saying, "David!" There was an urgency to her tone that concerned me. You may say it was a dream and that I knew Sadie's birth was coming soon, but it was as real to me as if JB had been in the room. I already had the air ticket to Hong Kong booked by the time the cable came through announcing Sadie's birth.

The British ruled Hong Kong fairly and efficiently, and no Chinese subject of Hong Kong in his right mind wanted to be ruled by Mao Tse-tung at that time. The one thing nobody in an official capacity ever talked about was, what if the Chinese decided to take Hong Kong? After all, the British were living "on borrowed time in a borrowed place," as the Australian newsman Richard Hughes had put it. The island of Hong Kong might technically have belonged to Britain in perpetuity, but the rest of the territory was on a ninety-nine-year lease with about thirty years to go. Unlike other colonies, there was no question about independence for Hong Kong. When the thirty years were up it would go back to China.

At one point during the Cultural Revolution it looked as though China's "People's Liberation Army" was advancing on Hong Kong, but a British helicopter pilot whom I knew tipped me off that the PLA was digging in facing the other way. Chou En-lai had reportedly decided to send the army to defend the colony from Red Guard hotheads. China would have Hong Kong in its own time, not in another Cultural Revolution spasm.

In 1997, just fifty years after Britain gave up India in bloodshed and tragedy, Hong Kong was returned to China peacefully, with the governor and the prince of Wales there in the pouring rain to see the British flag lowered on their last major overseas possession. The royal yacht was there, too, waiting to take the prince and the governor away, and late that night buses rolled across the frontier carrying the soldiers of the People's Liberation Army. I wrote in my rain-splashed notebook that I was seeing the final end to the British Empire, that great enterprise that had so absorbed the world for centuries for good and ill. From then on Britain's largest dependency in terms of population would be Bermuda.

Mao and the British had agreed on a historic compromise, "one country, two systems," whereby Hong Kong would revert to China but keep its own laws, customs, and capitalist system for another fifty years. In 1967, however, nobody knew whether Mao might decide to foreclose earlier.

One time a new British general arrived in Hong Kong and gave a press conference. He started talking about his Gurkhas, tough little soldiers from Nepal whom the British used to fight their colonial wars. He explained how he would deploy them along the border. Reporters gasped. Was the general raising the forbidden topic? Was he suggesting that Britain could actually defend Hong Kong against the overwhelming might of the People's Liberation Army across the border? "Perhaps not," said the general, "but we would give them an interesting afternoon."

Early on in Hong Kong we found our beloved amah, Ah Bing, who remained with us on three different continents until the end of her life. "Amah" on the China coast meant someone who took care of children, and Ah Bing treated ours with love and affection as if they were her own.

There were some journalists' wives who found Hong Kong boring with their husbands away in Saigon. This was not true of JB, who had majored in Oriental studies at Barnard and Columbia, but it was hard on others who were less resourceful. Once we took the wife of an Italian journalist to lunch at the Repulse Bay Hotel because we heard she was distraught over having to live in Hong Kong. The bay had been named for a British battleship that had once anchored there. The hotel oozed with colonial charm, and we ate on the veranda overlooking the blue waters of the South China Sea and the islands beyond. With fragrant frangipani growing and flame-of-the-forest trees coming into bloom on a bright sunny day, it was for us as pretty a picture as you could find anywhere. "Now, you have to admit this isn't bad," I said to my Italian guest as we looked at the view. She gave a deep sigh and said what has become for our family the ultimate put-down: "It is not Amalfi."

The author and his wife in Hong Kong, 1976.

We took wonderful weekend cruises in an old junk for hire, called the *Sea Dragon,* with our friends Nick and Sheila Platt and their boys. We would go out to the New Territories, where there were pristine beaches and clean seas.

One couldn't find a better way to get away from the war, but the war never completely left my mind. Nick, a diplomat in the American consulate, would go on to help open up America's Liaison Office in Beijing after President Nixon's famous visit to China and before there was a formal embassy. A generation of outright hostility between the two countries was brought to a close.

My times back with my family and friends in Hong Kong seemed all too brief and far between, and it always seemed to me I was back in the airport flying back to Saigon almost as soon as I had arrived. My eldest daughter, who was now in school, was asked by her teacher: "What does your daddy do?"

"He works at the airport," was her reply.

When I came back to Hong Kong as the *Washington Post*'s man on the China Coast in the following decade, and when I wasn't traveling, my main job was to report on what was happening inside that great mystery of China during the Cultural Revolution. Americans could not, in the early seventies, live in China, but even European and Canadian journalists who lived in Beijing found themselves greatly restricted.

The Cultural Revolution started when Chairman Mao decided that his revolution was getting too sclerotic and that what China needed was a fresh dose of rebellious upheaval. And with Red Guard youths terrorizing the cities and the countryside, a little like the Brown Shirts in Germany as Hitler was coming to power, upheaval is what Mao got.

Hong Kong was full of diplomats and journalists, and other experts on China, who tried to divine what was really going on among the fractious leadership in Beijing and the provinces. Shanghai could always be counted on to produce factions and personalities more red than even Beijing. We had access to Chinese provincial radio broadcasts, copied down and translated by CIA, and from these texts it might be possible to see one province putting out a different line from another. A master of this was an American diplomat at our consulate named Sherrod McCall. He had a sixth sense about who was trying to do in whom among the Chinese leadership and what each new political campaign, such as the one denouncing Confucius, really meant. It was

McCall who brought to my attention that one of the Chinese leaders, Deng Xiaoping, was saying that it doesn't matter the color of the cat as long as it catches mice. This appeared to be in direct contradiction to what Chairman Mao was saying, that it was better to be red than to be expert in anything.

Deng's statement turned out to be one of the most important pronouncements of the century, for it would be Deng who would eventually become China's paramount leader, virtually dismantling the Communist economic system and putting China on the road to being, at this writing, the second-biggest economy in the world after the United States. Mao had famously said when his guerrillas won China's civil war: "The Chinese people have stood up." But Mao would soon force them to their knees with an ideological tyranny that was worse than what had gone before. It was Deng who finally let them begin to stand.

During the harsh days of the Cultural Revolution, Chinese were always trying to sneak out of China into Hong Kong, some of them by swimming, and it became sort of a game. If anyone was caught trying to sneak in he was sent back. If he made it he could stay in Hong Kong.

Once in a while reporters, even Americans, were allowed to come up the Pearl River to the Canton trade fair for a rare visit inside China itself. You had to take a train to Lo Wu on the border, cross over a rickety bridge, and take another train to Canton. Today the border area is a vast industrial zone, but then it was nothing but open fields and poor farms. We were sequestered in the East Wind Hotel, which had sort of a cruise ship atmosphere, because you weren't really allowed out all that much, and if you were, it would be to some Potemkin industrial site or model commune.

With Deng in power I did get to go along on one of Henry Kissinger's frequent visits to Beijing in 1976. There was almost no traffic on the road in from the airport. The uniform blue suits that both men and women wore were everywhere in the streets. Bits of old China were still left in the byways of Beijing, most of them torn down later to make way for the modern. Visitors to China today cannot imagine how poor and behind the times China was thirty-five years ago. Most people traveled by bicycle and were afraid to even speak to foreigners.

When I visited Shanghai early in the twenty-first century, JB and I stayed in the old French Concession, by far the most charming part of Shanghai. But I could not help but marvel that China, after almost two centuries of suffering under foreign occupations of their coastal cities, the Japanese invasion, civil war, and Mao's misrule, had finally shucked all that off and was taking the place China held in the late eighteenth century, as one of the richest and most powerful countries in the world.

After five years of living in Hong Kong, it will always have a special place in our family. Our middle daughter, Alice, would return to the former colony to write for the *South China Morning Post,* and her first novel, *White Ghost Girls,* was set in the Hong Kong of the late sixties.

6

My Luck Runs Out

During the Indochina wars I was too seldom in Hong Kong. It was Vietnam that obsessed me then, and I acquired a certain reputation for being lucky. Some of my colleagues said that they felt safer on military operations with me. Mike Herr told me once that he could not picture me dead in the rain. Indeed I felt myself to be in a sort of time machine, as in the H. G. Wells story. With all my inoculations and malaria pills, I felt immune to the sickness I saw around me, and I just wasn't going to be shot. I felt as if I had come almost from another century and was walking through an ancient conflict from which I would and could soon return to the present.

In retrospect, 1967 was a fatal year for Vietnam, for it was then that the US command decided that Americans would fight the main force war while the South Vietnamese would take a secondary role in the defense of their own country. It sapped the will of the South Vietnamese, who always should have been at the forefront of their own defense.

In Saigon life was pleasant and safe enough for the moment. There may have been wire mesh on the outside of some cafés opening on the street, to deflect a grenade thrown from a passing motorbike, but that kind of incident wasn't happening anymore. Strangely, I used to wake up in the middle of the night with the smell of dead people in my room. I would turn on the light, and it would slowly go away. It happened often in those days. I am sure a psychiatrist would have had fun with that one, but I never told a living soul at the time.

There were parties and social gatherings, although the war was always present in conversation. A group of cynical young foreign-service officers sent out invitations saying, "Sir Cloudesley Shovell invites you to a light at the end of the tunnel party." "The light at the end of the tunnel" was a phrase used by an unfortunate French general, Henri Navarre, back in the fifties when France was trying to keep Vietnam French. Navarre, like Westmoreland, had been predicting that victory was just around the corner. As for Shovell, he was an eighteenth-century British admiral who led his entire fleet onto the rocks, losing many hundreds of lives.

Some Americans had Vietnamese girlfriends. There was a restaurant that had been a favorite of the French foreign legion during the last Indochina war. One sat on hard wooden benches and legionnaires had scribbled on the white walls. One hot, sweaty evening, with hot, sweaty customers making too much noise, the room suddenly fell silent. I turned around to see my friend Frank Wisner, a young Vietnamese-speaking foreign-service officer, come in dressed in a white linen suit, powder blue shirt, and black tie. On his arm was a stunningly attractive Vietnamese girl in a flowing blue ao dai, the becoming traditional dress of Vietnam.

In total silence, Frank and his lady mounted a ladder that led to a private dining room aloft. He shot us his signature grin as he rose above us. Once they had disappeared in the "*salle privée,*" the crowded room below exhaled in an audible sigh.

One of my friends in the Time-Life bureau, the photographer Dick Swanson, married his Vietnamese girlfriend. He dressed up in the traditional garb of a Vietnamese mandarin, run up by a Saigon tailor for the ceremony. Many of us bought clothes in Hong Kong or Saigon because they were inexpensive. Dick wore shirts with little Chinese characters under the breast pocket. People would ask him, "Is that your name in Chinese?" It was common to get your name translated into Chinese just for the fun of it, but no. Dick's shirts with the discreet Chinese characters said: "No Starch."

Swanson would return to Saigon as the city was falling to get as many of his in-laws out as was possible, and later the couple opened a restaurant in Washington that was a regular stop for the old Vietnam crowd.

Another memorable Saigon moment came at a diplomatic reception. *New York Times* correspondent Tom Buckley was chatting up one of the guests when his bureau chief, R. W. "Johnny" Apple, who was quite a bit younger than Buckley, bustled up to remind Buckley that he still had a story to write. Apple wasn't the rotund gourmand and bon vivant he later became. He was a skinny kid with a crew cut.

"Is that your boss?" asked Tom's interlocutor.

Buckley, who considered himself the real writer in the *Times*'s bureau, shot back: "Only in the sense that Pope Julius II was Michelangelo's boss."

Apple would become a good friend and a legendary *Times* reporter after the war. Many of the friends I made during the war became friends for life.

Later in the war, Al Schuster would become Saigon bureau chief for the *New York Times,* and under his administration the *Times* rented a new office, which was redecorated with bright Thai cotton curtains and other amenities. My friend Gloria Emerson, the only woman in the *Times* bureau, had complained to me that the previous *Times* office was disgusting. "Helmets, bayonets stuck in desks, jockstraps left in corners, horrible," she had said. So when the *Times* moved to better quarters I asked her: "How did you pull it off?"

"This new man Schuster is such a dear," she told me. "I explained to him that a new office in the same building could be obtained, and that it had two bathrooms instead of only one. 'I can understand how you might want a ladies' room, Gloria,' Al said to me. But I said, 'No, no, Al, one bathroom is for you and me. All the rest of the staff has this dreadful dripping gonorrhea.' Al signed the lease the next day."

Saigon in 1967 was just transitioning from white suits for men to dark suits, probably because of the increasing use of air-conditioning. Ambassador Henry Cabot Lodge, who had been a friend of my family, received me in a white cotton suit, and most Vietnamese officials wore the same at that time. But that was changing fast. Journalists, too often, wore silly little safari jackets known as TV suits, because television correspondents seemed particularly drawn to them.

My best Vietnamese friend was Pham Xuan An, who worked for *Time* and was in many ways a brilliant reporter. He gave me many insights into Vietnamese life and ways of thinking. He was also working as a spy for Hanoi, but I didn't know that until the war was over. He could often be seen at Givral, a coffee shop and bakery near the Continental, where he and his colleagues would discuss the latest political gossip. Some said that there was more intelligence exchanged in the smoke-filled air at Givral than at the entire CIA Saigon station. Alas, the old Givral is gone now, torn down along with the entire art-deco-style block, like so much of old Saigon, to make way for the new.

I used to bring An birds from the bird markets of Bangkok and Hong Kong. His thin frame and delicate hands, always with a cigarette between tobacco-stained fingers, made me think of an ancient Chinese mandarin. His deceptions only remind me that we Americans never really knew what was going on in Vietnam. We blundered in and blundered out again without ever really coming to grips with the society we were trampling underfoot.

It was An who suggested I go and see Edward Lansdale, who was attached to the American embassy. I had no idea that Lansdale was in Saigon, or even that he was still alive and active. Lansdale was a legend at the time. Some said that the Republic of South Vietnam was in good part his creation, although my friend and mentor Stanley Karnow, a Vietnam expert, said that Lansdale's role had been exaggerated by both friend and foe.

Lansdale, an air force intelligence officer, had served in the OSS, forerunner of the CIA. His new spy masters assigned him to be the liaison officer to the then–Filipino secretary of national defense, Ramon Magsaysay, in 1950. The newly independent Philippines was facing a Communist-inspired insurgency by a shadowy group called the Hukbalahaps, or simply "Huks." Lansdale specialized in psychological operations using techniques he had learned in the advertising business before the war. He urged on Magsaysay counterinsurgency tactics, winning over the peasants, and was largely credited with organizing Magsaysay's successful efforts in suppressing the Huks.

The Huks were based in central Luzon and never made inroads in other areas. Unlike other leftist insurgencies in those days, the Huks were never fully embraced by the Soviets nor by Mao. Later, with Lansdale's help, Magsaysay became president of the Philippines. As it would be in the following century, when General David Petraeus reinvented counterinsurgency for the Americans in Iraq, Lansdale was considered a messiah of how to conduct this new kind of warfare.

Lansdale had come to Vietnam during the French war as part of a Franco-American mission to help train what was then called the Vietnamese National Army to defeat Ho Chi Minh's Vietminh. When the Geneva Conference of 1954 resulted in the partition of Vietnam between a Communist north and the non-Communist south, Lansdale was in charge of dirty tricks, sabotaging facilities in the north that the Communists might use, even pouring sugar in the gasoline tanks of trucks the French were leaving behind. He also organized efforts to frighten Catholics into leaving the north and settling in the south in a population exchange permitted by the Geneva Accords. When a little-known figure, Ngo Dinh Diem, emerged as America's candidate to run what the Eisenhower administration saw as their new anti-Communist bastion in Asia, Lansdale was there to make him into a new Magsaysay.

An himself had been recruited by Lansdale into his intelligence network in the 1950s, though of course Lansdale never knew An's heart was in ridding his country of foreigners, nor that An's loyalties belonged to the Communists whom Lansdale and Diem were trying to destroy. But then neither did anyone else.

Diem was a true nationalist and anti-French, which pleased the Americans because they hoped to create a new order uncontaminated by French colonialism. Diem may have been a nationalist, but he was also a narrow-minded martinet as well as a devout Catholic in a country where the vast majority were Buddhists. He and his brother Ngo Dinh Nhu ran the new Republic of Vietnam almost as a police state, suppressing civil liberties and political opposition, and putting Catholic relatives and cronies in charge. When the Americans perceived that their new puppet wasn't all they had hoped for, Washington considered dumping Diem. But before that could happen, perhaps having been tipped off by Lansdale, Diem cracked down on criminal and religious sects whose militias were endangering his authority.

The crackdown was a success, and Washington began to see Diem in a new light as the strong leader who could build a regime to rival Ho Chi Minh's regime in the north, never mind that Diem became ever more dictatorial and isolated from his people. Diem was seen as Washington's golden boy, a great hero who was performing miracles in the anti-Communist cause. But Diem's repressive policies engendered so much dissent that Ho Chi Minh decided that there were opportunities that could be exploited, especially when it became evident that the election to unite the two Vietnams, as promised at Geneva, was never going to take place. Ho began infiltrating agents and supplies into the south, and by 1959 a new Communist insurgency in the south flowered.

Eisenhower upped the ante, increasing the number of American military advisers and amount of aid, but as the insurgency grew and grew, and Diem seemed increasingly incapable, America again grew tired of their puppet and encouraged a military coup that ended in Diem and his brother being murdered in the back of an armored personnel carrier. President Kennedy had wanted the Diem brothers not to be harmed and was ashen-faced when he heard of their deaths. Three weeks later he himself was assassinated in Dallas.

After that a revolving door of Vietnamese generals took power, and South Vietnam slid farther and farther downhill. America was not wrong to try to distance itself from French colonialism, but the Americans couldn't see that they themselves were becoming the new colonial masters in the eyes of the Vietnamese people, and that Diem and all the other South Vietnamese leaders would be perceived as tools of American power.

But by then Lansdale had long since departed to be deputy assistant secretary of defense for special operations, involving himself in attempts to kill Fidel Castro, and now was back in a vague advisory capacity to the American embassy.

I met Lansdale in what looked to me like a temporary building, surrounded by adoring aides. He was a fifties-type American patriot, so caught up in exporting American ideals that some said he was the model for Graham Greene's Alden Pyle in *The Quiet American,* although in fact this was untrue. Almost sixty now, he was no longer young and his eyes seemed dull and faraway. He was happy to see a reporter for *Time* magazine because the Luce publications had always been firmly in his camp, resisting defeatist talk. He didn't know that I, too, was a growing skeptic. I asked him about his successes in the Philippines and in the early Diem years, which he was happy to talk about, but he seemed to me listless and distant and out of touch with Vietnam as it had become. His glory years were behind him. The Magsaysay figure he had hoped to create in Vietnam did not live up to expectations. The Vietcong were far more formidable than the hapless Hukbalahaps, and it seemed to me that Lansdale was feeling sidelined—a spent force. He spoke very softly, so softly that I had to lean forward. In all it was a disappointing interview, and I went away feeling sorry for him.

He would suffer a further betrayal when his protégé, Daniel Ellsberg, turned against the war and leaked the Pentagon Papers to the press. And so Lansdale passed from the pages of history.

We came to save the Vietnamese from Communism, not exploit them economically as had the French, and there were many, especially among the propertied classes, who feared Communism and appreciated our effort. As for the peasantry in the countryside, they just wanted to be left alone.

The US military was always upbeat, and if you stayed in Saigon you might think the war was being won. If there was one trait that trumped all the others during the long war, it was American self-delusion. As Sebastian Junger would later write about Afghanistan, it wasn't as if American officials were actually lying to you about the progress of the war. They were just inviting you to join in a conspiracy of wishful thinking.

There was a daily briefing famously known as the "Five o'Clock Follies." There you could fill your notebooks with meaningless statistics on how many enemies had been killed that day or how many pigpens had been built. If you had just come in from reporting in the field you could but shake your head and wonder, for the war looked very different up close than it did in these Saigon briefings.

I once had an insight on how the wishful-thinking system worked. Once, following a firefight in thick country, we found three dead bodies after our attackers had withdrawn. The company commander, after talking it over with his platoon leaders, decided that there might have been twenty enemy killed, given the severity of the fight, and that the seventeen other dead bodies might have been dragged away by the North Vietnamese. So they decided on the figure twenty killed to report to battalion.

But when I got back to headquarters in Danang, I found that the figure sent to Saigon for this engagement had grown to thirty-two dead. Defense Secretary Robert McNamara had famously said: "Every quantitative measurement we have shows we're winning the war." And this was probably true, if only you could believe the quantitative measurements. In other instances the statistics might have been correct but they didn't mean anything in political terms. You could build a thousand pigpens for Vietnamese farmers, and they would be grateful to get them. But pigpens did not decide their politics. A farmer with a new pigpen might just as likely be for the Vietcong as against them. We could try to protect the population from Vietcong intimidation, but we couldn't protect their minds.

The war was all we reporters thought about in those days, and there was a certain comfort in that. None of the petty stuff of ordinary life concerned us. As my boss and friend *Time* bureau chief Simmons Fentress once wrote for a *Time* house organ:

Saigon is a one-subject town. You work the war, and you have it for lunch, dinner and nightcap. I used to do the civil rights beat out of Atlanta, and I thought that was the all-time topic A. It can't touch Vietnam. You pass a couple of guys at a restaurant table and you're apt to hear one of them saying, "the hell he was Viet Minh." A solid six hours of war talk isn't unusual here, and people seem never to tire of exploring how we got in and how we get out.

It was refreshing in Vietnam that none of us knew or cared about where we came from or what our backgrounds had been. We were all there because of the war, and what had gone before, where you went to school or college, did not matter in the slightest.

It was Fentress who took me around to a disreputable joint to play tic-tac-toe with a bar girl known as Foul Phuong—so named because of her colorful language. Her English was limited but loaded with expletives of excruciating vulgarity. She would play tic-tac-toe for her virtue. If you lost you would have to buy her a whiskey, known as a Saigon tea because the house would serve the girls tea masquerading as whiskey in order to charge more and keep the girls sober. If you won, Foul Phuong promised to take you home. "You go my how," she would pronounce it, but as far as I know she never lost a single game.

A Scottish reporter friend took a shine to a bar girl, and when she asked him where he was from he said: "I'm a Scot." It so happened that she had never heard of Scots or Scotland, so an English rival for her hand, knowing that the average Vietnamese looked down on the hill tribes whom the French called montagnards, quickly spoke up and said: "The Scots are England's montagnards." That was it, as far as the bar girl was concerned, and she turned her attention to the Englishman.

No doubt I was too obsessive about the war, feeling that no offensive or battle could go unreported by me personally, although *Time* would often mangle our reporting when it came out in the magazine. *Time* reporters seldom got bylines back then. Their dispatches became material from which *Time*'s rewrite men worked. But I didn't care. I had to be there. Looking back I think I had a touch of what we now call post-traumatic stress syndrome, and for years later I would have dreams of being trapped in a burning town. JB noticed that I would become nervous and irritable on anniversaries of Communist offensives long after the war was over. It took me years to get over it, if I have gotten over it.

As it had been in the Spanish Civil War, reporters and writers came to Vietnam with differing ideologies and political beliefs. Very few were as far to the left as in Spain, but there had long been tension within the press corps over the war. I always thought there were basically three generations of Vietnam reporters. The first, in the David Halberstam era of the early sixties, was made up of reporters who thought the cause was just but that the South Vietnamese were not pursuing the war properly. The criticism was tactical, not strategic. Later, my generation began to think the war wasn't worth the cost of fighting it but saw no virtue in the Vietnamese Communists either. Later, as the turmoil of the later sixties and early seventies began to break over the United States, some American reporters came out to Vietnam seeing virtue in the Communist cause just because American policy was so flawed.

Some old Asia hands, such as Joe Alsop, a tremendously influential columnist at the time, would come to Saigon and take a dim view of some of us younger reporters. Alsop was hook, line, and sinker for the war, but his eccentricities were always amusing. One time at a Saigon dinner party he described in his almost-British accent how, from the time he left Harvard until he joined General Chennault in China, he was never without a manservant. He went on to describe how he would hold out his arms in the morning for the manservant to help him into his jacket. An idealistic young foreign service officer, just up from the delta, began to sputter and said: "Goddamn it, Mr. Alsop, I prefer to dress myself!" Old Joe leaned back in his chair and drawled: "That's not quite true, is it? You nevah tried the othah."

Within the *Time* bureau there was often great tension with the home office. We often felt we were in a contest with the Washington bureau, which tended to give New York a rosy picture of the war compared with what we were reporting. But there was a sense of comradeship among us. Don Sider, a very good reporter who shared my obsession with seeing the war up close, became a particular friend. *Time* was good to its reporters. It treated them well, gave them frequent "R & R" (rest and recreation) breaks, paid them handsomely, and made them feel part of a greater enterprise. There were two *Time* reporters named Arthur Zich and Marvin Zim, and the saying was that you could always count on *Time* to stand by its correspondents through Zich and Zim.

In Saigon, one could drop around to the Circle Sportif, the French tennis club that had a swimming pool, and rub shoulders with some of Saigon's French community, which stood aloof from the vulgar Americans. Never mind that many of them were Corsicans; the French looked down on us as if they were Parisian aristocrats.

There were often evenings on the Saigon River. You could hire a small boat to take you out on the river as twilight settled on Saigon, and for a few hours war tensions slipped away.

There was a puddle duck in the little garden of number seven Han Thuyen, and to amuse my children back in Hong Kong I made up stories about "Saigon Duck." I sent them a picture of me holding up Saigon Duck as if we were in conversation, along with tape-recording cassettes. I found out that the duck would quack almost on cue if you put him in a bathtub. And so, with tape recorder in hand, I conducted long interviews with Saigon Duck in which I would translate for the girls his lengthy quacks, telling tales of mythical kingdoms and old Annamese legends with which Saigon Duck was familiar. When I got back to Hong Kong on a break from the war my daughter Alice, with some awe, asked me how I had learned "bird words."

But those relatively peaceful days in Saigon came to an abrupt halt early in 1968, during the lunar New Year holiday known as Tet. The North Vietnamese struck dozens of towns and cities simultaneously throughout the country, penetrating Saigon and even the walls of the American embassy. The Tet Offensive was a blow from which the Americans, who had been taken completely by surprise, never fully recovered—at least not politically. It would take weeks of bitter fighting before the situation was stabilized. The American public's faith in the war effort would never be the same.

True, the Tet Offensive failed in that the general uprising that the Communists anticipated never materialized. They took tremendous losses. True, also, that the indigenous southern Vietcong forces, as opposed to the North Vietnamese, never fully recovered from their losses at Tet. But on balance, when you consider that the United States then began the peace negotiations that would end its military involvement, and when you consider that General Westmoreland was fired, and that President Johnson himself declared he would not seek another term, then you have to give the strategic victory to Hanoi. It was hard for our military leaders to realize that you could win every battle and yet lose the war.

General Westmoreland would ask for two hundred thousand more troops after Tet, only to be turned down. More than one of the more literary correspondents in our midst recalled that Henry V, at least in Shakespeare's version, had told the Earl of Westmoreland to "wish not one man more" before the Battle of Agincourt.

I was in Hong Kong when the Tet thunderclap struck, and struggled hard to get back to Vietnam via a US military flight out of Bangkok. Commercial airlines were definitely not flying into Saigon for a while. I immediately left for Hue, the former imperial capital where my father had received his decoration thirty years before. Hue was the largest town to have completely fallen to the Communist forces, and the marines were fighting house to house, block to block, in street fighting they would not see again until Falluja during the Iraq War nearly forty years later.

We had been used to fighting in the countryside, even burning villages, but to see fighting in an urban area was something else altogether. In home after home, when we would take shelter with the marines, we would be among the shattered remains of urban life: a broken teapot, an abandoned doll, phonograph records and books, and sometimes terrified civilians in a cellar. Inside the citadel itself, the great enclosure that was imitative of Beijing's Forbidden City, the massive walls had been breached and broken by artillery and even naval gunfire from US Navy ships at sea.

At night there was always the problem of where we would bed down. You wanted to be near the command post so that you could keep in touch with what was going on, and you didn't want to be exposed to fire or an in-the-night attack. One evening we found the perfect place, a not-too-damaged villa right next door to where the colonel had set up command with his radio. We put blankets up over the windows so that light could not be seen and warmed our C rations in the fireplace, and I picked a handsome dining room table for my bed. But to our delight, we found an unopened bottle of Scotch whiskey that the owners had left behind in their flight. We finished the bottle before we turned in.

In the middle of the night, however, I felt a great urge to relieve myself, but the toilet was outside across the courtyard and potentially exposed to sniper fire. So I refilled the empty whiskey bottle and put it away in a cupboard. By the next morning I had forgotten about it.

Some days later, back in Danang, I overheard some of my colleagues having a hamburger at the next table. "Jeez," said one. "These Vietnamese are really weird. We holed up last night in some villa, right next to the command post, and I found this bottle of Johnnie Walker in a cupboard. You are not going to believe this, but . . ." I tiptoed away as I knew what the end of the story would be.

It wasn't easy getting in and out of Hue during the worst days of Tet. One time, to get back to Danang, I hopped on a landing barge headed down the Perfume River, which ran through Hue, to the open sea bound for Danang. On board were some International Control Commission personnel, who had been trapped in the fighting and were grateful to leave; some wounded marines; and a couple of correspondents like me. I never carried a weapon in Vietnam. It was against the rules for reporters to be armed. But as we headed downriver we began to take fire from the riverbank. I watched in horror as a rocket hit a boat behind us, which began to sink. Our petty officer skipper gunned his engines and called for every able-bodied man to man the rails and lay down suppressing fire. I could see North Vietnamese running along the bank, halting to shoot at us.

There were plenty of M16 rifles lying about on the deck, which some marines were too seriously wounded to use, and with the skipper telling us it was a matter of life and death, I picked one up and joined the passengers in firing clip after clip at the riverbank, first on the port side and then the starboard, as the captain directed us. I am not sure if I hit anybody. I hope not. But at the time, it reminded me of accounts I had read about China, about American gunboats steaming down rivers with the whole countryside up in arms against them.

I am not proud of that afternoon. My colleague Gene Roberts of the *New York Times*, who was aboard with me, refused to pick up a weapon, much less use it. Years later, Gene and I were having dinner together in New York and he told me he thought I had done the right thing under the circumstances. But I believe it was he who did the right thing. In any case, we were both very relieved to be quit of the river and out in the open sea, heading south in heavy weather with the salt spray breaking over us, and the International Control Commissioners at the rail throwing up.

On the nineteenth of February, 1968, my luck ran out, and the time machine I always imagined was there to take me away from the nightmare of

Hue was nowhere to be found. We had been following the fighting among ruined houses when a marine, standing beside a wall that once was a house, decided to look through a window in the wall. Firing broke out immediately, and the marine slumped to the ground, shot through the throat. A navy medical corpsman rushed to help him but was having trouble carrying the marine to the rear.

Rather than take another marine off the firing line, I got up from where I had been trying to stay as low to the ground as I could to help carry the wounded man. Even the two of us were having trouble carrying him, and a marine combat reporter named Steve Bernston was quick to come to our aid. A few yards farther back, Charlie Mohr of the *New York Times* and Al Webb of United Press joined our rescue effort. Without warning a rocket-propelled grenade came in and knocked us to the ground. I could feel a sharp pain in my leg and blood filling up my boot. Webb and Bernston were hurt worse than I, but, fortunately, Mohr was untouched. We managed to get far enough to the rear where there was an aid station, and the wounded marine was given an emergency tracheotomy, too late, as it turned out, for moments later he died.

My first reaction to getting shot was one of indignation. This wasn't supposed to happen to me! Wasn't I supposed to be lucky? Of course I was incredibly lucky that I wasn't killed or maimed for life, but that wasn't my thinking in the heat of the moment. I found out a long time later that the marine whom we had tried, and failed, to save was named Dennis Michels, a private first class.

My wound temporarily bandaged, I was taken to where a large helicopter was being loaded with wounded. As we took off and rose over the city crackling with gunfire, we could hear rounds hitting the fuselage. Luckily nothing vital was hit and we were soon at Hue Phu Bai, a landing field near the city.

There were too many wounded to be accommodated at the small field hospital, so the lightly wounded, such as myself, were left outside. It seemed like hours, although it was more likely only forty-five minutes. With a gentle rain falling, my teeth began chattering as if to break the enamel as I lay under a thin, rain-soaked blanket.

When I was finally brought inside and put on an operating table, the

American surgeon was in a white-hot fury. He said there were badly wounded Vietnamese soldiers being left out in the rain, but his orders were to take the Americans first. I feared for a moment he would be less than gentle with me, but he was a professional first and last, and he removed as much of the shrapnel from my leg as he thought advisable. To take out every bit of metal would do too much damage, he said.

The author, after being wounded during the fighting in Hue during the Tet Offensive in February, 1968.

For a long time, bits of metal would work their way out, breaking through the skin like boils on my leg. There is still some in there, and I have to be careful with hospital magnetic resolution equipment to this day.

Years later the Marine Corps would give Mohr, Webb, and me Bronze Star medals for trying to save the wounded marine. There was a grand show at the marine barracks in Washington, with the commandant of the Marine

Corps pinning the medals on our chests and the band playing the "Washington Post" march.

Some colleagues took a critical view of our getting involved in the combat instead of remaining observers. At the time I didn't really think about it. The guy was shot in front of me. The corpsman couldn't manage, so I lent a hand. My severest critic was Gloria Emerson, who had definite views on this kind of thing. When she heard about the incident she called up our mutual friend Ward Just and said: "Guess what Charlie and David have done now." I guess she didn't know Webb. Ward said he supposed we had just been trying to save a life, but Gloria would have none of it. "No," she said, "it was male hysteria," and that was the end of it as far as she was concerned. Gloria was one of the best war reporters of her day, specializing in what the war was doing to the Vietnamese. She would, in later life, growing old and sick, commit suicide. For Gloria, even death would be on her terms.

JB got word of my being hurt in a phone call from Lee Griggs, the *Time* bureau chief in Hong Kong. He had a bit of a stutter, and not knowing JB well, he was nervous about what her reaction would be. He hesitated to tell her, so JB said: "Lee, you are calling to tell me David has been hurt but not killed, right?"

"Ye—ye—yes, how—how—how did you know?"

"Because," JB said, letting Griggs off the hook, "if he were dead your instructions would have been to deliver the news in person, but since you are calling on the telephone, and not at my door, I assume he's wounded but not dead." Grace under pressure.

I was not to be the only *Time* magazine casualty of the Tet Offensive. John Cantwell, a genial Australian, went down the wrong street with some colleagues in Saigon, where they were all shot dead. He was married to a Chinese wife in Hong Kong and I was dispatched to bear the bad news. She took it very hard, and I feared it was going to be difficult for her financially because John had not been on staff. She might not receive any benefits. But Richard Clurman, chief of correspondents for the Time-Life News Service back in New York, called to say that Cantwell would be considered as if he had been on staff, and his widow would be treated accordingly. He said he would be on the next plane out. Clurman did this without getting permission from his superiors, which was so like him. I have often thought that there are very few Dick Clurmans in the news business anymore.

Clurman used to come to Saigon and ask to be taken out on military operations with ordinary soldiers, which was unusual for big shots, who usually just stuck to generals and their staffs. On one long patrol we stopped for the night near a dry streambed, and I put Clurman in the dried-up channel because it offered a few inches of protection should we be mortared in the night. Alas, a cloud burst with rain around one o'clock in the morning and sent a stream of water down upon my boss. Years later he would tell the story of his night in the field and it would be suggested that I had soaked him on purpose. But it was said with laughter and it added to his yarn.

Dick asked me to come back to New York for a week to talk to the editors. He was always trying to get *Time*'s editors to pay more attention to his field reporters. Antiwar demonstrations were building then, and I was also asked to talk to some groups interested in the war. It was an odd sensation, for I soon found that the peace demonstrators, at least the ones that I met, cared nothing about Vietnam for Vietnam's sake. They wanted to stop the war, but they weren't the least interested in the country in which the war was being fought. It was a disillusioning experience, and when it was over I was very glad to be back in Saigon.

Clurman would take an extraordinary step after the Tet Offensive. By this time Hedley Donovan had become editor in chief of Time-Life, replacing Henry Luce, who died in February of 1967. Luce, the old anti-Communist crusader, had always looked at Vietnam as another China, where he was born to missionary parents. To lose Vietnam would be akin to our loss of China in Luce's book. Donovan took a more nuanced stand, and on trips to Vietnam he would often solicit the opinions of his reporters over Saigon dinners. After Tet, Clurman instructed us to do a minimum of reporting and concentrate on writing critiques of the war for Clurman to present to Donovan. Although the turn against the war by CBS newscaster Walter Cronkite, said to be the most trusted man in America, is often cited as the turning point of American opinion, the influence of print was stronger then than now. The conversion of *Time* and *Life* against the war probably helped mold many an opinion.

Under Donovan, *Time* had begun to change its ever-optimistic view of the Vietnam War even before Tet. A cover story, which I reported from the marine fire base in Con Thien near the Demilitarized Zone in the north, had a photograph on the cover, taken by Dana Stone of UPI, of a marine in a fetal position in a foxhole, under shellfire from North Vietnam across the border. The words "Rising Doubt About the War" were slashed diagonally across the cover.

After a description of Con Thien under artillery attack, *Time* said: "In the US 10,000 miles away, Con Thien dramatized all the cumulative frustrations of the painful war. A long-rising surge of doubt about Vietnam was intensified for Americans as the bloody, muddy ordeal of Con Thien flickered across the TV screen." It was October 1967, three months before the Tet attack, at a moment when TV was well on its way to replace print as the way most Americans gathered their information.

In my post-Tet memo for Clurman, I said that fear of Chinese Communist expansion was a major reason, if not the major reason, we were in Vietnam. But history would suggest that the fiercely independent Vietnamese would resist China's intrusion into Southeast Asia, even though they were willing to accept Chinese help fighting the Americans and, before that, the French. China had occupied Vietnam for hundreds of years and Vietnam's patriotic legends all involved heroes who had resisted China. If one were looking for help containing China, the North Vietnamese Army was probably the best bet. China might have been giving the North Vietnamese immeasurable help in their war against us, but such a close relationship would likely not survive after we had left Indochina.

This became obvious several years later when Vietnam repulsed a Chinese punitive incursion into North Vietnam after the Americans had been defeated.

7

The South Vietnamese Hold the Line

In the spring of 1972 the North Vietnamese tried again with an all-out assault over the DMZ, called the Easter Offensive. By that time President Nixon's "Vietnamization" program was in full swing. American combat troops were mostly gone, and it was going to be South Vietnam's big test to see whether they could hold their own with American air and logistic support. A test soon came along the My Chanh River, which separated Quang Tri Province on the border with North Vietnam from Thua Thien Province north of Hue.

The North Vietnamese quickly took Quang Tri City and the entire province, and for a while the road was open to Hue. It looked as if the south was about to lose all of Eye Corps, and perhaps more. I ran into two friends in Hue on my way north, Peter Arnett and Horst Fass of the Associated Press. Peter, a jolly New Zealander, had won a Pulitzer back in the days when David Halberstam was becoming a legend, and Horst's photographs had won one too. Horst had been a boy in Germany during the last days of World War II and recalled being given a single-shot rocket called a Panzerfaust and told to shoot the first Russian tank he saw coming down the street. Luckily for him, none did. Horst and Peter were hatching a scheme to "rescue" Cham statues from the museum in Danang, ferreting them away to the south. The Cham were a vanished race in this part of Vietnam, but their beautiful statuary remained, reminiscent of the Khmer art of Cambodia. As it turned out the statues didn't need rescuing, as the South Vietnamese were about to hold their line on the My Chanh River.

The next morning I headed north to the My Chanh. I got there just in time for a decisive battle that saved Hue and the northern provinces. As night fell I was huddled next to a lone American adviser among a battalion of South Vietnamese marines. In the darkness we heard the unmistakable sound of tank treads clanking in the darkness. It was my first experience in a battle against tanks. Would the South Vietnamese hold, or would they flee as they had done at Quang Tri? In the next hours, as shells came down on our positions, the American adviser talked softly into his radio. I remember the American saying: "Lend me our assets." And within moments the assets arrived. Naval gunfire from American ships off the coast, planes screaming in from bases in Thailand lighting up the night with explosions. The South Vietnamese marines were armed with new wire-guided antitank missiles, and they used them well. There was no panic. The marines fired and fired again, and you could see North Vietnamese tanks going up in flames.

It was quite a night, but the My Chanh line held. The next morning I inspected the burned-out tanks on the plain ahead of us, littered with dead North Vietnamese. The American adviser told me that the North Vietnamese had not maneuvered their tanks well. They brought their tanks to a halt before they fired their cannons, and that had proved fatal time and time again during that long night. One dead North Vietnamese officer had a belt buckle with a red star. I contemplated taking it, but with a shiver I could imagine myself dead on another plain with someone taking that same belt buckle from my corpse. I left it well alone.

The South Vietnamese's holding of the My Chanh line has been used by revisionist historians to argue that if the United States had not taken away logistic and air support for the Saigon government when the final test came in 1975, maybe Saigon would not have fallen. It is an argument I do not buy.

After a break from the wars to take up a Nieman Fellowship at Harvard, a program for midcareer journalists, I was offered and accepted a job with the *Washington Post*. It was 1972, and the *Post,* under Ben Bradlee's editorship, was considered the writer's paper. It was then in its moment of Watergate glory. I had been unhappy with *Time*-style journalism for some time, and this was my chance to write for a newspaper.

8

The Americans Depart

Upon joining the *Post* in the summer of 1972 I moved my family to Washington. I hoped it would be a brief period before going back to Asia. I was aware that the *Post* had hired me with that in mind, but, as with all new recruits, I had to do my time in the home office.

JB had worked for the Graham family, proprietors of the *Washington Post,* for several of her college summers, looking after their children. I once visited their farm in Virginia before JB and I were married when I was still in the navy. Phil Graham was at his best then, active and in the thick of politics, before depression overcame him and drove him to suicide. Mrs. Graham had been gracious and charming, and after I had left JB asked Phil Graham what he thought of me. The reply was, "Well, he doesn't annoy me," which I suppose was the best I could hope for. But that had been years before, and I said nothing about it to my new *Washington Post* bosses and colleagues.

However, on my first day on the job Mrs. Graham sailed into the city room. She was now publisher in her own right and Watergate was the talk of the town. An editor said to her, "I'd like to introduce you to a new reporter we have just hired, David Greenway."

"Oh, I know David," she said. "He married my au pair girl."

One of my first assignments was to cover a press conference that Secretary of State Henry Kissinger had called in October of 1972 in which he stunned the world with the words "peace is at hand." At long last the North Vietnamese, after torturous negotiations in Paris, had agreed to a cease-fire on our terms, he said. For those of us in the audience who had reported from Vietnam it was an electrifying moment. But as it turned out, Henry Kissinger had misread the situation.

We didn't learn until later that Kissinger had so much trouble explaining the terms of his peace treaty to South Vietnam's president, Nguyen Van Thieu. When he did so, Kissinger cabled Nixon from Saigon to say: "We face the paradoxical situation that the North, which has effectively lost, is acting as if it won; while the South, which has effectively won, is acting as if it has lost. One of the major tasks now is to restore realities and get the psychological upper hand." Kissinger thought that Thieu did not understand the scope of Hanoi's concessions. But Thieu undertood the situation better than Kissinger.

"The issue is the life and death of South Vietnam and its 17 million people . . . ," Thieu told the American ambassador, Ellsworth Bunker. "Our position is very unfortunate. We have been very faithful to the Americans, and now we feel as if we are being sacrificed . . . If we accept the document as it now stands we will commit suicide . . . , and I will be committing suicide."[*]

Thieu was right. The fatal flaw in Kissinger's peace deal was that it allowed the North Vietnamese to maintain their forces deep inside South Vietnam, effectively outflanking the south and putting the Central Highlands in peril should the North Vietnamese decide to attack again in defiance of the treaty, which is exactly what they did.

To be fair to Kissinger, he was dealing with an America that was fed up with the Vietnam War. The US was not going to bulk up its forces and push the North Vietnamese back across the border. Kissinger thought that if the North Vietnamese cheated on the peace agreement the entire might of the United States could come down hard on the cheaters. But even as Kissinger was negotiating in Paris, the political will to continue the war was crumbling in the United States. American troops were leaving and the US Congress

---

[*] *New York Times*, "Word for Word: Nixon and Vietnam Grumbling Over an Unraveling War," by Tim Weiner, April 20, 2000.

effectively ended America's retaliatory capabilities by banning any further air strikes the following summer. As Kissinger would later acknowledge, "it was not Thieu's fault that we had simply come to the end of the road—largely as the result of our domestic divisions."[*]

After some months the *Post* named me as their new bureau chief in Hong Kong, where my family settled, but it was to Saigon that they sent me early in 1973. I soon discovered Kissinger's cease-fire was in name only. Vietnamese on both sides were still dying because each side was trying to consolidate its position and expand its territory at the expense of the other. The agreement allowed forces to stay in place, so both sides raised their flags over the territory they controlled. Traveling around the countryside, I was interested to see how many districts were flying Vietcong flags. Many of the areas that the Americans had thought pacified and solidly under government control were not. All the talk about strategic hamlets and protecting the population from the Vietcong and North Vietnamese had been a chimera.

The peace that was not a peace was to be supervised by the International Commission of Control and Supervision. The ICCS was composed of representatives of four nonbelligerent countries. Poland and Hungary were Communist countries. Canada and Indonesia were non-Communist countries. The Canadians would later be replaced with the Iranians, who, in the days of the shah, were considered reliably pro-Western.

None had been given much time to deploy, and although the Canadians had issued their men tropical shorts in the British tradition, their army underpants were of the boxer type and often hung down lower than the shorts, making a fashion statement several decades before such a thing became cool among teenagers.

ICCS teams were ready to move into the countryside in March of that year, but at least in one case that proved to be more difficult than had been anticipated. When asked to deploy in the ruins of Quang Tri City, near the border between the two Vietnams, the Poles and Hungarians complained

---

[*] Henry Kissinger, *White House Years* (Boston and Toronto: Little, Brown and Company, 1979), 1375.

of "vipers." Somehow this word got translated into "wipers" when it filtered down to Saigon, and at first the Americans didn't know what they were talking about. But the Poles and the Hungarians soon made it known that they were worried about poisonous snakes.

To us who knew Quang Tri, poisonous snakes had never been one of our worries. The Canadians came up with the statistic that, in all the years of war, only one American had ever died of snakebite in the entire country, but the Poles and the Hungarians still demanded viper traps. It turned out that in the vast arsenal that America had brought to Vietnam over the decades, viper traps had been overlooked. The Canadians solved the problem by finding an old World War II manual that said that spreading oil around the perimeter would keep snakes out. The Hungarians suggested that garlic would be just as good, which led to the inevitable rumor that the Hungarians were worried about vampires rather than vipers.

There was a Hungarian ICCS delegate—I have forgotten his name now—who was said to be willing to talk to Western reporters. A colleague, who was perhaps more sophisticated and had better linguistic skills than the rest of us, got into a conversation with the Hungarian about poker. The Hungarian waxed lyrical about the game and invited my colleague to come around that very night for a game.

"Did you listen closely?" asked my reporter friend. The Hungarian's rhapsody about the game, the four sides of the table and hidden cards, was a metaphor for the four-sided ICCS, and the four sides represented by the Americans, the North Vietnamese, the Vietcong, and the South Vietnamese, my colleague said. It meant that the Hungarian was willing to discuss inside information, and my colleague was going to harvest whatever scoops would be dealt at the poker table. He said he was sorry I had not been invited. The next day I asked my friend if the evening had lived up to his expectations. He said he didn't want to talk about it. But he finally confessed that what the Hungarian was talking about had not been a metaphor. The Hungarian simply wanted to play poker and had no intention of handing out scoops.

—

In accordance with the treaty agreed upon in Paris, American troops were to leave Vietnam forthwith. On March 30, 1973, the last contingent departed from Saigon's Tan Son Nhut Airport aboard a silver C-141 air force jet shortly after five p.m., bound for Clark Field in the Philippines, Honolulu, and home. It was a blazing hot afternoon. A North Vietnamese officer, part of North Vietnam's official delegation, which was also part of the peace agreement, recorded the event on a movie camera. It reminded me of the Communist film crews that had flown into Dien Bien Phu to re-create the French defeat nineteen years before.

Lieutenant Colonel Bui Tin, who had often acted as the North Vietnamese delegation's spokesman, was on hand in his well-pressed uniform. Bui Tin, Zelig-like, kept showing up at historic events. He had been at Dien Bien Phu, and he would be present again in 1975 to accept South Vietnam's total surrender. "This is an historic day," he said, addressing the departing Americans. "It is the first time in one hundred years that there are no foreign troops on the soil of Vietnam." It wasn't quite true. There was a small number of American military men staying on as military attachés, and a contingent of marines to guard the American embassy. But it was true enough in that there were no longer any foreign soldiers that could make any difference in Vietnam's future anymore. There were piles of helmets, combat boots, fatigues, and other military paraphernalia left about, which the departing GIs were leaving behind.

Bui Tin had a small bamboo scroll depicting a Hanoi pagoda and a pack of Ho Chi Minh playing cards to give the symbolic last soldier out. A sheepish master sergeant from Minnesota accepted them, red cheeked with embarrassment.

The South Vietnamese officers present seemed put out that a North Vietnamese was getting all the attention, and they pointed to a row of twenty-one coffins, draped in the red and yellow striped flag of the republic, some yards away. They contained South Vietnamese soldiers killed in the post-cease-fire fighting, and a woman kneeling by a coffin tried to straighten out one of the flags that kept blowing off in the wind.

It was a day of ceremonies and speech making. Upon closing down MACV, which had been established eight years before, General Frederick

Weyand stood at attention in a sun-baked parking lot while a recording of "The Star-Spangled Banner" was played over a loudspeaker. The general said that the US had accomplished its mission to "prevent an all-out attempt by an aggressor to impose its will through raw military force." He said that the "rights of the people of the Republic of Vietnam to shape their own destiny and to provide for their self-determination has been upheld."

None of us knew then that the rights of the South Vietnamese people were about to be extinguished in a show of raw military force only two years hence. Those "aggressors," however, would consider themselves liberators.

The South Vietnamese gave Weyand a stirring send-off, with a band playing "Auld Lang Syne." President Thieu thanked the Americans for all they had done in "this historic struggle."

An ugly scene, perhaps more rich in symbolism than the official speeches, took place when a couple of hundred Vietnamese civilians broke through the wire even before the last American had departed. They looted the commissary, and in minutes they had dragged out tables, chairs, fans, canned goods—everything that wasn't bolted to the floor, and some things that were. South Vietnamese military police helped them move the stolen goods through the wire. Eggs, flour, mustard, ketchup, cold cereal, and ice cream lay together on the floor in one gorgeous omelet. "I don't think they are trying to belittle us or anything," said a philosophical American. "They were just trying to get what they can while they can."

In describing all this I reminded our readers that seventeen years before, on a similarly hot spring day, the last of the French expeditionary force had departed Saigon forever. Wreaths had been laid in front of the monument for those who had died for France, and the departing troops had marched down Tu Do Street, which, according to a local French newspaper, "became rue Catinat again" for a few moments as the French colors passed. General Pierre Jacquot, commander of all French forces in Indochina, sailed down the Saigon River bound for France on the liner SS *Cambodge*. And now, another turn of the Vietnamese wheel was taking place.

America, too, following in the footsteps of the French, had gone to war to keep Vietnam in its orbit, and like the French were about to lose.

Because the Vietcong were anxious to legitimize their areas of control in that spring of 1973, there was an opportunity to interview them that hadn't been possible before. Frances FitzGerald and I hatched up a scheme to visit the Vietcong in their forest lair in the contested province of Chuong Thien, deep in the Mekong River delta. Tran Dung Tien, the *Post*'s able interpreter, agreed to come too, a courageous decision because no one knew how the Vietcong might react to a fellow Vietnamese whose politics were not theirs. Originally, Martin Woollacott of the *Guardian,* one of the best reporters in Vietnam, was to join us, but illness prevented him.

Frances FitzGerald, "Frankie" to her friends, was already a famous journalist. Her book *Fire in the Lake* had just taken America by storm, giving many their first insights into the Vietnamese culture and psyche in their clash with America's intrusive power. She was soon to be awarded the Pulitzer Prize, and the National Book Award, but that was some weeks away. She had come back to Vietnam on assignment for the *New Yorker.*

We drove the *Washington Post*'s car deep into the delta, and outside a small village called Long My, at the edge of the forest, villagers were watching a silver South Vietnamese jet bombing Vietcong positions away to the east. They stood silently as clouds of black smoke rose in the afternoon sky. This was a sort of no-man's-land between government-controlled areas and the territory of the Provisional Revolutionary Government (PRG), as the Vietcong called themselves.

We had sent a small boy into the forest to try to make contact for us, taking a message saying we were American journalists who would like to tell their story to the world. After a wait that seemed hours long, after I had begun to think this wasn't going to work, armed men began to emerge from the tall grass at the forest's edge. I was very nervous. My only sightings of Vietcong before had been in flashes of gunfire.

Frankie, however, was unconcerned. She assured me that she knew a Vietcong representative in Paris and that all would be well. I admired her sangfroid, but I was not sure these youngsters would care. Crossing enemy lines is always dangerous. You had to get beyond the first encounter and get passed up the line to more-senior officers.

A dozen or more appeared, most of them uniformed in dark green jackets and hats, although some of them wore the traditional black pajamas of the delta. Only a few carried AK-47s, the standard Soviet assault rifle of the North Vietnamese. Most were armed with captured American M16 rifles and grenade launchers. They carried American field radios, too, and most wore dressy Seiko watches with expansion wristbands such as could be bought in the better shops in Saigon.

They were surprisingly young, these men of the forest, and at first encounter they wore the exaggerated frowns of revolutionary posters. For half an hour there seemed to be some question of whether we were prisoners or guests, but eventually a girl cadre appeared with the red, blue, and yellow flag of the PRG and the tension broke as the daylight faded.

Here is what I wrote for the *Washington Post:*

> Pale lights bob and flicker like fireflies through the banana trees and over the rice paddies dry in the harvest now and white in the moonlight. The lights are dimmed US Army flashlights, but they belong to the Vietcong, who move through the countryside, as they have always done, long after the government troops have locked themselves up in their mud forts for the night. There is the sound of artillery in the distance, for the war in this contested province still goes on much as it has for the last 10 years.

Soon we were brought to a jungle camp, where a handsome man, obviously in authority, said: "We welcome you, and it does not matter if you are journalists or CIA because we have won the war." Just before midnight we were told that a senior PRG official would receive us now, and we left this time in a small boat, riding through the darkness farther into the interior with our boatmen singing revolutionary songs to impress us.

The senior official—we never knew his name—was clearly an educated man. His conversation ran from battle to Vietnamese poetry. He said he had been wounded nine times, and had once had coconut water put in his veins as an intravenous fluid—one of the many tricks Vietcong doctors had learned for saving lives despite the lack of modern medicine.

The drift of conversation during that long night with the enemy was their absolute conviction that they had won the war. The importance of the Paris agreements was that the Americans had admitted their defeat. As I write these words now, forty years later, I contrast this certainty on the part of the Vietcong with what the Americans were saying at the time. General Creighton Abrams thought Hanoi was agreeing to peace "because they [have] lost and they [know] it."* But the men of the forest thought otherwise. The Paris accords were just another milestone in the long history of Vietnamese fighting foreigners, said our host. The Americans were simply going the way of the "Mongols, the Chinese, the Japanese, the French," our PRG official said to us.

These Vietcong officials made no effort to hide the fact that the North Vietnamese Army was also in the region. The northerners had come to help their brothers in the south, they said, because there was only one Vietnam. We were given some food, and the talk went on and on into the small hours of the morning. When we started to nod, we were told that it wasn't every day we got to talk to a high official in the PRG, and that we should stay awake. But it did begin to feel like Scheherazade working on her nine hundredth tale. Faces gleamed in the light of the Coleman lamps, and the forest was alive with the sound of insects.

It was the antiforeign nature of the struggle with which they sought to impress us. As for Nguyen Van Thieu, the president of South Vietnam, "he is like a corpse being held up by the Americans," they said. "If the Americans should let him he would collapse." The Vietcong told us that they were willing to abide by the terms of the cease-fire but would fight if the South continued fighting. "Today you see us in the forest, but tomorrow you will see us in the cities," we were told.

For Henry Kissinger and Richard Nixon, the peace accords had awarded them peace with honor, or so they thought. But, as I wrote for the *Washington*

---

* Henry Kissinger, *White House Years* (Boston and Toronto: Little, Brown and Company, 1979), 1374.

Post at the time: "To the PRG of Long My it seemed that peace with honor meant nothing less than the completion of the Vietnamese revolution started so long ago by Ho Chi Minh, and that the American withdrawal and the cease-fire agreement were significant victories, but by no means the last step along that road." That last step was not far off.

9

A Curious Coda

When the long night in the forest was over, the Vietcong took us back to a main road where we could see traffic passing back and forth. It came home to me that this pattern, with the Vietcong owning the night and the government in control by day, had been going on for the better part of a decade and before that during the French war.

It was very much against the laws of South Vietnam to have anything to do with the enemy, and we were subject to arrest when we were back in government-held territory. And arrested we were, when we emerged from the forest, and taken to a military headquarters; I no longer remember where. This time it was Frankie's turn to be nervous and mine to assure her that, in the end, the South Vietnamese authorities weren't going to get rough with us.

In order to preserve my notes, I pretended to hide papers in my socks. "Aha!" said one of the soldiers guarding us, and a great fuss was made to make me take off my shoes and socks. I made the proper protestations but then gave in to force majeure. There was some disappointment when they found no notes in my socks, but this diversion distracted them from looking further, or in my pockets, where my notes were. In due course we were released and made our way back to our car, still on the road where we had left it, and then to Saigon.

I later heard from our friend Frank Wisner that there had been a terrific hue and cry when our car had been found abandoned by the side of the road. Frank, a foreign-service officer whose father had been a top CIA official along with Frankie's father, Desmond FitzGerald, in the glory days of the CIA, had heard that the agency was not going to let the disappearance of Frankie go unattended, or if necessary, unavenged. "You could have disappeared without a trace and it wouldn't have mattered, Greenway," Frank told me, but the daughter of Desmond FitzGerald was something else altogether. Thank God we showed up before a rescue mission could be organized.

My story made a bit of a stir when the *Post* published it, and I was woken in the middle of the night by an anxious William Shawn, a legendary and gentlemanly editor of the *New Yorker*. He was concerned about Frankie, and by the tone of his voice I could tell that he feared she had faced the fate worse than death at the hands of the dreaded Vietcong. I was happy to confirm Frankie's well-being.

A last, curious coda came about when a US army officer contacted me in Saigon with an intriguing deal. He said he could have us inserted by helicopter into the depths of the Ca Mao Peninsula, which had been in Vietcong hands for decades. No reporters, as far as we knew, had ever been there—certainly not in recent years. We would be allowed to talk to anyone we wanted, and afterward we would be brought out again by helicopter with a tremendous scoop for the *Washington Post* and a prize-winning article for the *New Yorker*.

I wondered, what was in it for the parties involved? We were told that the North Vietnamese and the Vietcong were anxious to show the extent to which they controlled territory in South Vietnam, and therefore were willing to receive us in their base camps. All the Americans wanted was for us to keep careful notes on any captured Americans or American graves. An exchange of prisoners was part of the peace agreement, and the Pentagon knew that the subject of prisoners would become a hot issue, as it later did.

The only fly in this ointment was the government of South Vietnam, the fourth party to the Paris Peace Accords. They did not want the North Vietnamese nor the Vietcong showing off how much territory they controlled in the south, and my *Post* article on our night in the forest had angered Saigon. They might try to shoot down the helicopter, so they were to be kept in the dark.

In the end we decided against it. We thought at the time that the trip would have been too much of a US government mission and not something an independent press should get involved with. Today, however, I think we might have been a bit too self-righteous, and it would have made a wonderful story.

Years later, reading Henry Kissinger's memoirs of the Paris negotiations, it struck me how much Nguyen Van Thieu and the South Vietnamese were the odd man out, just as they would have been should we have taken the US military up on its offer to visit Ca Mao. It was very much a Washington–Hanoi deal, with the Vietcong and the South Vietnamese left to do their masters' bidding.

Years later, Hamid Karzai, the Afghan leader whom America put in power, began to feel as Thieu had felt: that the Americans were trying to make deals with the Taliban behind his back. Karzai, like Thieu, could never escape the fact that he was America's man, and ruled only because of American support.

10

The Fall of Saigon

In the spring of 1975, on orders from the *Washington Post,* I came back to Saigon from Phnom Penh, where I had been for many weeks, just before that city fell to the implacable Khmer Rouge. South Vietnam appeared to be collapsing, and that was a bigger story in the eyes of the *Post* than even the impending fall of Phnom Penh. The entire American enterprise in Indochina was falling apart with a speed no one had anticipated.

President Thieu, without telling his American allies, had decided on a military evacuation of the Central Highlands to consolidate his forces. The evacuation was ill planned and ended in panic and rout. Soon Hue, Danang, Nha Trang, and all the coastal cities were falling as South Vietnam's once-proud army simply disintegrated.

Soon after I arrived, I quoted President Gerald Ford as having recently said that "the will of the South Vietnamese people to fight for their freedom is best evidenced by the fact that they are fleeing the North Vietnamese." "The opposite appears to be true," I wrote. "All over the northern part of the country the will to fight vanished when the panic struck, and some of the South Vietnamese army's best units dissolved without firing a shot. When discipline was gone some of the soldiers vented their rage and frustration by looting and killing people, and many of the refugees speak with contempt and hatred about the venality and corruption of the Saigon government. Many central

Vietnamese hate the Saigon government, but ran because of their fear and uncertainty for the future, and simply because everyone else was running."

As the North Vietnamese swept south in their final offensive, entire cities were abandoned by their defenders before the northerners actually arrived. The South Vietnamese defenders had simply deserted. Hundreds had tried to claw their way onto the last departing aircraft, some even hanging on to the wheels as the debacle spread southward.

For those like Joe Alsop and the now-dead Henry Luce, who had seen the fight for Vietnam through the lens of Chiang Kai-shek's defeat in China, their worst fears were being realized. South Vietnam was ending in much the same way as the better-equipped but less motivated Nationalist Chinese had lost to Mao's Communists a quarter century before.

With no Americans left in the northern towns, and the South Vietnamese command consistently unreliable, reporters turned to the food markets for information on what cities had fallen and which were still awaiting their fate. If shrimp was still available in the fish stalls, for example, it meant that the North Vietnamese had not yet arrived in Nha Trang, even though the city had officially fallen according to the South Vietnamese command.

Saigon, in those last weeks of war, had become a city of infectious fear and despair, of exhaustion beyond fatigue, of quick tears and tortured dreams. Vietnamese friends I had known for years would come with drawn faces to plead for help. It was hard to look into their eyes and not see an accusation of betrayal.

So tired and stressed did I become that I almost filed a dream to make the last edition of the *Washington Post*. I awoke from a shallow sleep early one morning in a panic. I had forgotten, I thought, to mention in my story sent the previous evening that President Thieu had had a meeting with the French and American ambassadors in which, against character, he had shown flexibility about making a deal with the Communists. No such meeting had taken place, but in my fevered brain I had dreamt it. Given the time zones between Washington and Saigon I could just make the last edition of the *Post*. So, throwing on my clothes, I rushed to the telegraph office.

As I started to write, however, the still-vivid dream began to dissolve in my brain and I stopped writing. I was shocked at how close I had come to filing a false story because of fatigue. Our editor, Ben Bradlee, was clearly worried about us and sometimes called us on the telephone from Washington to see how we were getting on. Finally we had to tell him, "Look, Ben, it is your lunchtime but the middle of the night here and we are dying for some sleep."

President Thieu was finally persuaded to step down, and flew away into exile, as the Americans tried to find a figure more acceptable to the Communists. But the Communists were having none of it.

As North Vietnamese forces drew closer, strangers would clutch at foreigners in the streets of Saigon begging to be rescued. Long lines of Vietnamese could be seen waiting at the gates of foreign embassies hoping for visas, while inside diplomats burned official papers in chancery gardens, the ashes floating out over embassy walls. The embassies were sending their staffs out. "The diplomats are going out all over Indochina," one said, paraphrasing Lord Gray on the eve of World War I.

Here is a dispatch I wrote for the *Washington Post* in those last despairing days when the corrupt, venal Saigon that had long ago sold itself to foreigners was dying.

SAIGON, April 25. When evening comes to Saigon, foreigners still gather on the open-sided terrace of the old-fashioned French colonial hotel, The Continental Palace, to drink an aperitif as they have done for 50 years. The lights begin to come on, the waiters in white suits take orders, and the slow fans on the high ceilings bring some relief in the tropical heat.

But when the hour of the curfew comes, and it now comes at 8 PM, the customers begin to wander away from the little tables and wicker chairs, and strange, and even terrifying, shapes begin to gather in the darkness outside. It is the hour when beggars, cripples, prostitutes, junkies and transvestites become desperate for one last pitch. There are children, dirty and un-cared for, whose only foreign words are "You, you give me money." Girls, some vacuous with narcotics, all of them begging and pleading, pulling at the last of the potential customers before the night and the curfew take all the foreigners away. Fear pervades all contacts and all conversations now, fear of the unknown, of what will come.

You could see the underlying tension in the puffy, drawn look on people's faces. Suicides spread like a virus carried by fear. A Saigon police colonel walked up to the South Vietnamese war memorial in Lam Son Square and saluted before he drew his pistol and shot himself. Mothers would offer their daughters in marriage in order to facilitate escape.

One Vietnamese acquaintance bought poison for himself and his family, but when the time came he couldn't do it. So he sent his children away to live with relatives who had not been "corrupted" by working with Americans.

Some Vietnamese had decided to stay come what may. "Perhaps it is better that you take away all the war profiteers, secret policemen and interrogators," a Vietnamese contact told me. "We Vietnamese make very bad exiles. Not as bad as the Russians, who cry even more than we do because of homesickness. But we are not like the Chinese, who can get along and prosper anywhere." Another friend had a place on a plane out but was told he could take only his wife and children. In the Confucian ethic of extended families, this was appalling to him. "One can have many children," he said, "but only one mother. Only a savage people would leave their mothers behind."

But they were in the minority. The vast majority were caught up in the infection of fear—fear of Communism, yes, but more just from fear itself. Time after time refugees would tell me that the reason they fled was that everybody else was fleeing.

It was at this time that the American press and television reporters in Saigon began a Scarlet Pimpernel operation to smuggle their staffs out of the country. We felt that our loyal Vietnamese employees would be in harm's way if the North Vietnamese took revenge on all those contaminated by working for Americans.

The American embassy was wise to our scheme, but the South Vietnamese authorities were not about to let this kind of evacuation go forward. So we had to work this in secret, taking employees and their families to the airport in ones and twos so that the authorities would not catch on. On a typical day a Vietnamese family might be told to wait in the cathedral until exactly five past eleven and then come out and wait until a van, circling the square, stopped for them.

Malcolm Browne, a *New York Times* reporter who had won his Pulitzer when he worked for the AP in the early sixties and was married to a Vietnamese, was often my partner in these people-smuggling operations. One time, with a couple of male employees whose families had already left for the States, we were turned back by the airport police, who were by now onto our tactics. We had the two of them in the backseat of a big American car with Mal and me in the front seat when we were stopped. What to do?

We shamelessly decided to play the colonial card. We went back, dressed up in suits and ties, and sat in the backseat while one of our Vietnamese drove the car. Seeing a Vietnamese driving two Americans, especially dressed in suits in the backseat, seemed right and proper to the guards, so they waved us through, never suspecting that it was the chauffeur who was about to board a plane for Clark Field in the Philippines. Then we drove the car back to Saigon and got in the backseat again while our second Vietnamese émigré drove the car. Years later the film *Driving Miss Daisy* reminded me of our role playing Daisy during the last days of Saigon.

The news organizations back home were responsible for these new refugees. The American authorities asked us to sign a statement that said: "The *Washington Post* guarantees onward passage and financial support for its employees and their families." And the *Post*, to its credit, did just that and found jobs for most of them too.

Our rescue missions had been just in time, for it was clear now that Saigon had very little time left to live. Here is another dispatch for the *Post* I wrote on the last evening before the American evacuation.

SAIGON, April 28. On the two-lane highway to Bien Hoa thousands upon thousands of refugees could be seen pouring in towards the capital. With darkness descending, under a rain-swollen sky pierced by lightning, the columns stretched away over the rolling countryside like a moving dragon in the reddish light of the passing day. Buses, cars, tractors and bicycles inched slowly forward with the noise of engines and the clashing of gears blending into a coughing groan. Police were out in force trying to prevent the refugees from coming into Saigon itself. People who live in shacks along the road were all out watching in silence as once again whole populations were on the move.

That same evening, as the sun set, Mal Browne and I saw a jet plane over Saigon in a steep climb. Mal, who knew more about aircraft than I, insisted it was a MiG, made in either Russia or China. We looked at each other in astonishment. I never had it confirmed that a MiG had appeared over Saigon that day, but I trusted Mal's judgment.

American officials, overworked, fatigued, and desperately in denial, had sought a third way during those last days and weeks. Maybe the North Vietnamese would agree to allow Saigon and a part of the south a temporary respite? Maybe, rather than the north trying to absorb too many unhappy southerners all at once, there could be a transition period, a coalition government in the south, at least for a decent interval. Who knew? The French held out some hope that a soft landing might be found for Saigon and the Mekong River delta. But it was all wishful thinking.

The result of all this wishful thinking was that plans for an orderly evacuation of Americans, and Vietnamese who had worked for us, kept getting delayed. Alcohol soothed American tensions, reminding me of stories of Berlin in 1945 as the end neared, with many of the inmates in Hitler's claustrophobic bunker slightly intoxicated much of the time.

America's last day in Vietnam began with artillery shells landing somewhere in the city, the sleep-destroying sound coming in through the open windows of my room early in the hours before the dawn. In the darkness my colleagues were gathering in the halls of the Continental.

Some had the sort of radio that could pick up radio traffic between the American embassy and the few remaining American marines at the airport. "Tan Son Nhut being heavily shelled," said a voice. "Four rounds in five seconds on the flight line." Two marines had already been killed. If Peter Dewey had been the first American to die in the Vietnam War in 1945, then Corporals Charles McMahon Jr. and Darwin Lee Judge were the last. Their bodies would be repatriated the following year.

As daylight broke on April 29, 1975, several of us went across the street and up to the roof of the Caravelle Hotel. It was one of Saigon's tallest buildings and offered a grandstand view. We could see fires burning out of control at the airport and a few South Vietnamese planes circling the city. With sinking stomachs we watched the lazy arc of a heat-seeking missile rise up and inexorably find its way to an airplane, which immediately disintegrated. None of us wanted to look each other in the eye, because we knew that very few of us would leave the city alive if the North Vietnamese decided to oppose the American air evacuation that was about to begin.

Years later the North Vietnamese commander, General Van Tien Dung, wrote that he had received instructions from Hanoi to press on with the attack on Saigon but not to interfere with an American evacuation—an order that he protested but obeyed.

Days before, Americans in the city had been given little maps with instructions telling them where to report "should it be felt necessary for US personnel to report to their designated assembly areas." Even in this last hour, the embassy had resorted to the same euphemistic style that had permeated the war. A style where every ambush would be called a "meeting engagement." Every junk that we sank at sea became a "water-borne logistics craft." Even at the end, language was used to mask the hard truth.

We had also been told to listen to the radio for a weather report. If we heard "One hundred five degrees and rising," followed by thirty seconds of Bing Crosby singing "White Christmas," we were to report to our evacuation areas, though the word "evacuation" was never used. I never met anyone who actually heard such a broadcast, but it was pretty obvious that we would have to make our way to the embassy now that the airport was under siege.

At the embassy itself we found marine guards furiously chopping down a tree in the courtyard behind the chancery in order to make room for a helicopter landing area. The tree had become something of a symbol. Ambassador Graham Martin had refused to let his staff cut it down before this moment, because he thought any sign that Americans might be abandoning Saigon would sow panic among the Vietnamese.

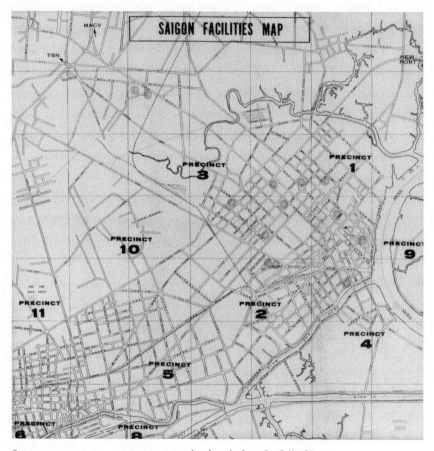

Saigon evacuation map given out in the days before the fall of Saigon.

Martin had held on to his delusions of a negotiated peace until the very end. As a result many Vietnamese who had worked for the Americans were left behind. Now, tired and sick with pneumonia, the old Cold War warrior was keeping up appearances till the end, even walking back to his quarters to fetch his dog in time to be evacuated.

Other Americans could be seen carrying out charts with red and blue arrows showing the irrepressible advance of the North Vietnamese. Others were burning thousands of dollars in US currency.

As morning turned to afternoon, the panic that Martin had feared came down upon us like a squall line. Hundreds upon hundreds of Vietnamese headed for the embassy, seething with the rolling-eyed fear of animals caught in a burning barn—all beseeching to be let in. They squeezed against the gates, tried to climb the fence, only to be thrown down by outnumbered marine guards.

A few were allowed inside. I watched a South Vietnamese general being squeezed in the main gate with a suitcase, while others were forced back. Some would try to press notes through the wire. "I am working for the Americans," said one. "Please tell Mr. Jacobson I am here."

I ran into the CIA's station chief, Thomas Polgar, who muttered darkly that radio intercepts indicated that the North Vietnamese were about to shell the embassy. Happily that never happened, even though a few helicopters did receive small-arms fire. That might have been from infuriated South Vietnamese. In any event, none were shot down.

Polgar, too, was the victim of self-delusions and, ignoring his less gullible staff, refused to believe their increasingly gloomy intelligence reports and kept thinking that a last-minute deal could be made with the Communists. A Hungarian-American, Polgar made friends with the Hungarian delegation of the International Commission of Control and Supervision (ICCS). Hungary, being a Communist country then, was more than willing to stoke Polgar's illusions.

As the republic's last afternoon progressed, the enormous crowd outside the embassy kept building. Keyes Beech, an American reporter caught outside the fence and trying to get in, would later write: "Once we moved into that seething mass we ceased to be correspondents. We were only men fighting for our lives, scratching, clawing, pushing ever closer to the wall. We were like animals." Vietnamese trying to scale the fence and embassy walls were brutally beaten back.

The *Washington Post* was down to two reporters, myself and the bureau chief, Phil McCombs. Midway through the afternoon, we realized that we could still file for the same day's newspaper on the American evacuation of Saigon. We fought our way through the ever-increasing crowds around the embassy and found our way back to the *Washington Post* office. Reuters, which was next door, usually transmitted our stories to Washington. But the Reuters office was abandoned, so we went back to the Continental, where *Time* magazine had an office.

There was An, my oldest Vietnamese friend, surrounded by family members who had not chosen to leave the country. I asked An if we could use *Time*'s telex to file for the *Post*. The Washington Post Company, which then owned *Newsweek*, was in competition with *Time*, but An said that Henry Luce would have wanted me to use the telex. So with the permission of An, and the ghost of *Time*'s founder, we filed a last story on the final American evacuation for the *Washington Post*. Getting back into the embassy, with so many fear-struck people trying to get in, was not an easy task, but we made it.

I toyed with staying on after the fall, as a few reporters did. But I thought it would end in a long house arrest by the North Vietnamese, locked up in a hotel, unable to file, maybe for months. I never suspected we would be killed if we got through the transition from one government to another, always the most dangerous time. But I didn't think I would be able to file. I was wrong. The North Vietnamese did allow correspondents to file their stories for quite some time after the fall before they finally shut that down.

With the choice made, I tossed the keys of the *Washington Post* car to James Fenton, a *Washington Post* stringer, and today a famous British poet, who was staying on.

When the helicopters arrived from the South China Sea, the wash from their rotors tore open the plastic bags awaiting burning, and thousands of papers flew into the air in a confetti of secrets. McCombs and I took our turn to get aboard a helicopter just as it was getting dark. A nervous door gunner asked me: "Where are they? Where are they?" I told him the North Vietnamese had not yet arrived.

I had a small bag of clothes in one hand and my faithful typewriter in the other when the door gunner said: "Only one bag." Without hesitation I threw away my clothes. I had begun to feel that it was my beloved typewriter that actually wrote my stories for me, and that I would be unable to write without it, so I clutched it to my chest and boarded the helicopter.

I caught my last glimpse of the dying republic out the helicopter window as we rose above the city in a sudden squall. I could see the rain-washed streets down by the waterfront, where masses of panicked people were trying to force their way onto overcrowded boats headed down the Saigon River to the sea. Away to the north I could see great ammunition dumps blowing up and raging fires in the distance.

We crossed the coast in the gathering dark. An American fleet lay waiting below us in the South China Sea. South Vietnamese helicopters, like butter-flies borne on an offshore wind, landed briefly on American ships before being tossed overboard to make room for more. Some crashed into the sea before reaching safety. All about us lay the flotillas of hopelessly overfilled boats packed with Vietnamese, like flotsam and jetsam left on the surface after a gigantic ship has gone down. These were the first of the "boat people" who would in years to come fill the refugee camps of Southeast Asia and beyond.

I jotted in my notebook a quote from a James Russell Lowell poem that can be seen inscribed near the graves of British Redcoats who fell at Concord Bridge back in Massachusetts in that same month just two hundred years previously, at the start of our own revolution. "They came three thousand miles and died to keep the past upon the throne." In our case we had come ten thousand miles to Vietnam to do the same thing.

After thirty years of first supporting the French and then fighting our own war, it was all coming to an inglorious and ignominious end. The evacuation went on through the night, the last being taken off the roof early in the morn-ing of the next day, when North Vietnamese tanks burst through the gates of Saigon's presidential palace.

Singapore's foreign minister S. Rajaratman would later say that the fall of Saigon marked the true close of the colonial era in Southeast Asia, the ef-fective and symbolic end of four centuries of Western political and military intervention in the region.

Many of the Vietnamese who tried to gain entrance to the embassy that day would spend years of hard labor in "reeducation camps," where many died. It was not like the evacuation of Phnom Penh in neighboring Cambodia, nor were the Vietnamese as hard on the losers as were the Khmer Rouge. But, nonetheless, it was a hard fate for those we left behind.

When we arrived aboard the USS *Denver* the correspondents were lined up to have an anal inspection with rubber gloves. They said it was to detect if we were concealing drugs, but at the time I thought it was the military showing its respect for the press. The ship was so crowded that there were no bunks for us, so lying down on the steel deck of a corridor, all the fear and tension of the last few weeks draining away, I fell into the deepest and soundest sleep I had had in a long while.

It was a time of drifting in the China seas, before we were transferred to the USS *Blue Ridge* and eventually flown ashore to Clark Field in the Philippines.

From Clark I got to Manila and the next flight out to Hong Kong, only to find that my family was out on our boat visiting a Chinese festival on a nearby island. Deciding not to wait for their return, I went down to the waterfront in Deep Water Bay, where we kept a small speedboat I shared with a British army officer. Happily for me, he was not using the boat, so I jumped in and headed for the island. I believe my family was astonished to see me coming up fast in a small boat. Back in our apartment overlooking the stunning harbor of Hong Kong, my helmet that I had brought home with me became a flower pot on the balcony. My war was over.

11

Returning to Saigon

Seven years after Saigon's fall I returned to Saigon, now officially called Ho Chi Minh City, although everyone still called it Saigon. My old haunt the Continental Palace had been turned into a school for government officials, and the famous open-sided Continental Shelf had been walled in. So I checked in to the Hotel Majestic, down by the waterfront. The last time I had seen it there was a big hole in the facade where a rocket had hit during the ancient regime's last days. Now, outside the front door, the abandoned legacy of America's lost war, the mixed-race children left behind, begged for coins. Upstairs, when the door to my room closed behind me and the bellboy departed, to my surprise I found myself in tears.

There was hardly any traffic in the streets anymore. Tu Do Street—"*tu do*" meant "freedom" in Vietnamese—had been renamed Dong Khoi, meaning "uprising." I noted this name change with irony, because the uprising that the Vietcong had always hoped for never materialized. Saigon fell to tanks, not popular ire.

As I made my rounds interviewing Saigon's new masters it soon became clear that southerners in what had been the Provisional Revolutionary Government, i.e. the Vietcong, had been shoved aside by the northerners and that everything was going to be done Hanoi's way. Wrongheaded agricultural practices, which Hanoi finally abandoned in later years, were being imposed on southern farmers. It was as if the southern revolutionaries, who had fought so hard for so long, were not completely trusted by Hanoi. One also saw signs that northerners were taking large quantities of luxury goods, fans, air conditioners, even refrigerators, away from Saigon to use in Hanoi and other northern towns.

I was surprised to see the Indian shopkeepers near the Majestic still in business under the new regime. They were from Pondicherry, the French colony on the Indian subcontinent, and had lived in Saigon for generations. While I was chatting with them a car backfired in the street outside. I flinched, and the giggling shopkeeper said: "*Beaucoup* VC, *beaucoup* VC," as if the Vietcong were still an enemy to be feared instead of the guys now running the country.

As I traveled around the country I saw that a huge business in exporting scrap metal was going on throughout the length of the land, with parts of old tanks, trucks, and airplanes being broken up to be sold abroad. It wasn't turning swords into plowshares, but tanks into Toyotas. You could buy a first-rate compass, torn from an abandoned American helicopter, for $10.

There was a brisk trade in cigarette lighters, Zippo rip-offs made to look as if they had once belonged to American GIs. They had corny sayings engraved on them, such as "I've done my time in Hell."

Outside of Danang, on that lovely stretch of coast once known as China Beach, I ran into some Russians who had earned a trip to Vietnam for exceeding their quotas in some Soviet factory—I've forgotten exactly what it was. One of them spoke English, and he asked me if I knew that this very beach was where American soldiers had relaxed on breaks from oppressing the masses. I didn't let on that I had spent some time on China Beach in the old days, but commented instead on what a wonderful beach it was. The Soviet worker allowed as how it was nice, but not as nice as Cuba, and the food was better in some of the Rumanian Black Sea resorts. It was my first indication that there existed an entire Communist beach scene different from the capitalist beach scene.

I spent Easter of 1982 in Hanoi, the first time I had been in the north. The city was run-down, with nothing for sale in the shops and depressed-looking people. But the old French colonial architecture was a delight. The Vietnamese today are tearing it down to make room for the new, but I would still rate Hanoi as the most charming city in Southeast Asia. I stayed in the once-elegant Metropole, where my parents had stayed in the thirties. Today it has been restored to its former glory, but in the early eighties it was run-down, with torn mosquito nets, no air-conditioning, plumbing that didn't work, and rats running around the halls. Downstairs glum Eastern Europeans sat about in the dining room sampling the thin soup and almost inedible meals. I soon found it was better to eat at a noodle stall outside in the streets.

Easter Sunday dawned to a steady drizzle, but to my surprise the Catholic cathedral was full to overflowing. I had expected religion to be suppressed, but clearly the Communist regime had decided not to be too strict in their official atheism.

One of the highlights in the local museum was a little model of the American embassy in Saigon, and the streets around it, as it was in 1975. When a switch was thrown, mechanical model tanks came down the side streets, and a tiny helicopter would come down on a string to the embassy itself. I had seen countless models depicting famous battles, but this was the first historical representation of an event in which I had participated.

The Russians were everywhere, and fast becoming the latest foreigners to be resented by the Vietnamese. When walking through the streets children would shout "Russian, Russian." One kid threw a bag of excrement at me. Happily he missed. The Russians, despite all they had done to help Hanoi during the war, were not popular.

A few years later I was back in Hanoi, with the usual "minder" that the foreign office assigned to visiting reporters. She would help me with appointments, translate for me, and of course keep tabs on me. I was expected to pay for any official cars that would take me to appointments. Since the price was exorbitant I decided to buy a bicycle. My minder was horrified. A foreigner traveling by bicycle? I was told that would be out of the question. But I held out until my minder gave up and took me to a shop that sold imported Five Rams bicycles from China. I said: "What about a Vietnamese bicycle?" No, she said, the Chinese bicycles were better. But I insisted on having a Vietnamese bicycle, a hero of the revolution. For did not heroic soldiers carry rice and ammunition on the backs of bicycles during the great patriotic struggle?

My minder relented, and so I bought a Vietnamese bicycle for something like $11. No sooner had I left the shop, however, than both tires went flat, the seat collapsed, and the handlebars wouldn't turn. But if socialist manufacture proved faulty, private enterprise was ready to step in. On every street corner one could find a bicycle repairman ready for business on the sidewalk. One of these entrepreneurs took my bike, sent a boy off for new inner tubes, fixed the seat and the handlebars with a small blowtorch, and sent me on my way in about twenty minutes for about $3.

My last trip to Vietnam, in 2000, as a new century dawned, revealed a country trying on the garments of capitalism while still keeping political control, much as China had done. Saigon was on its way to becoming a miniature Hong Kong with buildings sprouting ever higher. Its French past was fast disappearing. The young were studying English as a foreign language, not French. Motorbikes were fast replacing bicycles as the vehicle of choice, and there was a free-market bustle in the air. The iron fist was always there for those who stepped out of line, but the early clumsy mistakes of socialist economic planning had been scrapped and Vietnam was on its way.

Like all American visitors, I was surprised by the lack of bitterness. I got a good explanation of that when I met with Vietnamese officials, who were quick to say that it was important for Vietnam to have normal relations with the world's leading power, especially with a growling China next door. "And it helps to have won," said a veteran of that long war.

———

In the years since the fall of Saigon, revisionist theories have sprung up like weeds. Although there were no purges in Washington, as took place after the fall of China when State Department China hands were being fired, there were recriminations. It was said that we had actually won the war by 1972, that the

South Vietnamese could have held on even after our troops had left if only Congress had not closed down the war and refused to allow the United States to retaliate when the North Vietnamese broke everything agreed upon in Paris.

It is true that the cornerstone of that agreement was that the United States would retain the option to use force, and it is true that a war-weary Congress took away that option. But the South Vietnamese leadership was never able to instill a sense of dedication and sacrifice for their cause, as did the north. The Communists represented nationalism, while the south always appeared to be the puppet of foreigners, and steeped in corruption at that.

I had seen the South Vietnamese hold the My Chanh line against Communist attack in the Easter Offensive of 1972, with the help of American firepower but not American ground troops. Revisionists have used this battle to say if only we had supported the south in 1975 as we did in 1972, Saigon wouldn't have lost the war. But once the Paris Peace Accords had allowed the North Vietnamese to remain in the Central Highlands, outflanking the South Vietnamese, the country's fate was sealed. Besides, no matter how many times the North Vietnamese were halted, they always had the option to go home, lick their wounds, and prepare for yet another offensive.

America was not about to recommit ground troops, and as Ho Chi Minh had predicted, the Americans grew weary of fighting in a far-off land, as had the French. For America it was a distant war to support a distant cause—a colonial war to keep Vietnam in America's sphere of influence and deny it to Communism. For the Vietnamese it was always about their country.

Many years after the war I met the former secretary of defense Robert Mc-Namara, who had just written a book admitting that he and the Kennedy and Johnson administrations had been all wrong about the war. He said he had never understood that the war was more about Vietnamese nationalism than it was about Communism. Nor did he know anything about the Vietnamese, although God knows enough people tried to tell him. The trouble was that he had an unending faith in statistics and the belief that Americans could always win. After the war, he and a team of Americans journeyed to Hanoi to talk to Vietnamese about how it had all seemed from Hanoi's point of view.

The Americans had believed that if they inflicted enough pain on the Vietnamese—bombed them and killed them in great numbers—there would come a time when they would throw in the towel. When McNamara brought this up with his Vietnamese interlocutors, they told him, to the contrary, the bombing had actually increased morale.

One Vietnamese, Dao Huy Ngoc, put it this way: "When you look at this question of the sacrifices made by Vietnam in the war you must also consider the history of our country. When we gained our independence in 1945 we already had 4,000 years of history. For 1,000 years, we were under the feudalist control of the North [of China]. We had to fight in order to regain our independence. And 3,000 years later we had to fight to regain our independence again . . . we had to fight the French for nine years . . . Only then came the fight against the U.S."[*]

Michael Herr, in his masterpiece *Dispatches,* framed the conflict in another way. It was "a face-off between one god who would hold the coonskin to the wall while we nailed it up," Herr wrote, paraphrasing Lyndon Johnson's famous description of America's goal, "and another whose detachment would see the blood run out of ten generations, if that was how long it took for the wheel to go around."

After their conversations in Hanoi, McNamara and his colleagues came to the conclusion that any American strategy for Vietnam would have had to include a "viable South Vietnamese government with credibility in the eyes of the South Vietnamese people. No government in Saigon after November 1963, when [Ngo Dinh] Diem was assassinated, was credible in this sense. From 1965, therefore, when U.S. combat troops first arrived, the situation in Saigon was politically untenable. In the end, no American strategy could have reversed the outcome in Vietnam, because the NLF [Vietcong] and its North Vietnamese allies had committed to total war. Each was prepared to sustain casualties, far beyond American estimates, without giving up the fight."[†]

No strategy or tactic short of genocide, McNamara concluded, would have

---

[*] Robert McNamara, James Blight, and Robert Brigham, *Argument Without End* (New York: Public Affairs, 1999), 256.
[†] Ibid., 419.

won the war for us. I believe to this day that he was right, and thirty-five years after the fall of Saigon, I saw the same mistakes being made in Kabul, Afghanistan, with an American military that said if we can only inflict enough pain on the Taliban they will come around and talk peace with us. At this writing America is rapidly abandoning its nation-building and counterinsurgency goals, and is headed out the door, in Afghanistan, as it was in Vietnam in the early 1970s.

In Vietnam it was the other side who, in President Kennedy's words, were willing to pay any price, bear any burden, in defense of what they considered most important: the reunification of their country and the expulsion of foreign armies.

It wasn't until fourteen years after the war that I saw Pham Xuan An again. Every attempt to make contact with An before had failed. Finally, in 1989, he sent word that I might come to his house. He seemed frail to me, but he brought out his favorite Johnnie Walker whiskey and we soon got to topic A. Had he sought to deceive journalists, disseminate misinformation? Was that what Hanoi wanted him to do?

He said he had been working for the Communists since the French ruled Indochina. His reasons were nationalist rather than ideological. He didn't think foreigners should be running Vietnam. Mal Browne and I had gotten his wife out of the country just before Saigon fell, but she had since returned. I asked him why, if he was a hero of the revolution, he had sent his wife to America, only to bring her back.

"Yes, I am a hero of the revolution," he said with a touch of bitterness, but things hadn't worked out as he had planned. He said he had intended to move to America when the war was over and his duty done. He had spent time as a student in California in the fifties and loved America, he said. He had fully intended to join his wife in America as soon as his mother was well enough to travel.

But if he loved Americans, how could he betray them, I asked, and how could he possibly think the North Vietnamese would allow him to emigrate? He said it was his patriotic duty to oppose what America was doing in Vietnam, but that it had not lessened his affection for Americans. He had seen no reason why he shouldn't be allowed to leave once the war was over.

Saigon's new rulers didn't trust him altogether, he said. He had been tainted by having worked with Americans for so long. So he was sent to a kind of mini reeducation camp. "Maybe they were right," he said with a shrug. "I didn't know anything about Marxism. But I learned it was all about power, not ideals."

Disinformation was not part of his job, he insisted. He was told not to give us at *Time* any false information lest he blow his cover. His real mission, he said, was to use his press card to gain admission to South Vietnamese military circles. His masters wanted his assessment on which commanders might be sympathetic to their cause, who could be bribed, and who their unshakable enemies were.

I left thinking An had been a little naïve to think he would be allowed to go to America, but some say he thought he might be assigned to spy on the émigré community in America, to report back on what plots they might be planning against the Hanoi regime.

Only once had he risked his cover to help a friend, he said. When *Time's* Robert Sam Anson was captured by North Vietnamese in Cambodia, An sent word that he ought to be released. And he was. But I think he may have risked his cover another time. In 1971 the South Vietnamese tried to cut the Ho Chi Minh Trail, that vast system of dirt roads and paths down which North Vietnam sent supplies to the south through Laos. American troops had to stop at the border, to keep in place the fig leaf of Laotian neutrality, but they could and did supply air cover.

I had been up at the border watching the defeated South Vietnamese army stagger out of Laos. When I returned to Saigon to file my story, An told me that what I had seen was not the main South Vietnamese column. That was still trapped inside Laos and was still being mauled. What I had seen was a rescue column that had failed to reach the beleaguered main force. It was a bit of information that had not been disseminated by either the Americans or the South Vietnamese, who sought to cover up the extent of the failed operation Lan Son 719, as it was called.

There have been books written about An, one of them by himself, and many articles. But I cannot tell you to this day what was really in the heart of Pham Xuan An. He is dead now, but he remains a reminder to me of how little I really understood about Vietnam in all the years I lived and worked there.

Covering Southeast Asia

My travels in the late sixties and early seventies took me to Thailand, Burma, Malaysia, Singapore, the Philippines, and all across the Indonesian archipelago, crowding my notebooks with exotica from those enchanted lands. It was Laos and Cambodia, however, those two stepchildren of the Vietnam War, that most often filled my days. In 1968 I had been reassigned from Saigon to Bangkok, and a Communist-inspired insurrection was burning slowly in Thailand's northeast. Bangkok, by then, had lost much of the charm it had enjoyed in earlier times. Many of the "klongs," as the town's famous canals were called, had been filled in to make roads, and traffic was inflicting a gridlocked burden on urban life.

Yet there were quiet corners left in old Bangkok still untouched by the mounting chaos of the main thoroughfares. We found what could only be described as a Siamese-Edwardian house on the junction of two klongs next to a police station. "Siam" was the old name for Thailand, and this house belonged to an earlier time. It was large and spacious with highly polished wooden floors, and we soon took up the Thai practice of taking off our shoes before we entered. We learned not to sit with one leg crossed across the other, because displaying the sole of one's shoe is considered impolite in Thailand and other Buddhist countries in Southeast Asia.

Great rice barges would come down the network of canals from the Cambodian border into the capital and would tie up next to our house. At night kids who lived on these barges would sneak over to play on the swing set I had bought for my children. I remarked to a Thai friend that I was lucky living next to a police station as it meant the bargemen would be less likely to rob the house. He answered that I had it backward. I was lucky the barges tied up so close to the house because it meant that the police wouldn't rob me.

The author's house on a klong in Bangkok, 1969.

Although I much preferred Saigon to Bangkok, we did enjoy what Thailand had to offer: the exotic architecture of its temples; the sultry tropical nights, especially at the old Oriental Hotel on the Chao Phraya River, where many writers, such as Somerset Maugham and Joseph Conrad, had stayed. The Oriental was not the grand and expensive palace it is today. In the sixties it was a little run-down, only a couple of stories high, but evenings on the terrace with the wind off the river were lovely. In my parents' time the hotel had handed out bags for customers to put their legs in so mosquitoes wouldn't bite their ankles. The smell of a mosquito coil instantly reminds me of Bangkok even to this day, just as the smell of clove cigarettes will instantly transport me back to Indonesia in the sixties.

In those days Bangkok was filled with American military personnel on R & R from Vietnam, or down from the air bases up-country. Bangkok was the location of the headquarters of SEATO, the Southeast Asia Treaty Organization, which had been set up by John Foster Dulles as an Asian equivalent of NATO. Dulles's brother, CIA director Allen Dulles, also set up Bangkok as his spy center for Southeast Asia. SEATO never lived up to expectations because the Southeast Asian nations could never agree, but it was part of the web of alliances that Americans wove to contain Communism.

The Thai king, Bhumibol Adulyadej, was a beloved figure and the glue that kept the country together. At this writing he is the longest-serving monarch in the world, and the only one born in America. He was born in Cambridge, Massachusetts, while his father was a medical student at Harvard. He is old and frail, but forty years ago he had considerable political influence. Thailand is a constitutional monarchy, but such was the reverence shown His Majesty that he could stop a coup simply by letting it be known that he was against it.

Then as now, the lèse-majesté laws were very strict. You could go to jail for saying or printing anything deemed disrespectful to the monarchy. Movie theaters would play the national anthem before every show, with the king's image on the screen. Everyone was required to stand during the playing of the national anthem or risk arrest. To this day I can still hum the opening bars.

I had an occasion once to meet the king. Time Inc. was donating some money to one of his special charities, for the hill tribes, and I was designated to deliver the check. I was told that I would have fifteen or twenty minutes' conversation with His Majesty. When I presented myself to the palace a royal attendant briefed me on protocol. I was not to prostrate myself on the floor in front of the king, as Thai visitors would do, nor was I to place my forehead on his shoe. When dealing with foreigners, His Majesty preferred a simple handshake.

Since the king granted few such interviews, I planned my brief time to get some good quotes about the hill tribes that I could use in a story. Alas, it was not to be. One of his daughters was a student at Concord Academy in Massachusetts, and she was not behaving as the king would have liked. She was behaving too much like an American teenager, the king said, and it was all the fault of a permissive American culture that he deplored. His Majesty ended up giving me a full half hour, but it was taken up with invective against my country's dissolute ways and fretting about his daughter. We never did get around to discussing the hill tribes.

I don't think the king was the only Thai who felt put off by the American presence in those days, but everybody was making a lot of money out of the Americans and the war.

In 1969 Neil Armstrong made his famous stroll on the moon, and the event mesmerized the Thais. I went around some of the poorer districts of Bangkok seeking reactions, and from the little wooden houses hard by the klongs the blue glare of television screens appeared in the windows of those who could afford TV. But it was our Chinese amah, Ah Bing, who summed it up best in the pidgin patois of the China coast: "Man go topside moon? How can?"

My number two in *Time*'s Bangkok bureau was an old Asia hand named Peter Simms, a Brit who had forgotten more than I would ever know about the region. Peter was a relic of the British Raj, having served in the Bombay Sappers and Miners in British India, and I can still hear him saying, "Super," which he pronounced "*Soooopah,*" when he was especially pleased. He was married to Sanda, a princess from Burma's Shan States, whom he had met when they were both students at Cambridge. As a girl she had swanned around Inle Lake in a golden boat in the shape of a mythical duck, part of the trappings of royalty in the Shan States. Her father had been president of independent Burma. When the generals took over he was thrown in jail, and her brother killed, in what has too often been described as a bloodless coup. Peter and Sanda were no longer welcome in Burma after the coup, and Sanda was not to see her homeland again until 2012, when the generals began to relax their grip on the country.

Peter was as big and expansive as Sanda was petite and soft-spoken. We became friends for life. An annual event in Bangkok was the Oxford and Cambridge dinner; so many of the Thai elite had studied at those institutions.

Speeches were long and florid, and much was made of the dark blue flower in my buttonhole, as compared to Peter's light blue for Cambridge.

Peter would become the model for Jerry Westerby in John le Carré's *The Honourable Schoolboy.* Westerby may have had walk-on parts in earlier le Carré stories, but he came center stage in *The Honourable Schoolboy,* with many of Peter's characteristics and mannerisms. Le Carré had learned about Peter from his old intelligence sources, for unbeknownst to me at the time, Peter had worked for British intelligence. In later years, when I contemplated Pham Xuan An's career in North Vietnamese intelligence, I began to wonder if *Time* somehow attracted spies.

A few years later, when I was living in Hong Kong and working for the *Washington Post,* Peter sent me word that le Carré was coming my way and asked if I would see him. Le Carré, whose real name is David Cornwell, was looking for someone to guide him through some of the more exotic locations in Southeast Asia that were to provide the backdrop for *The Honourable Schoolboy.* Since I was a big fan of his books I readily accepted. But how to explain his presence if he wanted to sit in on my interviews? He was carrying some expensive cameras, so I asked him if he was a good photographer. He said he was, so we traveled together through northeast Thailand, Laos, and Cambodia, he as a *Washington Post* photographer and I as the reporter. His cover was perfect, because sources never pay any attention to photographers hovering about taking pictures during an interview, and soon his photographs started appearing along with my stories.

The *Washington Post* began asking to whom should they credit the photographs. Le Carré decided on a play on words. "Why don't we call me Janet Leigh-Carr?" he asked, feminizing "John le Carré." And so, in due course, Janet Leigh-Carr began to appear in *Washington Post* credit lines under his photographs.

My boss, foreign editor Lee Lescaze, was a personal friend of mine who had known JB long before I met her. Feeling protective, he sent me a marvelously stuffy letter. Far be it from him, he wrote, to pry into my personal life, but this woman I was traveling around Southeast Asia with was certainly not a photographer. I never told him the real story.

Our faithful Ah Bing, who had come with us to Bangkok from Hong Kong, had a healthy contempt for the Thais who worked in our house, but unlike so many other Southeast Asian countries, there was little anti-Chinese feeling in Thailand. Sino-Thais ran the economy, to be sure, but mostly they took Thai names, spoke Thai, and were pretty well, in some cases thoroughly, integrated.

Not so in Malaysia, where there was tension between Chinese and Malays and one terrible race riot in 1968. Indonesia, too, was always cracking down on their Chinese, who ran about 70 percent of the economy. At one point the Indonesians made the Chinese take Indonesian names. But many of them got their revenge by taking the names of famous kings and warriors, which annoyed the Indonesians no end. I remember one Chinese merchant in Surabaya handing me his card, which said, "Diponegoro"—the name of a legendary Javanese prince—"formerly Wu." It was as if, in America, he had changed his name to Thomas Jefferson, formerly Wu.

Thailand was the one country in Southeast Asia that had never been a European colony. Through clever maneuvering, Thailand had managed to remain useful as a buffer state between British and French territories. Traveling through the remnants of four former empires in Southeast Asia, however, British, French, American, and Dutch, one could see how different Western cultures had influenced their former colonies. In Indochina the French language and culture were still important. Young people in Vietnam, Cambodia, and Laos today cannot wait to learn English, but half a century ago you needed a little French to get by, and older Indochinese thought you uncultured if you faltered in French.

In Malaysia and Singapore the trappings of the British legal system—judges in wigs, the rule of law—were what you noticed. Malaysians and Singaporeans were joining British clubs, some of which had rejected natives only a decade or two before. They took their parliamentary procedures seriously even though, as the writer Dennis Bloodworth put it, democracy in Southeast Asia was a little like a bejeweled elephant—good for impressing people and on ceremonial occasions, but there should be no doubt about who rode whom.

The Philippines had belonged to Spain before Americans came in 1898, and the cliché was that Filipinos had spent four hundred years in a convent and fifty years in Hollywood. It was the Hollywood you noticed, except in the south, where a Muslim rebellion smoldered, just as it had when the Americans arrived at the end of the nineteenth century. America had given the Philippines its independence right after World War II and thus did not suffer the postwar anticolonial uprisings that the French, British, and Dutch endured. But in the late nineteenth and early twentieth centuries, America had put down Filipino yearnings for independence in a long, bloody, and cruel campaign against what we called the Philippine Insurrection.

The Philippines were dominated by Ferdinand and Imelda Marcos when I arrived. One year Imelda enticed a Miss Universe contest to Manila and, as part of the show, organized a parade containing all the different ethnicities and cultures of the islands. I was tipped off by a government official, who hated the Marcoses, to pay particular attention to the primitive tribesmen from the south who were to be seen hopping about with spears. It turned out they were university students dressed up to look like tribesmen, and they were hopping about because their bare feet were too tender to take the heat of the paved streets. Later, after Marcos was deposed, I was one of the gawkers who entered the looted palace to see Imelda Marcos's collection of a thousand shoes.

The Pacific island of Guam was another bit of the Spanish empire we picked up in 1898. Today, Guam is being built up as a major American base, but even forty-five years ago there was a noticeable American military presence. Guamanians liked to describe their island as "where America's day begins," because, being just the other side of the international date line, they could claim to be the easternmost American territory.

I was there to cover a brief visit between President Johnson and his Saigon team, but in my spare time I was asked if I would like to go on a "straggler bag" mission deep in the jungle. I had no idea what a straggler bag might be, but I was told that it consisted of a pencil, a pad of paper, and a note from the emperor of Japan saying: "If you are a Japanese soldier, please be advised that the war is over, and that, as your emperor, I request you to give yourself up and come home to the land of the rising sun." The Japanese had taken Guam soon after Pearl Harbor, only to lose it again as the Americans marched across the Pacific. If the soldier did not trust what the emperor was telling him, he was requested to at least leave a note on the pad of paper so that his emperor would know he was alive. All of this was put in a waterproof plastic bag and set out in the jungle near a stream or a pool where a straggler might come for water.

World War II had been over for more than twenty years, and at first I thought this was a snipe hunt designed to make a fool of me. But the Guamanians were serious, so off we went deep in the forest to tie straggler bags to trees. I could not imagine that there actually could be Japanese still hiding out who didn't know the war was over, but five years later, in 1972, long after I had departed Guam, never to return, a Japanese soldier, Shoichi Yokoi, who had been hiding in a cave for almost a quarter of a century finally gave himself up and was repatriated to Japan. Having been a tailor, he made clothes for himself out of wild hibiscus, and lived on coconuts, breadfruit, snails, and the odd rat that came his way. He explained that he had been led to believe that a Japanese soldier should never surrender, but in the end he was found by some hunters. He never answered his emperor's note in a straggler bag. Nor was he the last. Two more stragglers were discovered on other Pacific islands in 1974. Today, I am told, tourists can go and see the cave where Shoichi Yokoi hid out for so many years.

Indonesia, which the Japanese had hoped to make part of their empire, had been the Dutch East Indies for four hundred years. What struck me was how little Dutch influence there was left a generation after independence. Neither the Dutch language nor Dutch culture was noticeable. Just about the only reference to the Dutch I ever heard was when an Indonesian friend admonished me for standing with my hands on my hips. He said that was the way Dutchmen had stood when they were scolding the natives. He asked me not to stand that way again.

Although the virus of Islamic terrorism has reached the Indonesian archipelago in recent years, I never came across any hint of it. As my friend Jim Sterba put it, Islamic fanaticism lessens with humidity. The stern faith may flourish in the dry deserts of Saudi Arabia but lessens in the tropics. Indonesia may be the most populous Muslim country in the world, but the national airline, Garuda, is named for a Hindu god.

In the sixties and early seventies the tensions were political, not religious. General Suharto had recently taken over from the populist Sukarno, who had led his country to independence and spent the rest of his time in power living dangerously as a leader of the so-called nonaligned world. A pro-Communist coup in 1965 failed and was brutally suppressed. A wave of killing broke over the islands as people hunted down suspected Communists and settled scores. As many as half a million may have lost their lives. I interviewed a man in Bali, the one island with a Hindu majority, who told me how he would stand all day on a bridge chopping off heads into the water below. He said how tired his arm had gotten, but new victims kept being brought to the bridge for him to kill.

General Suharto is reviled today as having been an avaricious dictator, but in the late sixties he was seen as Indonesia's savior against Communism and chaos.

There was an undeniable fatalism in Indonesia. I attended the trial of a Communist leader in Blitar, East Java. It turned out the defendant had been to school with the military officer who was presiding over his trial. When asked if he had any last words before he was taken out and shot, the Communist leader said he held no bitterness, and told the officer that if the coup had succeeded he would have been sentencing the officer to death, instead of the other way around.

In those days the enchanting and hypnotic gongs of a traditional gamelan orchestra had not yet been overtaken by pop music. Shadow puppets, projected on a bedsheet by the light of an oil lamp, were more popular than movies in the countryside. The puppeteers could get away with sly political digs, masked as ancient legends, that would have landed them in jail if said outright.

Hong Kong was still a British colony when we lived there, and Macau, which we often visited, was still Portuguese. British colonialism in Hong Kong was seldom questioned by the citizenry in the sixties because the alternative was Communist China, then going through the convulsions of the Cultural Revolution. I always thought the British and the Chinese got along quite well in Hong Kong because each had an unshakable belief in their own racial and cultural superiority.

Half a century ago a colonial mentality still prevailed in Southeast Asia. It has vanished now with the passage of time and the rising confidence of Asia. But in those days many locals instinctively paid deference to white people, feeling that, somehow, white people knew best. Many of the newly independent elite had been educated in Europe, but even more humble people thought whites were on a different plane. When Ah Bing came to live with us in a Massachusetts suburb years later, she could not understand why we wanted her to lock the front door. "Why?" she would ask. "All Englisee people," meaning everybody was white, so how could there be thieves?

13

On the Opium Trail

Of all the countries in Southeast Asia, Burma was the most difficult from which to report. Visas were very few and far between, and the best I could do was get short, one-week tourist visas from time to time. Rangoon, which had rivaled Bangkok as an international air hub in the immediate post–World War II years, had by the late sixties advanced not at all. After Bangkok, Rangoon seemed frozen in the 1940s. The military coup that had killed Sanda Simms's brother and imprisoned her father had turned the country into an inward-looking backwater from which it is only now emerging.

More recently, the generals changed the name of Burma to Myanmar, and Rangoon to Yangon. But I have no doubt that one day the old names will be returned, just as the Khmer Rouge name for Cambodia, Kampuchea, was abandoned after the tyrants were gone.

The military dictatorship in Burma could be harsh and cruel, but in other ways a bit goofy compared to places like China and North Korea. I got to know a longtime newspaper editor in Rangoon named Sein Win. He had been sent to jail for a while, for insulting the government or some such thing. After he got out he found his telephone wasn't working properly. He could hear strange clicks on the line. Suspecting his telephone was being tapped, he marched down to the police station to complain. He said he had done his time in jail, and now the authorities should leave him alone. The police said: "Calm yourself, Uncle," "uncle" being a term of respect in Burma. "We only have a very few telephone taps in Burma, and you should be honored that we are using one on you."

Another time he sensed that he was being followed by two young men, obviously policemen. Since Burmese men wear sarongs instead of jackets and pants, they had to carry their revolvers in little cloth bags slung over their shoulders. The two undercover cops weren't very skilled in their tailing techniques, and one day Sein Win, walking down the street, stopped in front of a theater. The two cops came up behind him and said, "Oh, Uncle, have you seen that film? It is supposed to be very good."

Sein Win looked them over and said, "All right, boys, I have nothing better to do this afternoon." So in effect, Sein Win took the cops to the movies, where they sat immediately behind him, very much enjoying the film.

One time when my mother came to visit us in Bangkok I took her to Rangoon for a three-day visit. We stayed in the old Strand Hotel, where she and my father had stayed in 1939. It was a sad, run-down hotel in the sixties, not at all the expensive and modernized place it is today. A woman was playing old show tunes on a piano in the dining room. My mother said that she was absolutely sure that no paint had been applied in the Strand since her last stay, and pretty sure that the songs being played were the same ones being played on the same piano in 1939. Only the piano player was younger.

My last adventure for the *Washington Post* in Asia was a clandestine trip to Burma to visit the Shan State Army. Sanda Simms, with her family connections to the Shan States, had given me a few leads, and I was smuggled across the border to where I would meet the rebels. Like the Karens, whom I had visited farther to the south, the Shans were in a long-running rebellion against the majority Burman people and the government in Rangoon. Burma's ethnic minorities had been favored by the British for remaining loyal against the Japanese, which the Burmans had not always been. The British made some promises to the minorities that they could not keep. Aung San, father of the Burmese heroine Aung San Suu Kyi and father of independent Burma, had fought alongside the Japanese against the British. Once independence came, the majority Burmans took charge, and the minorities opted for armed rebellion.

By the time I got there, however, the Shan State Army seemed to be more interested in the opium trade than in actively fighting the Burmese army.

We started out at cock's crow, a heavily armed band of men, with the mist rising from the valleys and clinging like wool to the hilltops. We were in the high country of upper Burma, where the wooded hills stretch away toward China and the mountains of Tibet. Along the way we stopped at tribal villages where Chinese pharmacists from Hong Kong and Bangkok were busy refining raw opium into heroin. They were guarded by suspicious-looking characters who eyed me, the only white man, as if they were scowling extras in a bad Western.

The Shan commander asked me if I would like to ride a horse, but I said no, I was prepared to walk like everyone else. It was a matter of pride, but after the first couple of hours of up hill and down dale I was flagging. The short and indefatigable Shans strode on, each carrying automatic weapons, mortars, and mortar plates as well as hundreds of rounds of ammunition. Mercifully the Shan commander called a halt, and a horse appeared as if from nowhere. It was a small horse, a pony really, of the type common in those foothills of the Himalayas. It seems the Shan commander had foreseen my difficulty keeping up and the horse was surreptitiously being kept in reserve.

I tried to inquire how much it would cost me to rent the horse during my stay with the Shans, but the commander made a long face and said that it was impossible to rent the horse. But, he said with a beaming smile, I could buy it.

"Okay, how much?" I asked. The cost would be one hundred American dollars, but then he said he could keep the horse for me, without charge, to await my return, or the arrival of another *Washington Post* correspondent. I requested a receipt, and after a bit of consultation, great red seals saying "Shan State Army" were produced, and I was presented with the most official-looking receipt that side of Mandalay. When I later turned in my expense account for the trip, I listed the horse, which I had named Katharine, and submitted the price I had paid.

I later learned that you can rent anything on your expense account, but if you buy it, it becomes the property of the Washington Post Company, with all the accounting problems that entails. I was roundly admonished by the foreign desk, and when I returned to Washington on a home leave I was told that Katharine Graham, the proprietor, wanted to see me in her office.

At the time the *Washington Post,* and Mrs. Graham, were rightly enjoying fame for the Watergate story, which had unhorsed President Nixon. An obsequious magazine had labeled Mrs. Graham the most powerful woman in the world. When I was ushered trembling into the presence, Mrs. Graham asked only one question: why had I named the horse Katharine on my expense account? I said I had done so to curry favor with her comptrollers. I hoped that they might be less likely to reject my expense account if the horse was named for the publisher. "Case dismissed," she said. "I can only assume it is the most powerful horse in the world."

———————

"Give me an expense account and I'll cover anything."

—*Joel McCrea in Alfred Hitchcock's* Foreign Correspondent, *1940*

There were legendary expense accounts in those days. A *Time* magazine reporter, Jim Wilde, got a pad of blank receipts from his favorite restaurants printed up by a backstreet printer in Saigon. He also bought a rubber stamp saying "paid" in French. He would routinely write out some imaginary dinner order at whichever restaurant he chose, stamp it paid, and send it in to *Time.* He also had blank receipts for taxis, and one day Frank McCulloch, his boss, called him in and said: "Jim, I seem to remember you were out visiting an aircraft carrier in the South China Sea on these dates, but here I see you are asking to be reimbursed for taxis." "Oh," replied Wilde, "well, you know how big those flight decks are and I had to get around." Wilde told me years later that Frank burst out laughing as he tore Jim's expense accounts to shreds.

Another time I entertained an Asian diplomat at an opium den in Phnom Penh. He gave me a pretty good tip on a story, so I put his pipes of opium down on my expense account. I got a sharp note from my editor Lee Lescaze, instructing me to lie and call it whiskey. I would not be reimbursed for opium on his watch.

14

Laos: "The End of Nowhere"

I first went to Laos on a vacation break from Vietnam. JB had joined me in Bangkok for a brief "rest and recreation," or "R & R," in military terminology. We decided to visit Vientiane, the drowsy capital on a bend of the Mekong. It was the time of year for "slash and burn," as the Lao burned the grass, brush, and trees to make way for the planting of new crops. A great pall of smoke hung over much of the country during the burning season, and we landed in an old Royal Air Lao DC-3. We came in near darkness with the late afternoon sun showing only as a dark red ball in the smoke-filled western sky.

We took a taxi from the airport into town, and, compared to Bangkok or Saigon, we thought we had arrived in a different century. Motor traffic was at a minimum. Bicycles and bicycle rickshaws, known as cyclos, glided by. There were small kerosene lamps in the doorways and windows of small, low-rise buildings as we entered town. The Mekong was at low ebb, and great sandbanks spread out toward the remaining stream with the lights of Thailand blinking on the nether shore.

"The end of nowhere,"[*] as the country has been described, Laos is one of the few countries never to have had a railroad, although the Chinese are talking about building one now. And in those days there was no bridge across

---

[*] Charles Stevenson, *The End of Nowhere* (Boston: Beacon Press, 1972).

the Mekong either. You either flew in from Bangkok or Hong Kong, or you took a train up to the river's edge and took a ferry over from Thailand.

We headed toward the Constellation Hotel, a couple of stories high with a bar open to the street. The rooms were wood-floored and few, if any, offered hot water. You learned to get rooms on the second floor under the water tank, which would heat up under the burning afternoon sun and give you at least one hot shower in the evening. The Constellation became a home away from home during my Indochina years.

The owner was one of the more memorable Indochina characters. Half Corsican, half Chinese, Maurice Cavalerie had owned a hotel in the old days in what became North Vietnam. At the end of the French Indochina war, which resulted in a partitioning of Vietnam into north and south, Maurice joined the mass migration of northerners who opted to live in the about-to-be-formed Republic of South Vietnam. More than a million, most of them Catholics, moved south on ships provided by the Americans. Maurice, always with a cigarette in the corner of his mouth and eyes red from what I always suspected was too much opium, spoke often of his last night in the port of Haiphong, waiting for the last boat with the streets half-empty, abandoned dogs barking, suitcases full of money and gold at his side, and a submachine gun on his lap. He would complain bitterly that just because the French had lost at Dien Bien Phu, it didn't mean they had to give up the war and abandon the whole country.

Maurice made his way to Laos, where he became a friend to all the reporters who hung out at the Constellation over the years. The bar was always crowded, and you could get a rather tough water buffalo steak with French fries in the restaurant if you weren't going on to some better place. There were parties in the rooms upstairs reeking of marijuana, which was reputed to be of high quality, readily and openly available in the market. Vientiane was enough out of the war to still be on the hippie trail, and scraggly Westerners with no visible means of support were in evidence around town. There were crummy opium dens for expats, too, downmarket compared to Phnom Penh. You could get an opium addict's license in Laos, which made it legal to smoke opium. I never heard of anyone being asked to show their opium license.

Laos: "The End of Nowhere"

The great chronicler of the Indochina wars Bernard Fall said that Laos was "neither a geographical, nor an ethnic, nor social entity, but merely a political convenience." Over the centuries what is now Laos had been bedeviled by Burmese, Siamese, and Vietnamese. Hundreds of years ago hill tribes started moving down into the highlands of Laos from southern China, while the Lao, a people similar racially and linguistically to the Thai, dominated the lowlands. The country had always been a hodgepodge of ethnicities and cultures. The Lao, like their Thai, Burmese, and Cambodian neighbors, were Theravada Buddhists.

Laos, and Cambodia, were the "Indo" part of Indochina. Hugh Toye wrote: "For over a thousand years the Indochinese peninsula has been the scene of a conflict between the Indian-influenced kingdoms to the south and west of the Annamitic Chain [of mountains], and the Chinese-influenced Vietnamese, pressing southwards with their colonists from the over-crowded delta of the Red River." There were cultural, architectural, and linguistic differences, and also differences in the way they worshipped the Buddha. But in addition, there were differences in "manners, and ways of thought."

The thousand-year-old "yawning gulf that lies between the austere and self-contained civilization of China and the tolerant earthiness of Hindu cultures adds an inevitable measure of mutual dislike to the antique fears and ambitions of thirty generations," Toye wrote.[*]

The golden age of Laos came with the kingdom of Lan Xang in the fourteenth century, but eventually the territory broke into three kingdoms, one centered in Luang Prabang in the north, another in Vientiane in the center, and yet another in Champassak in the south. The French began absorbing these territories in the late nineteenth century as part of French Indochina. The French hoped to open the Mekong as a trade route into southern China but were thwarted by a series of rapids that defied navigation.

After a brief Japanese occupation in World War II, Laos emerged as a united state known as the Kingdom of Laos, under a bright red flag with a

---

[*] Hugh Toye, *Laos, Buffer State or Battle Ground* (New York: Oxford University Press, 1968), xiii.

white three-headed elephant in the center, symbolizing the union of three kingdoms. It was, and is, my favorite flag, but it flies over no public buildings anymore, having been abolished along with the monarchy when the Communists came to power. But it flies still in my cellar as I write as a reminder of that colorful and tragic land.

The French reasserted control of their Indochina colonies after World War II, but as they were facing defeat in Vietnam, Laos gained full independence in 1953. The army of France was finished in Indochina after the defeat at Dien Bien Phu in 1954, but America soon filled the vacuum left by the departing French.

Secretary of State John Foster Dulles, who was obsessed with the Communist threat, told the Senate Appropriations Committee that the red menace was about to engulf all of Southeast Asia. "Whether this can be stopped at this point and whether Laos and Cambodia and the southern part of Vietnam, Thailand, Malaya, and Indonesia can be kept out of Communist control depends very much on whether a dike around this present loss [can be maintained]," Dulles argued. The "domino theory" was born.

A civil war broke out among the Laotian factions, which a conference in Geneva in 1962 tried to fix. It established that Laos would be independent and neutral but didn't decide who would rule among the three princes: Boun Oum of Champassak, a right-winger under Thai and American influence in the south; Souphanouvong, the "red prince" who led the leftist Pathet Lao faction under North Vietnamese influence in the northeast; or the neutralist Prince Souvanna Phouma in the middle. It is no coincidence that the three princes mirrored the three-headed elephant on the Lao flag.

The three formed a coalition government in 1962, but it soon fell apart. What might have been a localized struggle for power became internationalized when John F. Kennedy took up where Eisenhower and John Foster Dulles had left off. I can still remember President Kennedy going on television with a map of Laos, which he mispronounced "Lay-oss," rhyming it with "chaos" rather than "mouse." Kennedy made it seem as if the entire free world depended on the fate of Laos, but John Kenneth Galbraith was closer to the truth when he said that Laos should be allowed to "return to the obscurity which it richly deserves."

Souphanouvong led his faction into resistance, the Americans decided that the neutralist Souvanna Phouma was their man, and the Laotian right had no choice but to go along with America's choice. The United States and North Vietnam pulled Laos into a proxy civil war within the greater struggle for Indochina. All the while King Sri Savang Vatthana, increasingly marginalized, reigned in name only from his palace in Luang Prabang.

The neutrality of Laos became a fig leaf, with neither the North Vietnamese nor the Americans paying much attention to it except to deny their involvement. Lip service was being paid to neutrality by the fact that the Americans had no overt military presence, no visible ground troops in Laos. The CIA ran America's war so that a thin veil of deniability could be maintained. The North Vietnamese needed the Ho Chi Minh Trail along the border with Vietnam, down which came the troops and supplies they infiltrated into South Vietnam. Farther north a shoulder of Laos around Sam Neau protruded deep into North Vietnam and was closer to Hanoi than to Vientiane. The North Vietnamese feared this was the back door to their country. Hanoi always maintained that their Lao allies, the Pathet Lao, were doing the fighting in Laos, but in reality Hanoi maintained several divisions on the Lao side of the border.

Senator William Fulbright, at a secret congressional hearing on Laos in 1969, asked the former ambassador William Sullivan, "Doesn't this ever strike you as sort of an absurdity? They are pretending they are not there and we are pretending we are not there. What does it all lead to?" But the pretense of Lao neutrality was deemed necessary for the Soviets as well as the Americans.

At first the Ho Chi Minh Trail consisted of paths cut through the jungle along which trudged Vietnamese troops wheeling bicycles laden with rice, ammunition, and supplies. Later the trail became a virtual highway with truck traffic moving south. American bombing raids were always a danger, and Laos quickly became the most heavily bombed country in the world. It was said that enough explosives were dropped on Laos to equal several Hiroshi-mas. But we correspondents seldom got to see that side of the war, in which hundreds of villages were destroyed and untold thousands killed, wounded, or displaced.

The Americans helped train the Royal Lao Armed Forces and left it to the CIA to run a secret war in Laos. By far the most effective fighters on America's side were the opium-growing Meo tribesmen—Hmong, as they like to be called today—who wanted to resist the incursions of the North Vietnamese into their mountain fastness. The Hmong consider the word "Meo" an insult. But the word "Hmong" did not come into common usage with Westerners until after the war.

The hill tribes in Laos were stratified vertically. Different tribes liked to live at different altitudes in the mountains. The Meo chose to live at the highest altitudes, and they were arguably the fiercest. They were led by a man named Vang Pao, and, for a while, they gave the North Vietnamese a very hard time.

The CIA would supply them by air, mostly, and if you got to know some of the CIA pilots in Vientiane you could sometimes hitch a ride in a Pilatus Porter, a single-engine Swiss plane designed for short takeoffs and landings on the glaciers of Switzerland. In Laos, the CIA built short airstrips on the steep hillsides where the Meo lived. The Porters would land uphill, which slowed down their speed, and take off downhill, which would accelerate their speed. There was a secret CIA base up in the mountains, which was the Shangri-la for the Vientiane press corps, called Long Cheng. Only a few ever wangled a visit there and I was never one of them.

The war in Laos followed a cyclical pattern. The government, and that usually meant the Meo, advanced in the wet season, while the North Vietnamese and their Pathet Lao pushed back again in the dry season. But neither side pushed too hard. A curious modus vivendi developed whereby the Pathet Lao and North Vietnamese held the eastern mountains and the Ho Chi Minh Trail, while the American-supported government held the Mekong River val-ley, where two-thirds of the population lived. The Americans bombed the

Communist-controlled areas, but there were no American ground troops involved in the fighting. Unlike in Vietnam, North Vietnamese and Americans never met in battle on the ground, nor would they give their surrogates on the ground enough material support to win their civil war. So underneath the greater Indochina-wide struggle between the North Vietnamese and the Americans, the Lao government and the Pathet Lao fought it out in an unwinnable, Orwellian war. There would be no end until their patrons called it quits. By the time I arrived, the Meo, masters of guerrilla warfare, were being pressed by the Americans to take on a greater role in harassing the North Vietnamese in more traditional set-piece battles. The results were disastrous for the Meo.

In an odd way the struggle for Laos was a resumption of a thousand years of struggle between the Sinocized Vietnamese and the Indian-influenced cultures to the west. French colonialism temporarily halted this older struggle, but now it was under way again under the auspices of Hanoi, backed by China, while Washington backed the royalist government.

Although the fighting was far from Vientiane, refugee camps for displaced highlanders were springing up all around the capital. All the powers had embassies in Vientiane, so it was possible to drop in on the Russians, the Chinese, and even the North Vietnamese, although they were never going to tell you anything. Vientiane was a nest of intrigues in those days, but it was said that the competing intelligence services had all agreed to keep the capital free from assassinations and terrorist attacks.

The American embassy was either helpful or unhelpful depending on who was the ambassador. I always found William Sullivan to be extremely helpful without losing sight of his mission to put the best face on what the United States was doing. G. McMurtrie Godley, who came to be known as "Bomber Godley" for his role in the air war in Laos, was decidedly less helpful.

A scourge of the American mission in Laos appeared in the form of a talented young journalist named Tim Allman, who had a well-jaundiced eye for the absurdities and deceits of the war in Laos. He became my stringer for *Time*. Another American, Fred Branfman, a Lao speaker and later a noted antiwar activist, devoted himself to chronicling the effects of American bombs on civilians in the northeast of the country, mostly by talking to refugees. Their primitive drawings of life under constant air attack were affectingly poignant. We learned how whole villages were living in caves and farming at night to avoid the bombs. Fred also incurred the ire of the American embassy but contributed a great deal to the journalism of that time. Ironically, primitive drawings of the type Fred had collected would turn up in later years chronicling postwar Communist atrocities.

Vientiane had a dreamy, otherworldly feel to it, heavy on Buddhism. But there was always some sort of political crisis to write about, even though it never meant very much. The standard headline, we used to joke, could be abbreviated to "LLKTOB," which stood for "Land-Locked Kingdom Teeters on Brink." The French used to say that colonial service in Laos ruined a man for more serious postings, because dreamy veterans of the colonial service in Laos were never able to reenter the real world again.

Both American and North Vietnamese trainers, trying to get the Laos to fight properly, complained that the Lao would deliberately aim high in order not to hurt the enemy. It was said that in Lao folklore an eclipse meant that a giant frog had swallowed the moon or the sun, and soldiers were said to fire at the sky in order to get the frog to regurgitate. I never saw this happen, but then I was never in Laos during an eclipse.

In Vientiane, reporters would get up not too early and have a coffee and freshly baked bread at some street-side café, often with an open sewer lending contrast to the sweet smell of croissants. Then you would make the rounds of diplomats, or visit refugee camps, or interview Lao officials. In the evening you might have a drink at the White Rose with an Air America pilot and try to get some information about what was happening up-country. The White Rose had an extraordinary floor show where Lao girls did things with cigarettes I never thought possible.

Air America was a CIA contract airline that transported personnel between the cities and towns under government control, as well as bases and clandestine airfields in the hill country. Its pilots came from the same mold as those who flew Civil Air Transport (CAT) in China in the 1940s, or Flying Tigers against Mao's forces during the Chinese civil war, or the Haiphong-based

Americans who flew for the French during their Indochina war, dropping supplies over besieged Dien Bien Phu. Indeed some had flown in those earlier conflicts and, like opium addicts who can't quit, were flying dangerously again in Laos.

Captain Fred Walker, for example, along with Mike Shaver, flew the last Air America plane out of Laos to Thailand on June 3, 1974. Twenty-one years before, Walker had flown one of the last resupply missions over Dien Bien Phu. And before that, he flew one of the last planes out of China's Yunnan Province one step ahead of Mao's Communist forces.[*]

There was one pilot—I believe his name was Neil Hansen—who used to take his place among the passengers in the plane he was supposed to fly that day. He would wait until the passengers started looking at their watches and wondering when the plane was going to leave. Then he would start complaining in a loud voice that Air America never left on time and, goddamn it, he would "just fly this sumbitch" himself. Whereupon he would unbuckle his seat belt, march up to the cockpit, start the engines, and take off, leaving the passengers biting their nails.

My favorite ambassador to Laos was Britain's Alan Davidson, who, besides being a professional diplomat, was also a well-known ichthyologist and food writer. He became fascinated with the great carp of the Mekong, the *pa beuk,* which can weigh nine hundred pounds and grow to enormous length. He sent word up-country that the British embassy would pay well if a fisherman could catch one, and when word came down that the fish was caught, he persuaded the Americans to bring it down to Vientiane by helicopter.

He couldn't wait to tell of his achievement, and he told me he was about to have a grand dinner party for the diplomatic corps, serving the *pa beuk* as the main course. I immediately asked to be invited, but he said his dinner was not going to be open to the press. I began to muse out loud about the story possibilities that his *pa beuk* offered. "I can see the headline," I said. " 'CIA Transports Large Fish for British Dinner Party While War Drags On.' "

---

* Jane Hamilton-Merritt, *Tragic Mountains: The Hmong, the Americans, and the Secret Wars for Laos, 1942–1992* (Bloomington and Indianapolis: Indiana University Press, 1993), 329.

"Hmmm," said Ambassador Davidson. "Perhaps a place could be found for the *Washington Post*'s fish and game correspondent, but not a political reporter." And so it was that I became a fish and game correspondent for an evening.

Most of Vientiane's diplomatic corps was there. I was seated decidedly below the salt, next to the female British courier who had brought the Stilton cheese out from London, and the French military attaché. The courier, who said her mission was to promote British exports, boasted that serving the Stilton was time specific, and that the cheese was timed to arrive on just the day of the party. The French attaché, unimpressed by English cheese, suggested that the British must have forgotten about the international date line.

The fish was dutifully served as the main course and tasted a little like veal. The pièce de résistance, however, was the severed head of the great fish, brought in on a big platter carried on the shoulders of several men, its carpy whiskers in repose and its dead eyes open. I wrote that it was a sight to make strong men gasp and women faint.

Later, an angry letter came to my editors from a woman who said my story was demeaning to women. Why should the outsized fish head make women faint while men only gasped? Did H. D. S. Greenway really think that women were more weak-kneed than men? The letter was forwarded on to me, and, since my byline is gender neutral, I was able to reply that I thought the writer was being presumptuous, and signed it Helen D. S. Greenway.

Many times I thought of my father, who, in his naturalist days, had visited northern Laos collecting birds in the 1920s and '30s, and received his medal in the royal capital. You could reach Luang Prabang by road or by air during the war when I was there, but mostly it was too dangerous to drive. The Pathet Lao kept cutting the road. But once or twice I did go by road, and, as twilight fell, I saw a tiger leap across the road. And if you flew anywhere in Laos you had to expect chickens and other animals aboard the plane.

There were no real hotels to stay in north of Vientiane. In Luang Prabang one stayed at a little guesthouse run by a French foreign legion deserter. There were no tourists then. The war was too close. We hired a boat, nothing more than a hollowed-out log with a long-tailed outboard motor, to take us up the

Mekong to where the Ou River joins the Mekong to see the Cave of the Buddhas, a cave in which there were hundreds of little Buddha statues put there by the faithful. My father had told me it was a sight to behold and not to be missed, the high, forest-covered hills and limestone outcroppings resembling Chinese scroll paintings.

There was an enchanting village on the other shore, which we visited. The houses were those half-timbered structures that were common in French colonial days, and people were carving a riverboat out of teak on the riverbank. The village bustled with life but was far removed from the commercialism of villages elsewhere in Asia. A couple of years later, when I came again, the village had been burned to the ground by the Pathet Lao.

At Sala Phou Khoun, a crossroads between Vientiane and Luang Prabang, there was also a lonely little French hotel with fireplaces in every room to ward off the cold of the highland winter. Everybody told me to stay there because of its charm, but by the time I got there it, too, had been burned to the ground in a Communist offensive.

It is not easy to beat the daily papers when you work for a weekly like *Time*, but Peter Simms and I did come across a genuine scoop. We found evidence of greater Thai involvement in the fighting in Laos than was generally known. A frightened Thailand had long been secretly helping the American war effort, and now Thai soldiers were being taken off the Thai army rolls to be considered volunteers fighting against Communism in Laos. We had interviews with Thai soldiers who had fought in Laos, but when the magazine appeared that week, our story wasn't there. I never found out exactly why or by whom the story had been spiked, but I decided then and there that I couldn't work for *Time* forever.

The Meo/Hmong were brave fighters, but as the war dragged on some of their soldiers were boys as young as ten. In the fall of 1969 Vang Pao and his Meo, with logistic support from the Americans, recaptured the Plain of Jars, that large upland plateau dotted with funereal urns from ancient times. In the spring of 1970, however, the North Vietnamese came roaring back, and an emergency air evacuation of Meo fighters and their families was quickly organized. I was up on the jar-covered plain at the time, and saw the big American C-130s come lumbering in from American bases in Thailand to hastily prepared dirt runways. Their markings were blacked out to observe the myth of neutrality, as if such aircraft in the middle of Laos at such a time could be anything but American.

An evacuation of tribesmen loyal to the United States from the "Plain of Jars" ahead of a North Vietnamese push in Laos in 1970. The author, reporting for Life *magazine, is visible at top left.*

Terrified women and children were herded aboard the cargo planes, their turbo jets screaming and their props whipping the plain with dust. The planes never cut their engines, landing and taking off again, transporting a mountain people away to exile, first in the Lao lowlands, then to Thailand, then later, for many, to the United States when the war was lost. In today's America the Hmong form a minority group suffering from being taken from the shaman-haunted uplands of Laos, and their preindustrial tribal society, to fend for themselves in alien and modern America.

At the evacuation site was the legendary American Edgar "Pop" Buell, the retired Indiana farmer who had served as the Agency for International Development's man for northern Laos for more than a decade. Buell had become a kind of Lord Jim to the Meo, but on this occasion he put his leathery face in his hands and said: "It's all just been running and dying, just running and dying."

Some say we took advantage of the Hmong, urging them to fight for our cause, which in the end destroyed them. Others say we were only arming them in their sincere desire to fight the Vietnamese, which they would have tried to do even without us. Both are true.

The Meo who couldn't make it out were abandoned to their fate, and as had happened at the end of the French war, pathetic radio calls for help kept coming in from the highlands. But the Americans were no longer taking their calls. The running and dying lasted long after the war's official end. Many Meo thought to be disloyal to the new Communist government were hunted down by the new rulers of Laos.

By the midseventies the American position in Laos was beginning to crumble, and the end came with the fall of South Vietnam. But Laos did not suffer the bizarre and horrible fate of Cambodia when the Communists took over. There was plenty of cruelty in the reeducation camps, where thousands died, including the king. But it was not as severe as Vietnam, or in the same league with the Cambodian holocaust, and the American embassy in Laos remained open, unlike in Vietnam and Cambodia.

I don't think Maurice spent his last night in Vientiane with suitcases of cash and a submachine gun, but Asian Communism had come once again to evict him. Maurice moved to Australia, where his daughter lived, married to an Australian correspondent. The Americans, like the French before them, had grown weary of the war, and people like Maurice were left in the lurch.

A coalition government was put in place after the Paris Peace Accords of 1973, but as in so many post–World War II coalitions, the Communist side encroached on all the agreements and assumed complete control in the months following the fall of Saigon. Many serving the old regime were put in camps, from which many did not return, or they fled across the river to Thailand. In December of 1975 the monarchy was abolished; the king imprisoned, where he subsequently died; and the Lao People's Democratic Republic was proclaimed.

• • •

When I returned to Laos years later after the war, many Hmong were being resettled in the lowlands by the Communist government. There they lived in misery away from their cool highlands. The reason given was that their slash-and-burn agriculture was destroying the forests, but I suspect there was an element of revenge in their handling of the Hmong, and a desire to keep a close eye on them. Vang Pao and many thousands of his followers may have made it to the United States, but many, many more were left behind to an uncertain fate.

The country had become a vassal state to Vietnam politically, but commercially the country was coming under Thai influence, which has continued at a rapid pace. In the future Laos seems destined to fall under China's sphere of influence.

Luang Prabang is a tourist destination now, and its temples are as beautiful as any in Southeast Asia. The passions that divided the warring princes, the hot war that served the Cold War and brought in the Americans to drop more bombs than were dropped in all of World War II, are gone. The long marches of North Vietnamese soldiers down the Ho Chi Minh Trail, the Air America flights into the mountains, are a thing of the past. But Laos, a prisoner of geography, because it borders on Vietnam, paid a dreadful price.

15

Cambodia: Between the Tiger and the Crocodile

Few countries were ever so dominated by the personality of one individual as was Cambodia under the late Norodom Sihanouk. "Mercurial" was the favorite adjective in press reports, but he was a patriot who tried his best to keep his country free and independent while the wars in Indochina raged around him. He failed horribly. His was a high-wire act in which he would favor the East one day and then the West the next. He would favor rightists in his own country and then the leftists. He tried to balance the interests of the Americans and then North Vietnamese and Chinese, until finally he fell off the wire. And, in one of the greatest miscalculations imaginable, after he was deposed and exiled, he threw his support behind the extreme leftist Khmer Rouge, or Red Khmer. By so doing he contributed to his country's descent into its darkest nightmare.

Cambodia, like Laos, is very much the "Indo" part of Indochina, and you felt it right away crossing the border from Vietnam. While Vietnam was under the cultural, religious, and linguistic sway of China, Cambodia was influenced by Hinduism and the Theravada Buddhism common to Sri Lanka, Burma, Thailand, and Laos. The Khmer people, as Cambodians are called, are generally darker skinned and stockier than the slender Vietnamese or the Lao.

Even the countryside itself changed the minute you crossed the Mekong.

The travel writer Norman Lewis got it right when he wrote: "On one bank of the river were the ordinary forest trees [of Vietnam] . . . The other bank bore sparse clumps of coconut palms . . . and beyond them, a foretaste of the withered plains of India."[*]

The Khmer empire reached its zenith in the twelfth century, when its territory spilled over into what is now Vietnam and Thailand. But in subsequent centuries, as its power waned, Cambodia has felt more like an Asian Poland, squeezed between, and threatened by, two more powerful neighbors. "Between the Tiger and the Crocodile," was the way Cambodians saw themselves.

Sihanouk had come to the Cambodian throne in 1941, after the fall of France, when his French colonial masters answered to the collaborationist Vichy government under the German thumb. The Japanese allowed the French to govern Indochina, as long as they collaborated, until the very end of the war, when the Japanese took direct control.

Sihanouk's eye was always on complete independence, which came in 1953 when French colonial rule in Indochina was in its death throes. In 1955 he abdicated in favor of his father, who had been passed over for king. Sihanouk wanted more room for political maneuvering and took the title of prince. He would take up the role of king again after the Khmer Rouge had been defeated and the monarchy restored.

Sihanouk was revered by his people as something close to a deity, and I watched worshipful peasants touch his shadow as he walked by. He would compose songs and both write and direct his own movies, in which he would take the leading role. He would press foreign diplomats into playing bit parts. *Shadow over Angkor,* a tale of CIA intrigue, which costarred him and his wife, Monique, was my favorite.

When I was first stationed in Saigon correspondents were barred from Cambodia, except on special occasions such as the national day, when Sihanouk would invite them in and put on a show.

The vast and flooded rice paddies of Cambodia reflected the sky from an airplane, so from above it looked as if a thin gauze was covering yet another sky

---

[*] Norman Lewis, *A Dragon Apparent* (London: Jonathan Cape, 1951), 193.

underneath, and when you saw the temples and pagodas of Cambodia, you knew you were in a different, and, before the war came, a more peaceful land.

Phnom Penh was a low-rise city, full of broad avenues and boulevards flanked by charming French colonial buildings—more gracious than scruffy Vientiane, and far less modern than Saigon. Foreign correspondents would stay in the sprawling, old colonial pile called Le Royal. Compared to traffic-choked Saigon, Phnom Penh had a languid air with few cars, so we glided around town on a three-wheeled bicycle rickshaw called a cyclopousse, or cyclo for short, basically a seat in front with a sunshade and a man pedaling behind. There were good French and Cambodian restaurants, some of the latter on floating barges in the Mekong River, where fresh fish could be had for a song.

In the 1960s Sihanouk was keeping his country out of the maelstrom that was devouring Laos and Vietnam. The Vietnamese Communists were using his forests to infiltrate their men and munitions into Vietnam. But that remained hidden in the midsixties, and visiting Cambodia then was to be transported back into another time, very different from bustling Bangkok or wartime Saigon. We would always make a point of visiting the great twelfth-century ruins known collectively as Angkor Wat, although Angkor Wat was but one of the temples in that vast complex.

On one occasion some American soldiers on a riverine patrol took a wrong turn up the Mekong River and strayed into neutral Cambodia's territory by mistake. They were arrested by the Cambodian authorities and thrown into prison in Phnom Penh. Washington expressed outrage, but before an international incident could get out of hand, Sihanouk decided to release them.

Being Sihanouk, however, he was not about to do this by a simple handover. He arranged to have them released during the ceremonies for the national day, when the world press and foreign diplomats would be gathered.

He sent his tailor around to the prison to have the bewildered Americans fitted for white cotton suits and shirts. When the national day came, Sihanouk had the wayward American soldiers up on the reviewing stand with him, looking quite spiffy, if uncomfortable, with bright neckties in the colors of Sihanouk's political party. He made a short speech, saying that the Americans were free to go. Their landing barge, however, would stay in Cambodia. "It has no heart, it has no soul. It will do very well here with our little navy," he said in his high-pitched voice. It was the kind of beau geste at which he was a master.

There would be enchanting performances of the court ballet, with the dancers, similar to those in Thailand, performing their graceful and stylized steps with fingers arched into seemingly impossible positions. We all believed that the Cambodians were a gentle people, beguiled as we were by temple bells and Khmer culture in this oasis from war. What we did not suspect was that the ancient torture scenes from the bas reliefs of Angkor would be repeated in the years to come under one of the century's cruelest regimes in a mad effort to turn back the clock to a pre-industrial, pre-urban past that would turn the entire country into a vast agricultural concentration camp.

That grim future would not come as long as Sihanouk was in power, as he desperately tried to balance the dark forces locked in a contest of wills that would eventually decide the fate of Indochina.

I happened to be in Laos on the ides of March, 1970, when Sihanouk was deposed while out of the country on a trip to France and Russia. I hurried to Phnom Penh. One of Sihanouk's top generals, Lon Nol, the only palindrome chief of state I ever met, had engineered the coup. Lon Nol impressed me then as high-strung, nervous, and perhaps a little frightened over the monumental step he had taken. Lon Nol abolished the monarchy, replacing it with the Khmer Republic, with himself as president.

Lon Nol and his officers had grown weary of the Sihanouk show. The prince had secretly allowed the North Vietnamese and the Communist powers to use the port of Sihanoukville to bring supplies to the Vietnamese, who were also using his eastern border as part of the Ho Chi Minh Trail. Sihanouk, also secretly, told the Americans that he would not object if they bombed the Vietnamese in his woods, as long as the bombs stayed away from population centers. The secret bombing of Cambodia was exposed in the American press, and the resulting White House effort to find who leaked the story resulted in the famous "plumbers" whose burglaries, authorized by the White House, contributed to Nixon's eventual downfall.

But now the balancing act was over. Lon Nol immediately ordered all Vietnamese Communist forces out of the country—an order he was pathetically unable to enforce.

I never found any evidence that the Americans engineered the coup, even though they, too, had grown weary of Sihanouk's maneuvers. The Americans were quick to take advantage of the coup, however, at first sending ethnic Khmer soldiers from South Vietnam to Phnom Penh. Soon General Ted Mataxis would arrive from the American army to help organize the war. But it would be a Cambodian war. America would supply the arms and ammunition, but, unlike in Vietnam, no American ground troops would be sent, except for a brief incursion in May of 1970. This incursion, although limited, caused widespread protests in the United States, culminating in the shooting of unarmed students at Kent State College.

Modern times have not seen such an army as Lon Nol organized in those early months of 1970. Patriotic youths flocked to his banner, for the Vietnamese were never popular with Cambodians. Waving flags, beating drums, brandishing swords as well as firearms too few knew how to use, Cambodian soldiers sallied forth to slay the Vietnamese dragon, putting little carved images of the Buddha in their mouths to save them from harm. Many adorned themselves with sashes sewn from prayer flags. They were shot to bits by the Vietnamese and sent reeling back from the frontier.

The North Vietnamese had no desire to take over Cambodia, at least not then, but they wanted to keep the Ho Chi Minh Trail open in order to resupply the forces in South Vietnam. Sihanouk took up residence in Beijing and recorded audiotapes inciting peasants to rise up against Lon Nol. The tapes were smuggled into Cambodia. In the forests, where antigovernment guerrilla groups had waxed and waned for decades, a new and fanatical resistance was formed, known to the world as the Khmer Rouge. At its head was Pol Pot, a semieducated schoolteacher who had garnered half-baked ideas from the French Revolution from studying in France. He married these with the most extreme Maoist doctrines to form a nihilistic jacquerie movement, a peasant uprising, the countryside against the cities, dedicated to the complete destruction of modern Cambodia with its Western influences.

In the first days of the new battle for Cambodia, when the front was very fluid, I ran into my old photographer friends from Saigon, Sean Flynn and Dana Stone, with whom I had worked before. Stone was a straightforward Vermonter, as different from the exotic and glamorous Flynn as Vermont cheddar is from Brie. Flynn was the son of Errol Flynn, the Hollywood actor who, as far as my generation was concerned, personified the word "swashbuckling." Sean looked a lot like his father in *Captain Blood,* and had been in a couple of minor movies himself. *Cinq gars pour Singapour,* starring Sean, had played in a dingy Saigon movie theater, and we all went to see it as the occasional rat ran over our feet. As Mike Herr described him in *Dispatches,* Flynn was special. "We all had our movie-fed war fantasies . . . and it could be totally disorienting to have this outrageously glamorous figure intrude . . . really unhinging." But Flynn had been in Indochina a long time, was used to long-range patrols where men would live in the jungle for weeks, and as Herr described it, soldiers knew that he was "a dude who definitely had his shit together."

Flynn had a scheme that didn't seem as crazy as it in fact was. Encounters between reporters and the Vietnamese Communists, North Vietnamese and Vietcong, had taken place with reporters living to tell the tale during those unsettling April days when the North Vietnamese were moving back from the border. The North Vietnamese were afraid of an American incursion into Cambodia, which soon came. Flynn thought if he and Dana could travel by motorcycle, allowing them to run on trails and tracks off the main roads, they might encounter Vietnamese who were moving back farther into Cambodia. It would make, with photographs, a great story, he argued. I felt it was far too dangerous, and, since Flynn was shooting for Time-Life, I tried to pull rank, saying I was the senior *Time* guy in Cambodia. I knew that if I could dissuade Flynn, Stone would follow.

Pulling rank on Flynn was like trying to talk down a cockatoo on the wing, but I tried. We went off to an opium "*fumerie*" frequented by a few Cambodians, French rubber planters, some foreign diplomats, and a few journalists. The drill was that you took off your clothes, put on a sarong, and lay down on a straw mat. A woman, usually an ancient crone, would roll the little balls of opium, which she would insert, with a needle, into the bowl of your pipe. She would help you hold the pipe over the flame of a tiny lamp while you inhaled deeply. Unlike other drugs, it was only mildly intoxicating, causing a certain drowsiness and a feeling of well-being. There were, of course, opium addicts. But with opium you really had to work at it. A few pipes a few times wouldn't do it. The expression "pipe dream" comes from the dreamy optimism opium gives you.

Sex was not part of the deal, although sometimes a young girl would walk on your back as a kind of massage. But Stone, the steady Vermonter who had never been to an opium den before, refused to take his clothes off, put on a sarong, or try a pipe. He sat with his knees up in a corner looking very suspicious.

For hours I tried every argument I could think of, saying their motorbike scheme was a very bad idea, but Flynn just laughed, said I was getting too old. I was thirty-five, only eight years older than he, but evidently an old coot who had lost his sense of adventure. Flynn wasn't going to back down no matter what I said. We parted in separate cyclos back to the hotel for a restless night's sleep. I n   ther of them again.

There have been books written about Flynn and Stone and their disappearance, and their fate remains an enduring mystery in journalists' lore. They were seen by other journalists coming up the road in a car behind them the next day. Flynn and Stone seemed to be motioning their colleagues not to come farther. The speculation is that they were captured by North Vietnamese soldiers and died in captivity. There were reports of radio traffic being intercepted, with the Vietnamese saying they had lost two white prisoners killed in a B-52 strike, but as far as I know it was never confirmed.

They were among the first of some thirty-four journalists to die in Cambodia, many of them in those first months when we didn't know the ropes. Journalists were captured and released by the Vietnamese, but later, when the Khmer Rouge took over the fighting against Lon Nol, no one captured by them ever came back. If you were caught by the Khmer Rouge you could count on being pulled out of your car and either shot on the spot or clubbed to death to save ammunition.

Once the restraining influence of Sihanouk had been removed, Cambodi-ans in the capital and elsewhere turned against the Vietnamese in their midst, some of whom had lived in Cambodia for generations. There were disgraceful massacres. No one will ever know how many Vietnamese were slaughtered in those distressing days. I watched scores of mutilated and swollen bodies floating down the Mekong. The ancient antagonism between the Cambodians and the Vietnamese was on the loose.

The war soon settled down into a kind of stalemate, with the Lon Nol government holding most of the major towns and cities, trying to keep the roads and the Mekong River open. The Khmer Rouge owned the forests and fought to keep the roads, and then the river, closed as they slowly tightened their grip around the towns.

To cover this battle for the highways, reporters would drive out of Phnom Penh in rented cars with their Cambodian interpreters and drivers, down roads leading away from the capital, like spokes on a wheel, looking for the war. Sometimes we could hitch a ride on Cambodian river gunboats to visit some of the besieged towns along the Mekong. You risked rocket fire from the banks on those trips, but the classic death in Cambodia would come to reporters on a lonely road with a Khmer Rouge ambush in waiting.

There were certain rules it was wise to learn. If there was no traffic coming in the other direction for a long while, turn around and go back. If no curi-ous children swarmed around your car when you arrived in a village, get out, and quick. For it meant the children were staying indoors because fear—or their parents' fear—had trumped curiosity. And that usually meant there were Khmer Rouge in the neighborhood. When you stopped to ask a farmer in the field about conditions on the road up ahead, you never asked too direct a question. You spent time with your interpreter, asking the farmer about his crops, the weather, his family, sidling up to the question about whether the road was safe. This way you were much more likely to get a straight answer instead of what the startled farmer might think you wanted to hear. It was time consuming, but there were more than a dozen reporters lost on the roads of Cambodia in just those early days, and I am convinced that these simple precautions saved my life.

On these trips out of the capital you might find the front line manned by only two or three bored soldiers washing their laundry by the side of the road with nothing happening that day. One time I went out with a British military attaché, and when we got out of the car a sniper took a shot at us, and missed. "Saucy of them," said the unflappable Brit.

Other times you would run into the back of a government advance, armored personnel carriers moving down the road with soldiers behind, and sometimes withering fire stripping the trees of their branches and leaves, which fell like confetti.

We were all very dependent on our interpreters, who, besides translating, could smooth over problems with the bureaucracy and find out valuable information. Many had been in the tourist industry before the war. When the war drove away all the tourists, many gravitated toward the capital, where, with their language skills, they could hire themselves out to journalists. It was dangerous work, and I often thought of them as similar to big-game hunters who had clients—sometimes foolish clients—who could get them killed. But like professional hunters, they were there to get their clients trophy stories and keep them out of trouble.

A very brave photographer and cameraman, an Australian named Neil Davis, once told me how he had been wounded in a firefight, and how his interpreter and guide carried him back to his car and put him in the backseat, where he drifted in and out of consciousness on the way back to Phnom Penh, losing blood all the way. Davis thought he was being taken to the hospital, but the car pulled up at the airport on the outskirts of the city. "Don't you want to ship film?" Davis's driver asked. Davis allowed as how this time it would be okay to go straight to the hospital and worry about the film later. Davis was later killed in Bangkok during a coup attempt, his dropped camera still running to film his own death.

The most famous of these Cambodian guides was Dith Pran, who was later portrayed in the film *The Killing Fields*. I had met Pran at Angkor Wat, where he worked before the war. He would arrange elephant-back rides to the temples at dusk. He became intensely loyal to Sidney Schanberg of the

New York Times, who would often yell at him in a way that would have been offensive to most Cambodians, but Pran would only smile.

Sidney was obsessed with the Cambodian story, and he made it his own, seldom leaving the country as the rest of us did from time to time. By the time I met him I had left *Time* and was working for the *Washington Post.* Even though our papers were rivals, I always enjoyed Sidney's company and admired his reporting skills. He was, like many *New York Times* men, very competitive.

One scoop that got away from both of us is also portrayed in *The Killing Fields.* Pran came to Sidney and told him that something horrible had happened in the Mekong market town of Neak Luong downriver. An American B-52 bomber had dropped its load over friendly territory with great loss of life. Pran got Sidney downriver in a boat, where he had the story all to himself but was detained by the Cambodian military. The rest of the press caught up with him when they were brought down by helicopter the next day—robbing Sidney of his scoop, even though his story was more complete and better than anyone else's.

When I say "the rest of the press," I mean all except this correspondent, who was nowhere to be seen. My interpreter, Yun, had also heard of the disaster, and like Pran, he smuggled me onto a boat headed downriver. Mine was a rice boat bound for Neak Luong. In the dark of night, Yun hid me among the bags of rice until we were clear of Phnom Penh. As we headed downstream I gloated that I would have the story all to myself, not realizing that Sidney was also headed downriver on another boat. But for me it was not to be. An hour out of Phnom Penh the engine quit and we drifted slowly until a Cambodian patrol boat took us under tow and brought us back to Phnom Penh the following day. I had not only failed to get there first, I had failed to get there at all. When I got back to the hotel, a "Why we no have?" telegram from my editor awaited me.

Telegrams were regularly left on the reception desk for reporters to pick up, mostly "play cables," saying things like "fronted your pagoda story," which meant it was on page one, or even "led paper with your Lon Nol." These telegrams were our primary source of communication with our home offices, as the telephone was notoriously unreliable, if you could get through at all. Sometimes to fool rivals, reporters would send themselves congratulatory telegrams about nonexistent stories.

A typical day reporting the war in Cambodia would often mean an early start and a day on the roads, trying to find out about how the ebb and flow of the fighting was going. At day's end I would come back to the Royal, which had been renamed Le Phnom after the monarchy was abolished. I would take a quick shower, which did little to cool me off in the exhausting heat, and sit down to write the daily story. Sometimes I would attend a government briefing, given by a Cambodian official who was appropriately named Am Rong.

I wrote my stories on that old Olympia typewriter that I had bought during my Oxford student days, stained with candle wax. Power outages were frequent, and I had two enormous, five-foot orange candles that I had bought in a Buddhist supply shop. Sitting in a sarong, which I always wore when writing in that climate, the candles casting giant shadows on the wall and sweat dripping on the copy paper, I typed out my pessimistic reports about a dying country. My stories were usually about the slowly deteriorating situation as the government's perimeter shrank and shrank. Roads were temporarily opened, then cut again, as the war dragged on.

I have a yellowing clip from the *Washington Post* of that year:

ANG SNOUL, September 19th, 1973—After three weeks of fighting, Highway 4 to the sea was cleared of insurgents Tuesday and Wednesday. Just off the road the government soldiers were sitting around in the ruins of the Kruos Pagoda burning bits of bodies.

First the government troops and then the insurgents had occupied the pagoda, and now it stands a tall ruin—its curling roof and red tiles holed by a hundred shells—stark white against the darkening, rain-swollen sky . . .

Outside the pagoda the insurgents had had to dig their bunkers in the rice paddy dikes because the paddies are flooded at this time of year. But pagodas always stand on high ground and they are well-built and solid. They make excellent positions from which to fight off an approaching enemy, and all over the country the fighting has often centered on pagodas like this one.

It is the insurgents' tactic to hold positions like this as long as they can and then to fade away in the night taking their dead and wounded with them whenever possible. The government soldiers said that this battle was no exception, and when the final assault was made the soldiers found the enemy gone.

For the first time in three weeks traffic was moving all along the road Wednesday, and the first truck convoys up from the sea have already reached Phnom Penh.

When we didn't run the roads, we would write stories about Phnom Penh, how much petroleum was left in town, what was the food supply. We tried to find out what the government might or might not be thinking, or just write human-interest stories about the hundreds of refugees pouring into the city each day.

We would take our stories down to the PTT, "Post, Telegraph, and Telephone," where they would be transmitted, very slowly, to Paris and then on to America. Colleagues, who were all filing at the same time, would go across the pretty little square, for all the world looking like a town square in the French Midi, to relax and have dinner together. My favorite restaurant was called Le Tavern.

It was a time to relax with your work done for the day. You had not been killed, and this was the moment to chat with friends and colleagues over a meal and some wine while your stories went out to the world. There was Jean-Claude Pomonti of *Le Monde;* John Swain, first of Agence France-Presse and then the *Times* of London; Schanberg; Elizabeth Becker, *Far East Economic Review;* Martin Woollacott of the *Guardian;* and the poet James Fenton, who was stringing for the *Washington Post,* to name a few. And who could forget Tiziano Terzani, a tall, mustached Florentine who wrote for the German magazine *Der Spiegel.* Tiziano always dressed in a white shirt and matching white trousers, and in conversation was a master of colorful hyperbole. We all basked in the sunshine of his personality and friendship. We were members of an informal club of sorts, held together by the all-absorbing story of a beautiful land coming apart. Of course none of us suspected just how terrible the end would be.

I did have one small glimpse of what was to come, however. I was told that a North Vietnamese adviser to the Khmer Rouge had defected to the government side and that I could interview him. He told me that he had fled from the Khmer Rouge because he feared for his life. He said that, unlike the Vietnamese Communists, who would perhaps come to a village and kill the head man if he was corrupt and hated by the people, or perhaps too well loved, the Khmer Rouge would kill people indiscriminately, despite his advice. Hanoi had sent him to help and guide the Khmer Rouge, he told me, but they, like many Cambodians, hated the Vietnamese and he feared they would kill him. Still, even his tale did not prepare me for the killing that was to come.

At night, often too tired to sleep well, we could hear the thunderous explosions from the B-52 bomber flying in from faraway Guam in the night sky, trying to keep the Khmer Rouge at bay. The shock waves rolling over the city would rattle the windows as if a demented intruder were running around the outside trying to get in.

Later in the war, when Khmer Rouge rockets were arriving in Phnom, I pulled my mosquito-netted bed away from the window in case a round should burst in the trees outside, sending shrapnel into my room.

On a hot afternoon, when I was writing a long article for the Sunday paper, I heard an incoming rocket burst not far from the hotel. There was a moment of silence, and then the high-pitched and desperate cries of children screaming—birdlike screaming in a way I had not heard before or since. The rocket had landed on a school, and the sight, when I went to see, of blood-soaked sandals lying in the dust, with small bodies torn to pieces, was heartbreaking. But it is the sound of those screams that I can sometimes hear still in my worst dreams almost forty years later.

One of the more dramatic stories of the Cambodian war was of the little tramp steamers, coasters, that would make the hazardous journey up the Mekong from the South China Sea. They brought vital food, fuel, and ammunition to besieged Phnom Penh. Once all the roads had been cut, this gallant flotilla became the city's main lifeline.

These little freighters and tugs pulling barges of ammunition were heavily sandbagged to protect their bridges. Their crews, representing all the races of the East, were well paid, but the voyage up from the sea was astonishingly dangerous. Many were holed by rocket fire from the banks, arriving in Phnom Penh very much the worse for it. Some were sunk along the way.

My friend Martin Woollacott wrote a story about the river sailors who made these parlous journeys. "The three captains, a wolfish Australian, a mustached Swede, and a dapper little Norwegian, stood on the quay above the broad Mekong River cursing the Khmer Rouge, their own crews and the port authorities. Drifters and fortune hunters right out of the pages of novelist Joseph Conrad, they were men who brought last Thursday's convoy up to Phnom Penh." Losses had been so heavy among the ships that the charter companies "had to put in some Goddamn round-eyes [white men] or else the Goddamn convoy never go at all," said the Swede. The Australian described to Woollacott "four bloody bad hours . . . I've never seen anything like it. It was four hours of continuous firing. Jeez, I thought Australians were popular everywhere, but we ain't got many friends on the Mekong, I can tell you."

The Norwegian captain told Woollacott: "It was incredible. The crew were screaming at me, one minute shouting at me to turn back, the next to keep the tug at full ahead. Everyone was shouting 'Beaucoup VC. Beaucoup VC.'" But they weren't Vietcong. They were Khmer Rouge.

When the river was finally cut off, it was clear to us that the city was doomed. I wrote a story for the *Post* about starvation breaking out in the city. I was later told that the story helped prompt Washington to begin bringing in food and supplies by air, as had once been done in Berlin when the Soviets tried to close off access to that city.

But there was no political will left in America to defend Cambodia. It was not Berlin. Congress cut off funding, ending the intense bombing campaign on August 15, 1973. It was a clear blue day when the bombing stopped, with the slightest suggestion of thunderheads forming up to the south. Perfect flying weather.

I could see American planes bombing and strafing away to the north, the jets pulling straight up from their runs at what seemed an impossible angle of ascent. On a little radio, of the kind that you could buy cheaply in Hong Kong, I could hear the pilots talking to each other and to ground control. Around eleven o'clock on that last morning, in that laconic manner in which American pilots talk, I heard: "You should not expend any more air. You should not expend any more air. Understand there is negative more activity for the facers [forward air controllers]," said another.

"That's affirmative on that," came the answer.

"Outstanding. Well we all enjoyed working with you. You did some fine work and we knocked their ass off more than once. We hope to work for you again," the pilot said, but it was not to be. America's air war in Indochina was over.

One of the spotter planes did a slow barrel roll. A pilot played "Turkey in the Straw" on a harmonica over the airwaves, as the planes broke off and headed west toward their bases in Thailand.

On the ground, a few miles outside the capital, I watched two government howitzers banging away at where they thought the Khmer Rouge might be, the soldiers bending to their task ramming rounds into the breaches. Farmers, ignoring the firing, were gathering rice stalks.

The Lon Nol government hung on for almost two years more and the war ground on. Thousands more refugees, with bullock carts looking exactly the same as those portrayed on the bas reliefs of Angkor eight centuries before, plodded down the roads toward the illusion of safety in Phnom Penh.

A couple of weeks before the Khmer Republic's end I was ordered to Saigon, so I missed the downfall. Schanberg and Dith Pran stayed, Sidney to win a well-deserved Pulitzer Prize, and Pran to endure his time in Khmer Rouge hell. Cambodia's four years of agony under the Khmer Rouge began with the "year zero," as they called it—taking their cue from the French Revolution.

Later, when the first shocking news of what life in Cambodia under the Khmer Rouge was like began to seep out, I visited the border refugee camps in Thailand and heard of how children were being indoctrinated to denounce their parents. People would be taken out and beaten to death. Anybody who could read or write was suspected of being a class enemy. An auto-genocide that would claim many more than a million lives through execution, starvation, and neglect was in full cry.

———

In 1979 the Vietnamese, finally losing patience with their erstwhile ally, invaded Cambodia and pushed the Khmer Rouge into the mountains and border regions near Thailand. In 1989 I returned to Cambodia again to write a story for the *New Yorker*. Normalcy was trying to creep back. But the horrors of Toul Sleng, the school that had been taken over by Pol Pot's people as a torture chamber and death camp, were terrible to see. The walls were lined with photographs of the condemned, which the Khmer Rouge had taken in a Nazi-like organizational effort to record their proceedings, each face showing the unbearable sadness and resignation of those who knew they were about to die. I searched in vain for any of my Cambodian friends, especially Yun.

Among the Cambodian faces in the photographs there was one of an American, an unsuspecting yachtsman who had been picked up off the coast and taken to the torture chamber to die. The thought of a carefree sailor, sailing way out in the blue sea, being snatched and ending up in this horror remains unbearable to me.

I wandered down to the little square where, years before, we had come to file out stories and share a meal. I found the building with the now-faded letters saying LE TAVERN. But the building had been burned out and was now just a hollow shell, as was Cambodia itself in the immediate post–Khmer Rouge years.

I went back to Angkor with some Australian aid workers, a quick visit, flying west in a terrifyingly decrepit Russian transport plane flown by Vietnamese pilots. We were told we had to be out by dark because the Khmer Rouge would infiltrate back into the ruins under cover of darkness. You could hear the rumble of artillery to the west where the Vietnamese and Khmer Rouge were still fighting in the mountains.

Our guide, in the course of visiting one of the temples, pointed out ashes in a corner where, he said, the Khmer Rouge had lit a campfire. I felt the ashes. They were still warm. The Air France hotel, I believe it was called l'Auberge du Temple, near the ruins where I had first met Dith Pran in happier times was burned to the ground. The old Grand Hotel d'Angkor in the town of Siem Reap was a mess, with blocked toilets and tattered mosquito nets and power failures. Vietnamese military officers lounged around smoking in broken armchairs.

The Khmer Rouge had been so efficient at wiping out Cambodians who showed any sign of education that there were very few left who could pass on the elements of Khmer culture to future generations. A search was afoot for old-timers who had survived, or had been living abroad, who could teach young girls the intricacies of Cambodian dance.

In Phnom Penh there were holes in the soaring yellow roofs of the royal palace, and the rusting hulk of a Philippine freighter lay beached on a nearby river bank. Little had been done to repair the city's water system, and foreign aid workers told me it was among the world's most polluted. Broken sewer and water pipes were leaking into each other, a constant source of disease. It was a measure of the horror in which traumatized Cambodians held their recent past that they would tell you that the real reason for the water pollution was that the Khmer Rouge had killed so many people that the water table itself was contaminated.

If the Khmer people are destined to choose between being eaten by a crocodile or a tiger, in 1989 the people of Phnom Penh seemed content with the Vietnamese tigers, who were by then planning their withdrawal, rather than Pol Pot's crocodiles whom they hoped would never return.

The United Nations was trying to prepare the country for its first postwar election. In one village not far from the capital, I watched as UN personnel tried to convince skeptical villagers that there could be such a thing as a secret ballot. They handed out pieces of paper to villagers and asked them to put them into a box. Then the box was opened, and the villagers were asked to find their particular piece of paper. The villagers could not, of course, but the UN people were missing the point. If the Khmer Rouge were to come back—and the Khmer Rouge were still holding out along the border with Thailand—they wouldn't be interested in which villager had voted for which party. They would kill the whole village for having anything to do with the voting. Against all odds the elections were relatively successful.

In 2000, more than thirty years since my first visit to Angkor, JB and I were back in the Grand Hotel d'Angkor in Siem Reap, now beautifully restored to its original splendor. There were hundreds of carefree tourists having a good time and visiting the ruins. I never thought I would be glad to see a site overrun with tourists, but after everything that Cambodia had been through in the intervening decades, the sight of foreigners having a good time—without a thought of what had transpired in that unhappy land— lifted my heart. A measure of normality was creeping back to a country that had been so abused.[*]

What made the Khmer Rouge so cruel and extreme, emptying cities and trying to erase every trace of Cambodia's culture, religion, even family life? Some blame it on Henry Kissinger and the intense American bombing, but I don't agree. Parts of Vietnam were also heavily bombed, and Laos even more, but the Lao and the Vietnamese did not revert to anything like the "year zero" of the Khmer Rouge.

Cambodian history is full of peasant uprisings, countryside against city, and the answer is more likely to be found deep in the Khmer psyche than in anything Henry Kissinger did.

---

[*] The monarchy was restored in 1993, and Sihanouk was back on the throne.

16

Indonesian New Guinea:
Stoning the Stone Age Men

A couple of notebooks in my cellar look more than usually tattered and sweat stained, and they contain some random information about cannibalism. They date from the sixties and seventies, when I made several trips back in time, or so it seemed, to an island in New Guinea where there were pockets of the population not far removed from the Stone Age. Lying north of Australia, it is the second-biggest island in the world after Greenland. The western half once belonged to the Dutch East Indies and is now a part of Indonesia. The eastern half was colonized in the north by imperial Germany and in the south by the British. After the First World War, Australia took over the entire eastern half until Papua New Guinea became independent in 1975.

With peaks as high as the Alps, with dark rivers, and jungles, and upland plateaus that look like they could be in Europe, New Guinea is altogether unique. The uplands are inhabited by a population that was all but hidden from the rest of the world until well into the twentieth century.

Although cannibalism and head-hunting had been largely suppressed by the time I reached those shores forty years ago, there were still a few pockets of backsliding despite the efforts of missionaries and governments. There were people who might have flown in an airplane but had never driven in a car. The coasts had been known to Europeans since the sixteenth century when the Portuguese began exploring the South Seas. The island was named because it reminded Portuguese sailors of the west coast of Africa. The highlands contained a population of almost a million people that were only discovered and exposed to outsiders in the 1930s when Australian gold prospectors made their way deep into the interior.

The photographs of those first meetings between white Australians and the darker Melanesian Papuans reveal what the indigenous peoples of the Americas must have felt when they first encountered Columbus and his crew. The photos show expressions of fear and utter amazement. They asked the Australian prospectors the exact same question that Columbus had been asked: "Are you our ancestors?"

Trouble came only when curious natives tried to snatch the Australians' gear. These misunderstandings about the nature of private property were similar to those between the early settlers in New England and the native population, and similar to Captain Cook's troubles in Tahiti. And, as in those previous cases, the natives were awed by gunpowder, which the Australians were not hesitant to use.

When Sukarno, the fiery first leader of independent Indonesia, took over from the Dutch after World War II he demanded control over every territory that had once been Dutch. The Dutch, in turn, regretfully left most of their island empire to Sukarno, but held on to New Guinea, claiming that the Papuans had no cultural or ethnic connection to the rest of Indonesia and therefore needed Dutch protection. The Dutch hoped to make New Guinea a model colony, an example of what enlightened colonialism could do. But in the end international pressure was too great and they had to hand it over to Sukarno.

When first I arrived the Dutch had just recently departed, and the provincial capital of Hollandia had been renamed Jayapura (Freedom City). The Indonesians had been getting some bad press for the way they had taken up the brown man's burden, which was being unfavorably compared to old-fashioned colonialism without any attempts at enlightenment. To counteract this impression the Indonesians took a chance and let some of the Western press in to take a look for themselves. We flew from the Indonesian capital, Jakarta, which the Dutch had called Batavia, to the island of Biak off the north coast of what was now Indonesian New Guinea. Biak had recently served as a landing field for the Dutch airline, KLM. But technology had extended the range of modern airplanes, and Biak was rapidly becoming a relic of the past, as remote from modern times as the old coaling stations that dotted the Pacific early in the age of steam.

In Jayapura we reporters were closely controlled, and there were few opportunities to do any hard independent reporting. But the anxious eyes of the local citizens and the messages on crumpled pieces of paper that they would furtively thrust into our hands told their own tales. They were tales of plunder and mistreatment at the hands of the Indonesians, who had more or less looted the model colony they found in Hollandia, taking refrigerators, air conditioners, and just about anything that wasn't nailed down back to Java. The Dutch had left behind, at least in the coastal towns, a much higher standard of living than existed in the rest of Indonesia, and the new masters from Java felt free to help themselves. The newly named Jayapura was sinking into what would become just another run-down Indonesian port.

Later, in 1969, Sean Flynn and I made a trip to Indonesian New Guinea to put together some stories on the lives of the highland natives whose way of life was still much as it had been for thousands of years.

Flynn told me that his film-star father, Errol Flynn, had once worked in the New Guinea goldfields and had killed a man. Flynn senior had had to leave the territory in a hurry and that's why he ended up in Hollywood.

While still on the coast we ran across an improbable—at the time he seemed preposterous—character of the kind one might have met in a South Seas story by W. Somerset Maugham, except that he came from Yonkers. When this bizarre fellow learned we were journalists he began insisting that we write a story about him. He attached himself to us in an annoying way, but he was pleasant enough that we didn't want to hurt his feelings by telling him to buzz off. It became apparent to me that he was developing a crush on Sean, but Flynn was oblivious to that.

He plied us with ever more fantastic yarns of traveling into the Hindu Kush mountains of Afghanistan and up the Amazon looking for more and more remote populations and unknown diseases that he could study in isolation.

He told us tales about riding down New Guinea rivers with cannibal raiders who would hamstring their victims so they couldn't run away, but keep them alive so that their meat would still be fresh by the time the cannibals reached home and were ready to eat.

He said he would one day be famous for having discovered a hitherto-unknown disease that, like the gods, made people mad before it destroyed them. He called it a "laughing disease" because of the hideous grin on the victims' faces in the last stages of the illness. You could only contract this disease, he said, by eating and smearing yourself with the brains of those whom you were about to devour. He thought a big spread in *Life* magazine would be just the thing to cement his fame. Flynn and I were looking for good stories, but we weren't about to fall for this blarney. We decided he was either the world's greatest bullshitter or simply mad, so we declined his offer to write him up and moved on. His name was Carleton Gajdusek.

Nearly ten years later there were press reports about Gajdusek. He had just won the Nobel Prize for medicine for discovering a mysterious disease called kuru that you could get only from eating and smearing yourself with the brains of others, just as he had said. The disease had nearly wiped out the Fore tribe in New Guinea, who, after eating their victims, descended into trembling madness and death. The practice of mortuary feasts had all but vanished in New Guinea since the 1940s, suppressed by the authorities, but it had lingered on in remote places. The disease turned out to be related to Creutzfeldt-Jakob, or "mad cow," disease. Apparently the annoying Gajdusek had been right all along, and I longed to call Flynn to tell him of the scoop we had missed. But by that time Flynn had met his own untimely death in Cambodia.

Alas, Gajdusek was accused of molesting boys from New Guinea whom he had adopted and taken home to Maryland. It caused considerable scandal at the time, but he insisted that sex with young men was an ancient tradition going back to classical Greece. When he died, in 2008, he was better remembered for his considerable scientific achievements than his unconventional life.

Flynn and I were headed for the highlands, where an altogether more primitive people were to be found than those living on the coast. The highland women wore only grass skirts, and the men wore only "phallocrypts," intricately engineered gourds to hide the penis. We were told that they liked a cheap tobacco called "shag" that could be used as currency. Their other currency consisted of cowrie shells. How these seashells ever found their way into the highlands remained a mystery. They were in use when the first outsiders arrived, but then no highlander had ever seen the ocean and their languages had no word for the ocean. Even by the time Flynn and I arrived, many had no idea they lived on an island.

The only practical way to reach the highlands was by missionary air flight. At one end of the runway were the Catholics, mostly Dutch and French, jolly priests who gave you a glass of wine and would entertain you royally before flying you to their remote airstrips in the interior. At the other end of the runway lived the Protestants, mostly Bible Belt Americans who wouldn't give you anything to drink and were dour company. But the Protestants were known to be superb bush pilots and better mechanics who regularly took apart their new Cessnas and put them together again to make sure they were working properly.

We decided to fly with the Protestants on the way up and with the Catholics on the way down. It was better not to talk too much about your plans, because if either end of the runway knew you were flying with the other, both might refuse to take you at all. I have often thought that in that land of exotic races with outlandish practices, perhaps the best anthropological study would have been the Protestant and Catholic missionaries and their rivalries at opposite ends of the airfield.

The flight up from the coast took us through thick clouds before we broke out into the cool upland sunshine. We said good-bye to our taciturn pilot and started walking. We wanted to find a village that had no metal objects in use because we wanted to walk back as far in time as we could. In the end we had to settle for a village in which the only metal in use was the headman's belt buckle. But he was the only guy in town wearing short pants instead of a phallocrypt. We found villagers using axes made of a jadelike stone bound to a wooden handle, living in houses in which there were no nails.

We settled in for a few days with hospitable people who were living a life of subsistence farming and a little pig hunting with stone weapons from another age. They had periodic wars with other villages, but given that they fought with primitive bows and arrows with no feathers to guide them, casualties were few in any one battle. How different their warfare seemed from Vietnam, from whence we had come, with its whole-scale destruction of villages by fire and bomb. But villagers in New Guinea lived in fear of each other, and, over time, casualties could take a big chunk out of their populations. Peace talks were difficult because it was said that there were at least seven hundred different languages on the island.

Sean Flynn in New Guinea with the "stone age men," 1974.

We discovered that the men and teenage boys of our village lived in long-houses separate from their women and girls. The guys were grateful for the shag tobacco we had brought them and smoked it in cone-shaped rolled-up leaves. We had been told by missionaries that shag was the expected house present we should bring. Our hosts seemed healthy enough, except for chronic respiratory problems. They killed a pig for us, a great honor, and with no common language we communicated our gratitude in sign language, at which Flynn excelled. They seemed never to have seen a camera before and were never sure what Flynn was doing. Cameras in those days had no way of showing the pictures you were actually taking, so Flynn, to show them how it worked, took off the lens and bade them peer into the camera's innards as he held it to his eye. Then, when he released the trigger, they could see his eye looking at them, and they invariably jumped back in alarm.

We spent evenings in their smoky houses sitting around the fire and puffing on our shag and listening to their songs. It was then that Flynn had his bright idea. He had brought some marijuana with him, and he suggested we stone the Stone Age men. I was not thrilled.

"What?" said Flynn. "You believe all this 'reefer madness' crap about grass making people violent? Here's a chance to prove in field conditions that marijuana makes people jolly."

"Yeah, but what if making them jolly means eating us for dinner, Sean?" I said. But I was having no more success with him now than I had later when I tried to talk him out of his fatal motorcycle trip in search of the Vietcong in Cambodia. So I asked him to give me half a day's head start out of the valley before he lit up our hosts.

I made my way down to the airstrip a day later just as a Catholic plane was landing. An amiable French pilot took me back to semi-civilization, where I downed a good bottle of Burgundy with the priests. When I caught up with Flynn again he told me that his experiment had been a total success. He had mixed the pot in with the shag and watched the male population of the village get high. He swore that they had never seemed more friendly, that their songs had never been better sung, nor louder, than on his last night in the Dani highlands of New Guinea.

17

Australian New Guinea: Missionaries, Cannibals, & Cargo Cults

I wasn't to see New Guinea again until 1974, when the *Washington Post* assigned me to write some stories about the Australian half of the island. Papua New Guinea was being prepared for independence, the latest in the long process of decolonization that had so indelibly marked the second half of the twentieth century. Australians had ruled Papua New Guinea since World War I, when the League of Nations had mandated both the German half in the north and the British southern half to them.

I learned that Papuan delegates had gone to my managing editor, Howard Simons, and persuaded him that the *Post* should take a look at the newborn country on the eve of its birth. Few countries have had to make the leap from near Stone Age conditions into the modern world so quickly, and this appealed to Simons. When I arrived 96 percent of all managerial and executive positions were still in the hands of expatriates, mostly Australians, and more than half of all wages and salaries went into their pockets as well. You couldn't say that Papua New Guinea was actually ready for independence, but it was coming, ready or not.

I would spend six weeks traversing the emerging country in the twilight of colonial rule, from the coasts where Australians and Americans had turned back the Japanese in World War II, to the highlands where tribes still fought their wars with arrows and spears. Whereas American doctors in Vietnam could boast the most advanced gunshot-wound treatment in the world, the coffee-growing town of Mount Hagen had the world's best arrow-wound hospital.

Australia was working diligently to train Papuans to take over, but it was obvious that a certain amount of chaos was bound to follow independence. Away from the major towns the country was run by Australian district commissioners whose word was law over vast territories. These colonial officers were known as "outside men" in the former British south, and "kiaps" in the former German territory in the north. The word "kiap" was a corruption of "*Kapitän.*"

Up in the highlands I found white coffee and tea planters playing tennis dressed in whites and sipping gins in their clubs while Papuans looked on in a bemused way. It was a perfect picture of colonial society that had not changed all that much since the British Raj. Now, however, a form colony was preparing another colony for independence.

One week I went on an overland trek with a twenty-seven-year-old assistant district commissioner named David Bawden, whose subdistrict contained eight hundred square miles of jungle-covered hills and about twenty-four thousand people. He was acting magistrate, senior police officer, tax collector, postmaster, banking agent, and coordinator for all government services. Under his command were seven constables of the Royal Papua New Guinea Constabulary, and five jail wardens. He communicated with his subjects in that curious mixture of corrupted English with a little Spanish, German, Portuguese, Malay, and Melanesian thrown in called "pidgin." It was the lingua franca of the islands and the only way that people speaking more than seven hundred different languages could communicate.

In Bibles, which missionaries translated into pidgin, the Lord's Prayer begins: "*Papa bilong mipela yu stap long heven.*" The Gospel According to Matthew, chapter 2, verse 22, tells how "*Herodes I kilim ol pickinni belong Bethlehem.*" The universality of pidgin was driven home to me when I heard a parrot say: "*Mi laikim kaikai,*" "*kaikai*" being food. It was the closest it could get to "Polly want a cracker."

Bawden and I set out walking at the head of a long line of prisoners who were carrying our camping gear balanced on their heads or between poles on their shoulders, like a scene out of David Livingstone's Africa. The purpose was to touch base with remote communities, hear their grievances, and moderate disputes. Bawden could hear court cases, short of capital offenses, and those convicted would join the end of our foot caravan and be taken back to a jail. The equipment these prisoners carried was not the lightweight fare you can buy at Eastern Mountain Sports. Our tents were made of old-fashioned weighty canvas. The tables and chairs were of heavy wood, and even the crockery was thick and heavy.

It was as tough a walk as I have ever had, and I didn't have to carry anything. Up steep hills we went on jungle tracks, and down again into sunless valleys, only to ascend again to another ridge. One day we were walking up a shallow riverbed when Bawden told me to empty the water from my canteen and fill it up with river water. I did, and that night when our camp was set up and the whiskey was uncorked for the usual "sundowner," he told me to put my canteen water into my glass and hold it up to the dying light. It was flecked with gold dust. I am not sure it made the whiskey taste any better, but I am prepared to say that it did.

At one sparse settlement clinging to the side of a hill, Bawden heard a case of a highlander who had struck his victim with an ax, causing grievous bodily harm. Bawden took testimony from witnesses and proceeded as if he were a bewigged barrister from Lincoln's Inn. The trial took all of twenty minutes, however, and the shackled perp took up the rear as we marched on to the next village. He would spend six months in jail when we returned to base.

An educated Papuan later told me that he did not resent what the "outside men" were trying to do. The kiaps had opened the country, he said, and brought peace and a measure of impartial law to people who for centuries had lived cramped lives in fear and constantly at war with their neighbors. "The kiaps were doing what they thought was right," he told me, "but they destroyed our minds, our ability to think things out for ourselves. The great disservice the Australians did us was to restrict different alternatives and options. They wanted to bring development but only on their terms, never ours." It was as good a rundown on the advantages and disadvantages of colonialism as I ever heard.

Bawden knew that the old paternalism was coming to an end. On his wall back at base he had tacked Lawrence of Arabia's famous dictum: "Better they do it imperfectly than you do it perfectly, for it is their country, their war, and your time is limited." More than thirty-five years later I would see that on the wall of an American billet in Afghanistan.

Ever since the Melanesians of the South Pacific first came in contact with Europeans there had been an undercurrent that the white man, with all his conspicuous wealth and chattel, had somehow managed to cheat the native out of his share. From time to time, especially on the north coast of New Guinea and surrounding islands, this feeling surfaced in the form of cargo cults—the semi-religious belief that a group or individual has found the magic formula to ensure that all the white man's "cargo" will at last be delivered to the indigenous natives as their ancestors had always intended.

"Look at it from the native's point of view," an American missionary said to me. "He sees that the white man doesn't seem to do much work, at least not what he would understand as work, and yet whenever a ship or a plane arrives the cargo is always consigned to the whites, never to him. Naturally he asks himself, why is it that the whites have so much and the blacks so little?"

Cargo cults began flourishing soon after World War II, when the Americans went home and took their jeeps, generators, radios, and Coleman lamps with them. Whatever they left behind soon fell into disrepair. It wasn't fair. So cultists began to build imitation piers out into the ocean to lure in the ships that had once come with such plenty. They hacked imitation airstrips out of the jungle to lure down planes they saw flying overhead. From time to time the Australians would fly some cult leaders to Sydney to show them where cargo really came from—that it was the product of industry and not magic. But they weren't always believed.

One cult that was still being talked about ten years later when I arrived was inadvertently started by an American survey team working on the island of New Hanover in the Bismarck Archipelago in 1964. It appears that one of the team said in jest to one of the natives that the key to wealth and prosperity— and to all their tantalizing equipment—was to vote for Lyndon Baines Johnson, who was then running for president back home.

Unfortunately it was taken seriously by his rapt audience. For when the

Australians started to teach people about democracy and holding local elections, there were New Hanoverians who said they would have no one but LBJ as their postcolonial leader. The Aussies tried to explain that LBJ could not be their candidate, but New Hanover wasn't having any of that. Had not the Australians told them that democracy meant choosing their own leaders? And was the white man now telling them they couldn't vote for the man of their choice? And the man of their choice was LBJ.

Thus was the LBJ cult born, and quickly did it spread to neighboring New Ireland. Would-be Johnson voters started collecting "LBJ taxes," money that would be needed to bring LBJ to their islands. Word went out that the Australians were deliberately keeping LBJ away in order to keep all the cargo for themselves, and, of course, the tax collectors were getting rich.

When a government boat came to explain things, it was met by a hail of arrows. Fourteen constables were injured. The cult was finally suppressed, and so it was that the Great Society never reached the islands of the Bismarck Archipelago.

Forty years ago Christian missionaries had great influence in New Guinea. They had been coming since the nineteenth century and had faced many hardships, diseases, and hostile tribes. A missionary had been killed and possibly eaten only a year before I first visited the Indonesian side of the island. Despite the many good deeds missionaries had accomplished, the downside was their intolerance of what they considered paganism. They had tried to forbid the magnificent erotic carvings of the Sepik River country, bullied natives into destroying their culture, and burned their spirit houses. By 1974 missionaries were running two-thirds of the primary schools and nearly half of the high schools in Papua New Guinea.

I sought out the Catholic archbishop, an American from Illinois named Adolph Noser. He told me of a time, thirteen years before, when he had arrived to conduct a mass in a small and remote village. One convert to Catholicism asked Noser if he would please kill a black rooster for them. Noser, not understanding what was about to unfold, told the man to go kill a rooster himself. After the mass, the man who had asked for a black rooster to be killed selected a man from the congregation, and in front of the archbishop, asked the man to lift his chin. He then calmly cut the man's throat.

The horrified Noser thought back on what he had said the last time he had been present in that same village. He had said that Christ had died for the sins of mankind. Somehow the Catholic convert had come away with the impression that someone needed to be sacrificed for the sins of that village. "They interpret things in the light of their own thinking, desires, and wants," the archbishop said, "and sometimes it causes a lot of confusion."

An Australian judge, presiding over another murder trial, was quoted as saying: "I incline strongly to the view that over-rigid teachings and non-comprehending acceptance of the Bible is at the root of this quite unnecessary death."

Another missionary told me that it made him nervous trying to explain to his parishioners about the wafer representing the body of Christ and the wine his blood. It might be interpreted as condoning cannibalism, he feared. When he started to explain the Eucharist the look of understanding that came over the faces of his parishioners made him nervous.

One of the questions the Australians were worrying about was, what should be their attitude toward liquor for the natives? One school of thought was that it was condescending to say the Papuans couldn't hold their liquor, and that the country was soon to be free to make its own choices. The other school said that the natives clearly couldn't hold their liquor and it was destroying them. The same had been true of our own native populations in the American West. I once visited a mining camp on the island of Bougainville and saw firsthand how drunk the native workers got on paydays. It was the habit of the mining camp just to turn the fire hoses on the workers' barracks to clean up the vomit.

I left what was soon to become the new nation of Papua New Guinea with the feeling that the island was ill prepared to go it alone and that the Australians should have stayed for a few more years. But when I said that to an Australian he said: "Trouble is we bloody well should have started preparing these Kanakas for independence long ago." "Kanakas" was a none-too-flattering word for the Papuans.

18

Muhammad Ali's Holy War

It was a restless time after the fall of Saigon. I still had my China-watching duties in Hong Kong, but for those of us who had been totally absorbed with Vietnam, the ignominious end left a big hole. As it happened, Muhammad Ali, heavyweight boxing champion of the world, was scheduled to fight the heavyweight champion of Europe, an Englishman named Joe Bugner. The fight was to take place in the Malaysian capital of Kuala Lumpur. No one thought Bugner had much of a chance, and so the *Post* decided to send me from Hong Kong instead of one of their Washington-based sports writers. I was told later that Ben Bradlee had said: "We have to find some postwar violence for Greenway."

The *Post* didn't know it, but a cousin of my father's had married a previous champion, Gene Tunney, in the 1920s, and so we grew up with boxing lore. There is a certain honesty about boxing. After all is said and done the purpose is to knock the other man down—no nets, balls, rackets, or sticks to disguise naked aggression.

I had seen Ali fight before in Madison Square Garden in New York. My friend Terry Smith asked me to dinner and to the fight with his dad, the famous *New York Times* sportswriter Red Smith. At dinner, Red Smith gave us a detailed and reasoned prediction of how and why Ali would win. When Joe Frazier won I looked out of the corner of my eye to catch Red Smith's reaction. Without looking directly at me he said, out of the corner of his mouth, "My boy, crow is an acquired taste."

Ali was blessed with a gift of gab, and those of us gathering in Kuala Lumpur looked forward to his imaginative and colorful hyping of the fight. It had been the "Rumble in the Jungle" against George Foreman in the Congo, but here in Muslim Malaysia Ali was dubbing the fight a "holy war." Ali was saying that Allah would protect him. Now, some of us knew that there had been terrible communal riots in Malaysia a few years before, Malays against the Chinese minority, with hundreds killed. The jihad talk was making the authorities nervous. A senior policeman told me, "Some of our people here are very simple and they take their religion very seriously." This was in the days before Muslim extremism as it is today, but the possibility of rioting was uppermost in police minds.

A couple of us scheduled a prefight interview with Ali, but he was out when we arrived at his hotel. Angelo Dundee, his trainer, sat and talked to us until the champ showed up. We tried to explain to Dundee why the holy war hype was a bad idea in this particular country, and that the authorities were very nervous that Ali's remarks could start trouble. All police leaves were being canceled. I was probably a bit long-winded in my presentation to Dundee, but he boiled it down to a few words when the champ walked in. "We got to cut the holy war shit, Ali, they already had one here."

Another colorful character in Ali's corner was Bundini Brown. Brown loved his drink and was upset to find that there would be no liquor served at the sultan's dinner. I overheard him on the phone making plans for that night's banquet. He had figured out the seating arrangement, and he was giving instructions that a tumbler of clear gin be put at his place at table instead of water, surreptitiously in order not to offend Muslim sensibilities. "And," he admonished, "hold the olive."

Dundee had predicted a knockout in the ninth round, but in the blazing heat of the Malaysian summer Ali could only muster a decision. There were no knockdowns, which disappointed the spectators, but Ali had dominated the ring, and in October he would meet Frazier again in the "Thrilla in Manila." Alas, this was considered too good a fight for the likes of me, but I was glad to have had my first, and last, chance to cover a prizefight.

I ran into Ali many years later in Havana, Cuba, but by then his trade had taken its toll, and his gift of gab was sorely diminished.

19

Bangladesh: Birth of a Nation

Some of my notebooks from 1971 show the stains of monsoon rains. For when civil war between East and West Pakistan broke out in the early summer of that year *Time* sent me to Calcutta, India, to cover one of the great refugee crises of the twentieth century. Almost seven million people, many of them of the Hindu minority, poured out of Pakistani East Bengal into Indian West Bengal that summer to avoid the fighting. It was a humanitarian catastrophe unequaled in my experience.

The origins of the crisis went back to the bloody partition of British India in 1947, perhaps the greatest failure of Britain's attempt to divest itself of empire. The new state of Pakistan was carved out of India's northern provinces to give Indian Muslims a homeland of their own, separate from the Hindus who make up the majority on the subcontinent. The disparate peoples of West Pakistan, Punjabis, Baluchis, Pashtuns, and Sindhis, had their own problems getting along together. But putting them together with Bengali Muslims in East Pakistan, who had no linguistic, cultural, or ethnic ties with West Pakistan and were separated by more than one thousand miles of Indian territory, created, as *Time* magazine aptly put it, "a geographical curiosity . . . and a political absurdity."[*] Now, a quarter of a century after partition, there was further sorting out to be done.

---

[*] *Time,* August 2, 1971. Cover story, "Pakistan's Agony."

East Pakistanis outnumbered their countrymen in West Pakistan seventy-eight million to fifty-eight million, but resources and industrialization always flowed to the west. The Bengalis in East Pakistan were becoming an angry agrarian backwater.

From the beginning, the United States had a complicated and unrealistic relationship with the two successor entities to British India. Upset by India's relationship with the Soviet Union, and put off and at the same time intimidated by India's claim to moral superiority, we tried to enlist Pakistan as an ally in the struggle against Communism, flooding the country with arms and money, only to turn off the spigot periodically whenever we thought Pakistan was not sufficiently doing our bidding.

Henry Kissinger put the problem well when he wrote: "We treated Pakistan simply as a potential military ally against Communist aggression. There was no recognition that most Pakistanis considered their real security threat to be India . . . We also sought to include Pakistan in a concept of containment that it did not share."[*] Kissinger's words apply just as well to today's tortured relationship with Pakistan. We seek to enlist Pakistan in a policy of containment against Islamic extremism in Afghanistan just the way we wanted them as an ally against Communism. Both were concepts that Pakistan never really shared, believing throughout that the real enemy was India.

As can so often happen, it was a natural disaster, and the government's inadequate response to it, that triggered the political turmoil that resulted in the birth of a separate Bengal nation, Bangladesh. In November of 1970 a cyclone came up from the Bay of Bengal and devastated the low-lying lands of the delta where the Ganges and the Brahmaputra Rivers meet. It left somewhere between two hundred thousand and half a million dead.

In addition to other grievances, East Pakistanis were further angered by a painfully inadequate response to the cyclone from the central government. President Yahya Khan took thirteen days before visiting the devastated region. Food and shelter came too little and too late. Pakistani helicopters that could have helped stayed in West Pakistan. The Pakistani navy made little effort

---

[*] Henry Kissinger, *White House Years* (Boston: Little, Brown and Company, 1979), 845–46.

to search for victims. Bengalis overwhelmingly expressed their discontent in an election, and a move toward autonomy, and then outright independence, gathered speed.

West Pakistan sought to put down these independence yearnings by brute force, committing atrocities that shocked the world. A civil war between the two halves of Pakistan followed. President Nixon and Henry Kissinger made their famous "tilt" toward Pakistan partly because, unknown to the world, Kissinger was planning his famous secret trip to Beijing to realign the Cold War, and he needed Pakistan to pull it off.

By the time photographer David Burnett and I reached Calcutta in July, a Bangladesh provisional government had been set up. Refugees were on the move in the hundreds of thousands seeking safety in India. We rented a jeep and drove out into the countryside to find them. It wasn't hard. All you had to do was to follow skies full of vultures that hovered over the long columns of misery, waiting for some of them to die. We were working on a cover story that would be entitled "Pakistan's Agony."

Here is a dispatch I wrote for that story:

Across rivers, down roads and along countless jungle tracks, the population of East Pakistan continues to hemorrhage into India. At most border crossings there are no checkpoints, no defined frontiers, just mud tracks leading out of Pakistan like pores in the skin.

At one such crossing we watched them come—an endless, unorganized column with a few pathetic kettles, boxes, bits of cloth on their heads, carrying their sick children and their old, their bare feet padding on the track, with the mud sucking at their heels in the wet parts. They were silent for the most part, except for a child whimpering, and their faces were blank. Many were sick and covered with sores, and in under the trees there were groups of hundreds that had stopped for rest. But along the track the column never ended, night and day pushing on into India.

They bring the cholera with them, and when they die by the road no one buries them. A corpse lay half on the track, the people stepping over and around him, and a young boy sat beside him selling chapatis. Further on an old man lay on his back with a pack of dogs snarling and fighting over him. His body heaves and bucks, can he still be alive? No, he is dead and he heaves only because the dogs are worrying at him. They have eaten open his groin and are pulling out his innards. Some in the long column put a piece of cloth over their noses as they pass by.

It has been months now since it all began and still they come—50,000, 100,000 per day? No one knows. They are all terrified. They all have heard tales of rape and murder at the hands of the Pakistani Army. Some of them take us for light-skinned Punjabis from West Pakistan and bolt from the path. One of us stops to photograph a cripple who has been crawling on his hands and knees. He sees the camera pointed at him and asks, quietly, without emotion, if we are going to kill him.

At Boyra there is a landing where high palm trees bend gracefully over the river. Across the stream is East Pakistan and nothing moves except the bands of refugees making their way through the jute fields to the water's edge. Boatmen will bring them over. Women wash and children splash in the river and a few feet from them, where the ducks are swimming, there is a body of a child bobbing swollen among the water weeds. It has been there since yesterday. Should I wade in and lift it out of the river? But what would I do with it then? What can anybody do?

In actual fact the Indian government was doing a good job, given the circumstances, housing and feeding the refugees, but the scenes of suffering we witnessed that summer were appalling. The United States took up much of the financial burden, but still the strain on India's resources was severe. Indira Gandhi, for whom the very concept of Pakistan was an affront, contemplated a lightning invasion of East Pakistan, but her military persuaded her to hold off—at least until the Himalayan passes were snowed in so that China wouldn't be tempted to intervene on Pakistan's behalf. China was just as affronted by India's close relations with Russia as were the Americans.

We all wanted to make contact with the Bengali rebels in East Pakistan, and there were endless intrigues in Calcutta to that end. Finally, Burnett and I found people who could smuggle us across the border, avoiding Indian security, to make contact with a rebel band. We went by jeep and boat across monsoon-swollen streams, finally to be received by a company of "Mukti Bahini," as the rebels were called.

The rebel commander was full of bluster and told us of successful ambushes against the "Punjabis," his term for the Pakistani army, which was indeed made up almost exclusively of West Pakistanis. The East Pakistan Rifles, raised locally and consisting of Bengalis, had mostly defected to the rebel cause.

We had heard rumors in the refugee camps that the Indians were training refugees to go back and fight in East Pakistan, and that they were giving them weapons. Hoping to confirm the rumors, I had memorized what weapons were Indian army issue and what were weapons carried by the East Pakistan Rifles.

The author with rebel soldiers in East Pakistan during the insurrection against Pakistan in 1971.

So having spotted some Indian weapons in the hands of his rebel soldiers, I asked the commander where his weapons came from. "All from East Pakistan deserters or captured," he said as he described a recent raid on a Pakistani army arsenal.

"But then why are some of your men carrying Indian army rifles?" I asked.

"Oh, sahib, please do not be printing that," he said, but I duly reported to *Time* that India was indeed supplying weapons to the rebels.

Later that summer the Pakistanis allowed me to visit Dacca, the capital of East Pakistan. JB flew over to join me and we stayed at the Intercontinental Hotel, which was swarming with Pakistani military, and I was delighted to run into a truly legendary British reporter named Clare Hollingworth. Clare had been in Poland when the Germans invaded in 1939 and managed to get through to her editor by telephone to tell him that the war had begun. Her editor told her that he was sure there would be no war, so she held the telephone out the window so he could hear the Stukas screaming by in the sky overhead.

Clare had covered General Montgomery's Eighth Army in the western desert of North Africa during World War II, and had met many of the Pakistani generals and colonels when they were young officers in the British Indian army. She had been out on operations with them fighting the very Mukti Bahini I had visited, and so we agreed to have a drink and exchange impressions. I told her that I thought the rebels were disorganized, but as long as they had help from India they couldn't in the end lose.

I asked her if she thought India would intervene, and she said, "Yes, but no war until Christmas." She unrolled a large topographical map and said: "Here the Brahmaputra, in flood wide as the English channel." The Indians would wait until the dry season so that they could better maneuver their tanks, she said. "But by Christmas there will be war." And she turned out to be absolutely right. Before the year ended Mrs. Gandhi could no longer resist the chance to dismember the hated Pakistan. She sent her army in just before Christmas and quickly defeated the Pakistani forces. Bangladesh became a reality on the points of Indian bayonets.

By the time India invaded, however, I was out of the war due to circumstances beyond my control. I had been typing a story for *Time* up in my room in Dacca when I ran out of smokes. Telling JB I would be right back, I went down to the cigar stand in the lobby. The last thing I remember was the wall behind the cigar stand disintegrating and bricks and plaster flying over my head. The Mukti Bahini had planted a bomb in the men's room behind the wall, hoping to kill some of the Pakistani military. I was actually saved by being so close to the wall, because the blast knocked me down and sent most of the bricks over my head to spread mayhem throughout the lobby farther away.

JB, still upstairs, heard the blast and, looking out of the window, saw smoke pouring out of the lobby and glass on the lawn outside. Not knowing quite what to do, she went out into the hall. There she met Clare coming out of her room. "Come, my dear," said Clare. "I was in the King David in '48." She was referring to the hotel in Jerusalem blown up by Jewish freedom fighters cum terrorists during the British mandate. "It's time to go. There's always a second bomb." Luckily for us there wasn't a second bomb, but I had a concussion and was seeing double.

My bosses at *Time* told me to come home but said I could stop off anywhere I pleased on the way back for a rest. We caught a Pakistan International Airlines flight from Dacca to Karachi in West Pakistan, but because India was no longer allowing Pakistani flights over their territory, we had to fly all around the subcontinent over Sri Lanka and up the west coast of India to reach West Pakistan. The plane was full of Pakistani military, and we watched boxes of fresh melons being loaded aboard. We both thought it a high probability that one of the melons would turn out to be a bomb, but it was not the case.

Three years later I returned to Bangladesh because a famine had overtaken the country. It turned out to be the last great famine on the Indian subcontinent, and there were trains coming into Dacca station full of people who had died from hunger on the journey.

The Russians had sent giant helicopters to Bangladesh to help distribute food to starving communities. I soon found that the best way to get around the country was to hitch a ride with the Russian pilots, who were friendly and willing to take a capitalist along with them. Early in November of that year the Russians took the day off to celebrate the October Revolution of 1917. They invited me to celebrate with them, and try as I might, I could not avoid drinking enormous quantities of vodka. Every time I tried to avoid taking yet another drink, the pilots would say: "David! In 1945 Russians and Americans are meeting on the Elbe. Drink," and yet another linked-arm toast had to be made to the enduring friendship between the Russian and American people. The next day I could not get out of bed, but neither could the Russian pilots.

On one of those Russian mercy flights I reached the town of Rangpur up in the north of the country. There I met the local Bangladeshi official in charge, and to my amazement it turned out to be the same commander of the Mukti Bahini rebel band I had met three years before during my Calcutta summer. I congratulated him for surviving all the political turmoil that had followed Bangladesh's independence, and he invited me up to his official bungalow. Not being a very observant Muslim, he offered me a whiskey.

As we settled down to reminisce about the old days of the struggle he said: "I remember now, you were the fellow that caught me out with Indian weapons."

"Yup," said I, "that was me," thinking myself clever to have caught him out in a fib about the Indian rifles his men were carrying.

"What you didn't know," he said, "was that those were Indian soldiers carrying them." I was floored. As happens so often in journalism, you think you know the story, only to find out later that the situation was far more complicated and devious than you had ever imagined.

Getting our stories out in Dacca and Calcutta meant taking a taxi or a rickshaw late at night to a telegraph office somewhere in the depths of the city. The one in Calcutta looked like an industrial nightmare, with shirtless telegraphers, sweating profusely in the heat of a Bengal summer, accompanied by what I remember as a great deal of noise and clatter of the telegraphy machinery.

Journalism is a matter of three different processes: gathering the information, writing it, and then getting it out to your paper, in my case across the seas. Nowadays the latter two are conjoined, and reporters simply write and press a key to send their words out over the Internet. But in my early reporting years getting the story out could be more daunting and sometimes more time consuming than either the reporting or the writing. If your hotel was fortunate enough to have a telex machine, you could laboriously type it out on telex tape and transmit it. But if not, you had to find a telegraph office somewhere.

Different telegraph offices had different procedures, and with some it was useful to find out what was expected by way of a tip. In Vientiane, Laos, the telegraph operator was on the second floor, and a basket was lowered down from a hole in the ceiling. You would put your copy in the basket, along with a tip, and tug the string for the copy to be lifted aloft for transmission. If the tip was not enough, the basket would come dropping down again for more money.

Sometimes, especially if the story was politically sensitive, it was wise to take the copy out of the country for filing. You could send it out with some willing person who happened to be leaving, and this was called "pigeoning" the story, as if it were being sent by carrier pigeon. You couldn't be sure if your pigeon would actually take your story to a telegraph office upon arrival, and many a pigeoned story never reached the home office. Once someone who I thought was a friend simply threw away a story I had asked her to take from China back to Hong Kong for transmission. She said she didn't want to risk offending the Chinese. Mercifully, the Internet has taken most of the risk out of filing stories, and the days of treacherous pigeons are no more.

20

The First *Washington Post* Bureau in Israel Since 2000 Years

With the war over, and with my tour in Hong Kong coming to an end, I began lobbying for an assignment in Jerusalem. In those days the *Post* had only one news bureau in the Middle East and it had been in Beirut. With the onset of the Lebanese civil war the *Post* had decided to move the bureau to Cairo and open up a second bureau somewhere in the region. Just where this second bureau should be was being hotly debated.

Phil Foisie, the foreign editor, invited me to fly from Hong Kong to Paris, where he was meeting with his foreign-bureau chiefs. Foisie was being advised by a correspondent more senior than I that the second bureau should be in Amman, Jordan. The argument was that Amman was a good place to jump on a plane and go anywhere in the Arab world. It was too difficult to get from Israel to other Arab countries, he said, because no Arab country then recognized Israel and there were no flights between Israel and any Arab land. And if there was a big story in Israel I could pop across the Allenby Bridge over the Jordan River and take a taxi to Jerusalem.

I argued that for an American paper, there was no choice but to put a second Middle East bureau in Jerusalem. Israel was simply too big a story, and too important an ally, for an American paper to do otherwise. And if I was needed elsewhere, I could cross the Allenby Bridge the other way and fly anywhere from Amman. Or I could fly to Cyprus or Athens and do the same.

I lost the argument and was told to go back to Hong Kong via Amman and find myself a house and a school for my children. I accepted the decision, of course, but didn't believe for a moment it would stand. Not to cover Israel with a resident correspondent, especially now that the *Post* was expanding its foreign bureaus, would be journalistically unacceptable, I thought. But I wasn't going to make the mistake of appealing the decision over Foisie's head. As it turned out I didn't have to.

I did go to Jordan and found that there were plenty of houses to be had, and room for my children in the English-speaking school. But I slipped over the Allenby Bridge to Israel and looked up my old friend Terry Smith, who was the *New York Times*'s man in the Holy Land. The *Times* had had a bureau in Jerusalem since the British Mandate, before the state of Israel was declared in 1948, and neither he nor I had any doubt that the *Post* would follow suit. I found a house for rent in what had been an Arab section of Jerusalem under the British and before that the Ottomans. Now it was in West, or Jewish, Jerusalem. It was a dream: whitewashed walls, high ceilings, arched windows, lemon trees in the garden with towering cypress trees as well. I signed a three-year lease without telling the *Post*. I was willing to risk losing the deposit and absorbing the cost myself if my gamble failed. It didn't. When Ben Bradlee, the *Post*'s editor in chief, heard of the decision to send me to Amman he said: "For Christ's sake, Foisie, send him to Jerusalem," and that was that. Foisie sent me an embarrassed cable telling me of the change of plans, and I wired back that I would have no trouble finding suitable quarters in Jerusalem and would not have to make a special trip to Israel to search for it. No one at the *Post* ever knew that I had already rented a house on their behalf.

The *Post* was closing its bureau in Belgrade, and I was instructed to stop off there en route to my new assignment to take the office car to Israel. I did, via ship from Greece to Haifa. I drove down the coast road and up to Jerusalem, passing the wrecks of old trucks that the Israelis had kept as mementos of the 1948 war. Seeing those battered frames of armored trucks left over from Israel's heroic past never lost its impact on me.

For the next two and a half years I drove on Yugoslav license plates. Since the occupied territories had different license plates than Israelis had, it was good to have neutral foreign plates to keep me out of trouble. And every time I got a parking ticket I would simply mail it to the Yugoslav embassy in Tel Aviv. Since there was no Yugoslav embassy in Israel, there being no diplomatic relations between the two countries, I have no idea what happened to the missent tickets.

Israel in 1976 was becoming disillusioned with its long marriage to the Labor Party, which had been in power since 1948 but didn't know yet that divorce was just around the corner. Yitzhak Rabin, a hero of the 1967 Six-Day War, which gained Israel the West Bank, Gaza, the Golan Heights, the Sinai, and Arab East Jerusalem, was prime minister. Many of the old heroes of the independence struggle, founding fathers such as Moshe Dayan, Abba Eban, and Yigal Allon, and a founding mother, Golda Meir, were still alive.

The world had thrilled to Israel's lightning victories in the Six-Day War, but only a few recognized that these new conquests would turn out to be a curse, creating a cancer within the bowels of the Jewish state. Israel's long occupation of the Palestinian people has harmed the Jewish state in incalculable ways.

Israelis were wont to point out that the Palestinians had never been an independent people. The West Bank had been part of Jordan and Gaza part of Egypt after the British left. Israelis argued that they were not alone in absorbing territories and peoples by war and boundary changes. Look at the number of Hungarians who were forced to live under Rumanian rule after World War I or the parts of Germany transferred to Poland. Why couldn't that be so with the West Bank and Gaza? But Palestinian nationalism rose as a mirror image of Zionism, and no matter what you call it, the occupation of Palestinian territories remains just that today: a military occupation going on now for almost half a century.

Israel's tragedy was that it acquired an alien and hostile people just when colonialism was discredited and dying all over the world. What was once acceptable to the world no longer was. Today Palestinians remain a subjugated people deprived of civil rights and citizenship. Many observers have pointed out that Israel cannot remain a democracy and a Jewish state until the Palestinians are set free and have their own country, but at this writing there is no sign that Israel is ready to disgorge its 1967 conquests. Jewish settlement goes on unchecked, so the chances of a viable Palestinian state on contiguous territory grow ever more remote.

One can never discount the fear factor when it comes to Israel and the occupation. With the most powerful army in the Middle East, backed up by atomic bombs, Israel may seem the mighty Goliath to its neighbors. But Israelis see themselves as the young Jewish David surrounded by millions of Muslims who wish them ill. The events of the Arab Spring have only increased this sense of dread. Considering Jewish history how could it be otherwise?

After the '67 war Israel thought it could give the captured territories back in exchange for peace. Israel was just waiting for "the telephone call" from Arab leaders, it was said. But the telephone call never came. The Arabs hurled their defiance in Israel's face. The three nos of Khartoum, no recognition, no peace, and no negotiations, became the Arab order of the day.

In time Egypt and Jordan would recognize Israel, and the Palestinians finally agreed to settle for just the West Bank, Gaza, and East Jerusalem, and forgo their claims on Israel itself. The three nos of Khartoum finally became yeses, and the Arab world offered recognition and peace in exchange for setting the Palestinians free. But by then it was too late. Israel had grown used to its conquests and could not bring itself to give back its captive peoples and territories.

The Palestinians, in turn, never could bring themselves to completely give up violence as a way of prodding the Israelis toward an agreement, nor did they always grasp a chance for dialogue when it was presented. Abba Eban wasn't all wrong when he famously said the Palestinians "never miss an opportunity to miss an opportunity."

When I arrived in 1976 Israel was still a bit in shock from the 1973 Yom Kippur War, in which Egypt's Anwar Sadat had caught the Israelis napping in the Sinai with an armed crossing of the Suez Canal. For a moment Israel reeled from the attacks, not only in the Sinai but in the Golan Heights, too, where the Syrians had attacked. Moshe Dayan told me that bringing out an atom bomb, which Israel had never admitted having, was under active consideration in the darkest days of '76. But Israel regained the initiative, and both the Syrians and the Egyptians were pushed back.

The day I arrived as the *Post*'s man in Israel, the country had just carried out a successful raid on Entebbe, Uganda, to rescue Jewish hostages in a hijacked plane. I was at first overwhelmed, but Terry Smith advised me to "just dig into the story and by the time it is done you will know everybody in the country."

Official Israel seemed pleased to have a *Washington Post* correspondent assigned to Israel, and because of the *Post*'s prowess during Watergate the paper no longer took second place to the *New York Times* when it came to access and telephone calls returned. Few countries are as adept as Israel in handling the foreign press, and mindful of the sometimes heavy-handed pressure to absorb Israel's historical narrative, I would be introduced as "the *Washington Post*'s first bureau chief in Jerusalem since 2000 years."

Israel then had about a third of the population it has today. The Russians had not yet arrived en masse, and under the mild, rather Scandinavian-style socialism of the Labor government, there were not the disparities between rich and poor that one sees in today's Israel. Traffic jams were few and far between in the midseventies. Jerusalem, then, was a bit shabby compared to the glittering capital it is today, with fewer first-class hotels. In the seventies some of Jerusalem, just outside the old city walls, still consisted of Ottoman buildings with red tile roofs still holed by artillery fired in the '48 and '67 wars.

Palestinians chafed under occupation, but their resistance had not yet hardened into the "intifadas," the uprisings that were to come. Suicide bombings were unheard of.

The Labor government forbade Israelis to settle in the West Bank, lest that complicate returning it one day to Arab hands. But exceptions were made, especially in Hebron, where Arab riots during the British Mandate had killed Jews and forced them to leave what Jews considered holy sanctuaries.

Ze'ev Chafets, who later became head of the government press office, told a story of how some black people from Detroit and Chicago had claimed to be a lost Hebrew tribe. They called themselves Black Hebrews, perhaps as a counterweight to the rising Black Muslim movement in America. Claiming the "right of return," which all Jews enjoy if they want to emigrate to Israel, they showed up at Ben Gurion Airport in Tel Aviv and threw their American passports away. They said that they would now live in Israel as Jews. The government didn't know quite what to make of them. Their claims to Jewishness might have been flimsy, but nobody wanted to seem racist, so the Black Hebrews were given housing down in the Negev desert. There they resided quietly until one day some of them decided to move to Jericho in the occupied West Bank.

The government came to Ze'ev and said: You are from Detroit. You know these people. Would you please go down to Jericho and explain to them that they are not allowed to live in the occupied territories? The Israeli government didn't want any trouble, nothing that might fuel the fires of the "Zionism is racism" talk that was prevalent at the time. They just wanted Ze'ev to sweet-talk the Black Hebrews out of the West Bank and back into Israel proper.

Ze'ev went down to Jericho as bade and found where the Black Hebrews were living. He knocked on the door, which was opened by a very large man in Moses-like robes and carrying a huge stick. Ze'ev laid some jive talk on him for a while, and the Black Hebrew responded well to this amusing Detroiter at his door—that is, until Ze'ev brought up the subject of not being allowed to live in Jericho. With that the large black man flew into a rage, slammed his stick, and said: "The white man has taken us from Africa into slavery! And now the white man is telling us we can't live in Jericho?"

Ze'ev replied weakly with a shrug: "It's not because you are black. It's because you're Jewish."

But Labor's not-too-successful attempts to keep Israeli Jews from living in the West Bank crumbled when the opposition Likud Party came to power, and today multiple Jewish settlements dot the West Bank hilltops like ancient Crusader fortresses. There is little or no political will in Israel to take on the sometimes fanatical settler movement.

Ever since Israel's founding fathers wrested independence from the British and defeated the combined Arab armies that sought to abort the birth of a Jewish state, every Israeli government had been dominated by the Labor Party and its allies. Traditionally, Labor could always count on cornering close to 50 percent of the vote, making it easy to put together a ruling coalition.

Moreover, the Labor Party had enjoyed strict party discipline, with party lists of candidates being drawn up in back rooms.

Anything resembling primaries did not exist, and voters had little to say about the candidates for whom they were asked to vote. But this cozy arrangement began to slip after the 1973 war, when the Labor alignment's share of the vote began to drop. By the time I arrived in the country the ruling party was in serious trouble.

The demographics of Israel were also changing. The old Ashkenazi, or central and eastern European, elite that had founded the state was beginning to be challenged by Sephardic Jews from the Middle East and North Africa. Although the rival and right-wing Likud Party was dominated by Ashkenazim, they appealed to the newer Sephardic Jews, who were increasing in numbers.

The general election of 1977 that brought Likud to power ended the reign of the Labor Party. The left-wing vote was split between Labor and a reformer and former general in the 1948 war for independence named Yigael Yadin. As an archaeologist Yadin had led expeditions that uncovered the ancient cities of Megiddo, Hazor, and Masada, where the Jewish "Zealots" of the first century had committed mass suicide rather than submit to Roman rule. Yadin contended that the Labor Party had become lazy and corrupt and that it was time for a new party, the "Democratic Movement for Change." But his run ensured that the right-wing Likud would slip into power.

Yadin was not all wrong. Rabin, who was later assassinated by a right-wing fanatic for trying to achieve a peace with the Palestinians and a two-state solution, had run out of political steam in 1976. Buffeted by repeated scandals and whiffs of corruption in high places, Rabin had already gotten into trouble over his wife's illegal bank account when he was ambassador to the United States. He was forced to resign early in 1977. His defense minister, Shimon Peres, took his place at the top of the Labor ticket hardly a month before the election. Peres went on to lose the first of many bids for power. He later became president of Israel, a largely ceremonial position, and a respected senior statesman, but he was never very good at persuading voters to give him political power.

Menachem Begin, who emerged from the elections as prime minister, had been in opposition all his political life. He came from the so-called Revisionist wing of Zionism, more militant and nationalistic than David Ben-Gurion, Israel's first Labor prime minister. During the struggle for independence, Begin presided over the Irgun, considered a terrorist organization by the British and resented by the more mainstream resistance army Haganah. Along with the so-called Stern Gang, led by future Likud prime minister Yitzhak Shamir, the revisionists, inspired by Vladimir Jabotinsky, tended more toward assassinations and bombings of civilians than did the Haganah. When Ben-Gurion settled for half of British-mandated Palestine for his Jewish state, Begin split with him, saying Ben-Gurion should have held out for all of Palestine from the Mediterranean to the Jordan River. Some revisionists said that what is now Jordan, too, should be part of the Jewish state.

I asked Begin once if he thought he had committed acts of terrorism against the British. "We did what was necessary," was his answer. If ever there was an example of the old saying that one man's terrorist is another's statesman, it was Menachem Begin.

Now, after twenty-eight years in political opposition, Begin was in power, and his Sephardic following was calling him "King of the Jews." He asked Labor's Moshe Dayan to be his foreign minister, and Yigael Yadin's party joined Likud in coalition as well, despite its leftist sympathies. Getting Dayan was a spectacular political coup, as the one-eyed military hero with the black patch was a towering political figure and one of the best-known people in the world. Dayan accepted on the condition that Begin hold a referendum before any attempt to change the status of the occupied territories.

For us American journalists the Likud victory was an opportunity. Our bosses back home all knew Israel's old leaders by their first names and had become used to Labor always being returned to power. But few in Washington knew Begin or the Likud. A new page had been turned and we were on the spot to write about it.

Discovering a new story in a new place is one of the joys of being a foreign correspondent, and I threw myself into it. I loved Jerusalem and its "old and scarred hills," as Melville once described them. The breadth of history going back through Crusader and Roman times was breathtaking, and nothing pleased me more than to get lost in the old walled city with its spice smells, merchants hawking their wares, and cobblestoned alleys flowing with humanity where robed Arabs and Armenians jostled with Jews in their seventeenth-century hats and dark coats.

We had to wait a bit before we could move into our new house, so we spent a month or so at the American Colony Hotel, located in a Turkish pasha's house outside the walls of the old city. It had been started by Americans from Chicago in the nineteenth century who had been drawn to the Holy Land. The Colony was not the expensive, four-star hostelry it is today. It was run by Horatio Vester, grandson of the hotel's founder, and his wife Valentine, "Val" to everybody, a Yorkshire lady of the old school.

The founders of the American Colony had been persuaded to open a hotel in Jerusalem by the grandfather of the actor Peter Ustinov. The senior Ustinov had been a Protestant in the Russian czar's cavalry. He was willing to swear allegiance to his czar, but when he was required to swear allegiance to the Russian Orthodox Church, that was too much. So he resigned. He moved to the Holy Land, where he opened a hotel in Jaffa. He needed a sister hotel in Jerusalem to lodge his guests when they made the then-not-altogether-safe journey up through the Bab el-Wad to the Holy City.

We became close friends with Val and Horatio, and years later, when I would come back to Jerusalem as foreign editor of the *Boston Globe,* I would always stay at the Colony. One time I wrote to Val saying I was coming for a conference and was being put up at the Hilton, but that I would come and pay a call on her. I arrived at the Colony and was told Val would be back in an hour. So I had a beer in the garden, smelling the lemon blossoms and looking at the palm trees that old Ustinov had planted. The gallant trees had shrapnel in them from previous wars. I thought: I shouldn't be staying at the Hilton even if it is paid for. So I went to the desk and said that I knew it was the height of the tourist season, but would there possibly be a room for me at this last minute?

"But, Mr. Greenway," the desk clerk said, "Mrs. Vester reserved your favorite room for you."

"How could that be? I wrote and told her I had to stay at the Hilton this time."

"I know," said the desk clerk. "She didn't believe you."

Terry Smith introduced us to Father Jerome Murphy-O'Connor, a Dominican priest and expert on the history and geography of Jerusalem and its surrounds. A noted Paulist scholar, Jerry led a Sunday group that took day trips to different sites where we would hike, have a picnic lunch, and listen to Jerry explain what once had happened there. I was not always able to go because Israel's holiday was Saturday, the Jewish Sabbath, not Sunday, but whenever the story would allow it, JB, the children, and I would meet with the group for a pleasant Jerry outing in the hills.

Jerry and my youngest daughter, Sadie, then age nine, seemed to form a special bond, teasing each other unmercifully. One Sunday Jerry led us down to Jericho, where Joshua blew his horn, and for some reason we walked down in the desert toward the Dead Sea. Suddenly we came upon an old, British-style helmet that could only have come off a Jordanian soldier in the 1967 war. How had no one found it before? Suddenly we realized we were in an old minefield. It was Sadie who suggested that Father Jerry should lead us out, and we all agreed as he had a much better working relationship with God than the rest of us.

Winters could be cold and rainy in Jerusalem, and sometimes a blanket of snow would set off the city's astonishing beauty. You could drive down to Jericho by the Dead Sea and enter a very different hot and sunny climate for lunch. And there was no danger in those pre-intifada days.

The girls entered the Anglican International School of Jerusalem, which was one of the very few places where Christian kids, Arabs, and some Jews went to school together. My daughter Alice, who would later become a journalist before she turned to writing novels, started a school newspaper, which shocked the Brits who ran the place. Crusading articles about how the space heaters were endangering the health of students were not well received by the faculty of the Anglican school.

Often, in those days, Israel's northern border would come under rocket attack from Palestinians in Lebanon, and I, along with Bill Farrell of the *New York Times,* would drive up in the early morning to report what was going on. Our bosses in New York and Washington might not have been altogether happy if they had known that we were doing the story together, but we would divide up the people we were interviewing so that our quotes would not overlap.

One such morning, to keep myself awake as dawn was breaking, I was singing songs from *Brigadoon* when rockets began to land on either side of the car. I had to make the instant decision of whether to stop the car and get out into the ditch, or floor it, hoping to outrun the rockets. I floored it, and when the dust had settled Farrell said he didn't know whether the rockets had been fired by Palestinians or by outraged music critics from Metulla, the Israeli town under fire.

Violence between Arabs and Jews was endemic then as now, and some of my old news clips look as if they could have been written today. Consider this story from 1976.

> HEBRON, Israeli occupied West Bank, October 3—Arabs desecrated holy scrolls in the Jewish section of the Tomb of Abraham today in retaliation for Jews having trampled on the Moslem holy book, the Koran. This is the latest act in the steadily mounting conflict accompanied by riots and stone-throwing demonstrations in several Arab towns on the occupied West Bank . . .

I could not have operated in Israel as I did without the help, wisdom, friendship, and guidance of Yuval Elizur, a veteran Israeli journalist who had been the *Post*'s stringer in pre-bureau days. He and his wife, Judy, became my life-long friends. Elizur, a "sabra," meaning that he had been born in Israel, was originally named Silberstein. His father, Reuben Silberstein, was a successful contractor during the British Mandate after World War I. As Jewish desire for independence from Britain grew after World War II, Elizur joined the Palmach, the elite strike force of the Jewish resistance movement Haganah. The British authorities got ahold of the Palmach's membership list, so the Palmach issued everyone false identity cards.

Yuval showed his father his false identity card, and his father strongly objected to his son's move. It was a crime to have a false identity card, and if Yuval was caught it would bring shame on the family name. Not wanting to be disloyal to his dad, but determined to stay in the Palmach, Yuval had his name legally changed by deed poll to match his false identity.

As Washington was unsure of what to make of Begin, Israelis were just as unsure of what to make of President Carter. They remembered and appreciated the Nixon administration, which had stepped in to resupply Israel during the Yom Kippur War in 1973, and they were used to the histrionic style of Henry Kissinger. An Israeli told me how Kissinger always arrived in a state of high drama. Motorcades would roar up from the airport with sirens screaming and Kissinger would arrive giving the impression that Israel would have to give him what he wanted and quickly, as he was about to dash off to Damascus or Cairo. Cyrus Vance, Carter's new low-key secretary of state, came in quietly and spoke quietly without much fuss, and Israelis were unsure what to make of it.

But Carter went right to work on trying for a comprehensive peace. "The Israeli cabinet's unanimous approval of the joint US-Israeli conference represents a procedural concession in that Israel is now apparently willing to sit down with Palestinians at Geneva," I wrote for the *Post* in October of 1977. "Yet Israel has already set up so many preconditions as to who may be considered an acceptable Palestinian that the United States may find it very difficult to sell this paper to the Arabs. Israel's apparent refusal to even discuss a Palestinian entity at Geneva also makes it doubtful that last night's action can be considered a major breakthrough."

President Carter wasn't shy about turning the thumb screws. Dayan released a previously classified document describing a meeting between himself and Carter that Dayan described as "brutal." Dayan said that Carter had threatened Israel with "total isolation" if an agreement could not be reached. The controversy largely revolved around Palestinian participation. Israel's position then was that Palestinians could sit with other Arab delegations, but that Israel would not negotiate on the question of a Palestinian entity on the West Bank or in Gaza. But history was about to turn away from Washington's efforts and toward an enigmatic figure on the Nile, Anwar Sadat.

One of the better calls the *Washington Post* made that year was to have the Cairo and Jerusalem bureau chiefs switch places for a couple of weeks. I had not been in Cairo since the summer of 1956, when all Egypt was in thrall to Nasser's seizure of the Suez Canal. One of the Egyptians I wanted to look up was Boutros Boutros-Ghali, then a columnist at *Al-Ahram,* and later to become Secretary General of the United Nations. He was a Coptic Christian, that ancient branch of Christianity centered in Egypt. The Copts had fared well when the British were in charge, but today they feel threatened by the rising tide of Islam. Ghali admitted that his French was better than his Arabic, but he was fluent in English, too.

"When you were here in 1956, Cairo was like Athens and Alexandria like Marseilles," he told me. But today, he said, his country was sinking deep into third-world status. Two things contributed to Egypt's decline, he said: "Overpopulation and this endless quarrel with Israel." Egypt had been at the forefront of every war against Israel, he said, had taken the most losses and suffered terribly. It was not Egypt's quarrel, he said. Egypt was a Mediterranean and an African power, not just an adjunct of the Middle East, and needed to be concerned with bigger issues such as the sources of the Nile. It was Nasser with his vainglorious pan-Arab dreams who had dragged Egypt into wars with Israel.

But had not Anwar Sadat just fought a war with Israel three years before? I asked. Yes, Boutros Boutros-Ghali replied, but that was to take back lost Egyptian land in the Sinai, to restore Egypt's pride. Now, he said, Egypt must move away from confrontation with Israel, which was sapping its resources. Sadat was moving toward the Americans and away from the Russians, who had always been Egypt's backers in Nasser's day.

Were there others who felt that way? I asked. Yes, he said, quite a few, and I could expect some changes soon.

I went back to Israel and went to see Shlomo Avineri, then the secretary general of the Israeli foreign office and later a respected columnist and political observer. I told him that I thought I had detected a new thinking in Cairo, perhaps a new opening toward Israel to reduce, or even end, confrontation.

"You Americans are so naïve," he said. We didn't speak Arabic. We didn't know the meanings of the different and nuanced Arabic words Arabs used to describe peace, he said. "And no Arab country will ever make peace with Israel."

I went away thinking that perhaps what I had heard in Cairo was wishful thinking on the part of a few intellectuals in Boutros Boutros-Ghali's circle, and that I mustn't make too much of it. So when Anwar Sadat made his announcement that he would come to Jerusalem and change history, I was as astonished as everyone else.

Sadat Comes to Jerusalem

Sadat's decision to visit Israel created an explosion of joy not seen in the Jewish state before or since, perhaps even more than at the creation of the state in '48. For that event promised more war and great apprehension, while Sadat brought with him the promise of peace between Arab and Jew, for which Israelis so longed. Egypt sent an advance party a few days before Sadat himself came, and their Boeing 737 became the first Egyptian aircraft seen over Tel Aviv since the Egyptian air force bombed the city in 1948. The Egyptian delegation was put up in Jerusalem's King David Hotel, the very building Begin had blown up, killing ninety-one people, just thirty years before when he was leading the Irgun against the British.

"Israelis are in a fever pitch of excitement," I wrote for the *Post,* "and there was literally dancing in the streets by dozens of people here in the capital last night. 'I just cannot believe it,' is the comment most often heard. The Hebrew-language newspaper, *Maariv,* printed 'Welcome Sadat' in Arabic over its nameplate . . . Some Jews from Arab countries sounded the traditional Arab ululation."

Sadat had surprised everybody by making war to make peace. His crossing of the Suez Canal had had an initial success, and for a time Israel's army was in retreat. But General Ariel Sharon eventually got the upper hand, cutting off the Egyptian army in the Sinai and then crossing the canal himself into Africa. The United States brokered a cease-fire and saved the trapped Egyptian army in Sinai. A series of military disengagements followed under American supervision.

It was that initial success of Egypt's army against Israel in the canal crossing that restored Egypt's pride and allowed Sadat to make the political overture toward Israel that he was now making. Like the Tet Offensive in Vietnam, the 1973 war in the Sinai may have technically ended in defeat for Egypt, but Sadat turned it into a political success. It was a war that gave Sadat the cover to pledge, "No more wars," to the Israeli Knesset (parliament).

Israel had had all the intelligence it needed to thwart Sadat's surprise attack, but the Israelis simply could not believe the oft-defeated Egyptians had it in them to make another try. The initial shock within Israel that the Egyptians had crossed the canal and surprised Israeli forces was never quite overcome by Israel's later battle successes. It lessened the average Israeli's confidence in the leadership and contributed to Menachem Begin's coming to power.

But now the world was turning upside down and Sadat was actually coming to Jerusalem. Earlier, Prime Minister Begin had responded graciously to Sadat's initiative and issued a formal invitation to the Egyptian president. Since there were no diplomatic relations between Israel and Egypt, the invitation had to be passed between American ambassadors Sam Lewis in Tel Aviv and Hermann Eilts in Cairo, where Sadat was telling visitors that the "vicious circle" of conflict with Israel "has to be broken."

Not only had my Cairo source Boutros Boutros-Ghali been right, but he was about to arrive as acting Egyptian foreign minister. The previous foreign minister, Ismail Fahmi, had resigned in protest over Sadat's overture to Israel, so Boutros-Ghali got the job.

When Sadat arrived on Israeli soil he quickly asked: "Where is Ariel Sharon?" When Egypt's nemesis was produced, Sadat said to him, with a big smile: "I wanted to catch you."

Reporters began to flow into Jerusalem by the hundreds, and the government hastily set up press centers for reporters to work and file their stories. There were more than eighty telex machines and four hundred telephones made available to the visiting press, all in about thirty-six hours. When I congratulated the press center for its quick work I was told: "We Israelis are good at innovation. If we had had months to work on this we would have screwed it up." It was indicative of the times that both Sadat and Begin had already been interviewed by CBS's Walter Cronkite before they met each other.

Sadat's actual arrival caused even greater celebrations in the streets of Jerusalem and other Israeli towns, and I can remember people joining arms and singing: "All we are saying is give peace a chance." One of the Egyptian president's official stops was the Yad Vashem memorial to the six million Jews killed by Hitler in the holocaust. Sadat, as a young officer in Cairo during World War II, had been a member of an anti-British, pro-German underground, and was jailed for it. But that was then, and this was now, and the Jews of Israel had nothing but praise for the Egyptian leader.

We reporters were working very long hours, and JB was in America with her ailing father. My daughter Julia's sixteenth birthday coincided with that climactic week and she joined in the festivity by holding nonstop parties in our house over which I had very little supervision. Now that she is in her fifties, she remembers it still as one of the great blowouts of her youth.

Almost forgotten today is that Sadat fully intended his peace deal to include the Palestinians. In his address to the Knesset he offered Israel complete acceptance to "live among us in full security and safety." The price, he told the Israeli parliament, would be an Israeli withdrawal to the pre-1967 borders and the creation of a Palestinian homeland. "No one can build his happiness at the expense and misery of others," he told the Israelis.

In Begin's reply one could sense that the outcome was not going to be everything Sadat had hoped. Begin stressed the persecution of the Jews throughout history and the hostility of the Arabs in modern times. Declaring that the Jews had a God-given right to Palestine, he vowed that Israel would "never again put [its] people within range for extermination." He never mentioned the Palestinians once in his speech.

It eventually became clear that Begin was willing to give back the Sinai in exchange for peace with Egypt, but not the West Bank or even Gaza. Perhaps he felt that giving back the Sinai should be enough of a gesture for peace, and that by making it happen he would lessen international pressure to give up the Palestinian territories. To this day I don't believe that a Labor government, had it remained in power, would have agreed to giving back all of the Sinai as Begin was now doing.

Sadat had put too much on the line to reverse his peace initiative just for the sake of the Palestinians, but he and Begin's failure to achieve anything for the occupied territories damaged the cold peace that followed. It would be years before the rest of the Arab states forgave Egypt and eventually made their own offer to Israel. Two Palestinian uprisings and endless efforts by American presidents and world leaders to obtain something for the Palestinians have come and gone in the ensuing decades, but at this writing Israel, under Benjamin Netanyahu, seems more determined than ever not only to keep the West Bank but to people it with Jewish settlements.

With Egypt no longer a belligerent, Israel would go on to fighting wars in Lebanon, first with the Palestinians and then with the militant Shia group Hezbollah. It seems that the prediction made by an Arab historian in 1905—I forget now his name—holds true today. "Two important phenomena of the same nature, yet antagonistic, manifest themselves nowadays in Turkish Asia . . . They are the awakening of the Arab nation and the latent efforts of the Jews to reconstitute on a large scale the ancient kingdom of Israel. These two movements are destined to fight each other continually."

But what Sadat and Begin did achieve that day was no small thing: the first peace between Israel and an Arab state. For Egypt it meant it could concentrate on other things besides battling Israel, and for Israel it meant that its southern flank was now secure. Without Egypt, any attempt to take on Israel militarily was, from then on, off the table.

Because there were so many reporters in town for Sadat's visit, a "pool" system had to be devised. A "pool report" means that one reporter is assigned to an event, but he shares his copy with the rest. My pool assignment was the Church of the Holy Sepulchre. I was told to be there an hour early because of tight security. I waited in the gloom near where, according to tradition, Christ was crucified, when all of a sudden there was a commotion and there was Sadat standing before me. I had been told I had but one question, and that he would give only one answer. So I had given the question some thought.

I said: "Mr. President, what does it mean to you, a devout Muslim, to be here in the very heart of Christianity?"

He looked me up and down and said: "Young man, I will have you know that there are more Christians in my country than there are Jews in Israel." And with that he was gone.

When Begin made his reciprocal visit to Cairo, a press plane was arranged so that we could be on the ground when the Israeli prime minister landed. We were to be the first Israeli plane to land in Egypt. I was suffering from a reoccurrence of a neck injury from a helicopter crash in Cambodia a few years before, and I showed up at the airport in a neck brace looking like Erich von Stroheim in *Grand Illusion.* Concerned colleagues asked me what I would do if it got worse in Egypt. The irrepressible Bill Farrell said: "Simple. A Cairo-practor."

If I had thought Jerusalem joyful, Cairo was no less so over the prospect of peace. Cairenes would not let an Israeli buy a drink or pay for a taxi. A bemused Dutch couple said that they had been driven all over town and shown the sights for free because their Dutch had been mistaken for Hebrew.

Yuval Elizur, who remembered traveling between Jerusalem and Cairo freely in British Mandate days, wanted to head straight for Café Groppi in Talaat Harb Square, a famous Swiss confectionery shop and tearoom he remembered from his childhood. Another Israeli correspondent headed straight for Shepheard's Hotel, not realizing that the famed original had been burned down by rioters in the early 1950s. As she boasted about how her father had stayed in this exact same place during the parlous days of World War II, I had not the heart to tell her that the new Shepheard's was not even in the same location.

The fallout from Sadat's visit would occupy much of the next weeks and months. I traveled across the Allenby Bridge for an interview with King Hussein of Jordan, and almost missed my appointment because of a passport misunderstanding. In those days Arab countries would not accept a passport that had an Israeli stamp in it. Therefore I had two passports, one an Israel-only passport issued by the American consulate in Jerusalem that contained all my Israeli residence stamps. The other, my old passport, was for the rest of the world. The Jordanian border guard, thumbing through my rest-of-the-world passport, came across a visa for Laos left over from my Southeast Asia days. "Aha!" he said. "This is an Israeli stamp." I tried to tell him it was from Laos, but he said he knew Hebrew writing when he saw it. Finally, I took my Israel-only passport out of my other pocket and said: "That's what Hebrew looks like."

"Put it away," he said, "put it away," shielding his eyes as if he had seen the mark of the devil, and I was admitted to the Hashemite Kingdom of Jordan.

I interviewed King Hussein several times, and he always seemed to me reasonable, even wise in some respects. He had made a terrible mistake joining Nasser to attack Israel in 1967, which lost him the West Bank. Nonetheless, Israeli leaders were often making secret visits to see him, and many wished they could have given the West Bank back to him. But back in the sixties I had visited the West Bank when Jordan ruled, and I knew that, sooner or later, Palestinian nationalism would have risen against King Hussein as it has against Israeli rule.

22

Coming Home

It was in 1978 that Tom Winship of the *Boston Globe* made me an offer: come home to Boston and be the national and the foreign editor of the *Globe.* There were no *Globe* foreign or national bureaus, save a very good Washington bureau, but Winship had it in mind to build up a foreign service and maybe a couple of domestic bureaus in Washington and on the West Coast. American newspapers were entering a belle epoque in the last two decades of the twentieth century, before everything changed. They were making more profit than most of their advertisers, and there was enough money around to fuel dreams of expansion.

Feeling that my children were growing up not knowing really where they belonged, and with my parents getting old, I decided to make the move. Ben Bradlee couldn't have been nicer about it. So I moved home to become an editor.

Winship was a beloved figure, and largely because of his personality the *Globe* punched way above its weight in the world of American journalism. From my point of view, the *Globe* had an advantage that other provincial papers did not have. With Harvard, MIT, Tufts, Boston University, and other institutes of higher learning in its circulation area, international news was both appreciated and expected. Winship knew there was a vacuum to fill, that the *Globe* would never be the *New York Times,* but that a small but talented foreign staff could make its mark just as his Washington bureau had done.

I had oversight over the national news, of course, but with the talented leadership of Washington bureau chief Marty Nolan and his staff, I knew that a light touch was in order. My job there would be to make it possible for the reporters to do their best and make sure their stories played well in the paper. It was building a foreign staff that was a challenge.

I was in the unusual position of being a writing foreign editor, so I made many trips overseas in those days hiring good stringers and making contacts. Once, when I heard my old overseas colleagues complaining about their editors around a dinner table in Beirut, I said: "Just a minute, guys. I'm an editor now." One of them said: "Oh, Greenway, you're just a mouse studying to be a rat."

Nineteen seventy-nine was an extraordinary year for foreign news. Margaret Thatcher came to power in Britain, and soon, as the *Economist* magazine put it, "she sent Britain upstairs without its supper" when it needed it. The Egypt-Israel Peace Treaty was signed in Washington. Anastasio Somoza of Nicaragua fell, to be replaced by the left-leaning Sandinistas. Franklin Roosevelt had famously said of Somoza, "He's a son of a bitch but he's our son of a bitch." The shah of Iran, in whom the United States had invested so much, also fell that year, to be replaced by an anti-American theocracy. The taking of our diplomats in the American embassy in Tehran would consume and ultimately destroy the Carter administration. To top off that bad year for the United States, at Christmastime the Soviets invaded Afghanistan.

Also, in an event the importance of which has always been underestimated, the Great Mosque at Mecca was taken over by Islamic extremists—a shocking event in the very heart of Islam, undermining the legitimacy of the Saudi state. It was an early warning of religious extremists for whom not even the Saudi dynasty was sufficiently Islamic and Wahhabi. I happened to be in Saudi Arabia at the time and got word from Boston that I should proceed to Mecca at once and report from the scene. Alas, the *Globe* didn't seem to know that non-Muslims are not allowed in Mecca.

A recurring theme of America's post–World War II history has been the sound of our sons of bitches falling from power, from Ngo Dinh Diem in Vietnam, through Somoza and the shah, up through Egypt's Hosni Mubarak in the Arab Spring, men on whom we had spent much money and political capital to keep the past upon the throne.

I took many trips in those days. One was to Nicaragua, where Stephen Kinzer was representing the *New York Times.* He is today a distinguished author of many books. But he had originally worked for me when I was first starting to organize foreign bureaus and had done distinguished work for the *Globe* in El Salvador. Back then he was just about the only correspondent in Central America who had been in Nicaragua when Somoza was in power, and had become a sort of dean of American reporters in Central America. I was happy for him to land a job with the *Times.*

The best story, the one that told the most about Nicaragua under the Sandinistas, was one I did not write. It involved a search for a parrot. Kinzer lived in a house that had been rented from a Nicaraguan exile in Miami. With its generous verandas it seemed to me that a parrot would give the place a certain touch. So with Phil Bennett, our new man in Central America, I slipped off to the local Managua market to buy him one. At the first stall we stopped at the merchant got extremely huffy. "We don't buy and sell animals anymore the way they did in Somoza's time," he said. "We don't exploit animals as playthings. Exploitation is over. This is the new Nicaragua!" So we slunk off to the second market stall.

"Parrots," said the proprietor, "there aren't any parrots here. Look around you. There isn't anything worth buying. This isn't like the old days. The entire country is being impoverished. No, you won't find a parrot or anything else in this market anymore."

At the third stall, the owner put his finger to his lips for silence and pointed to his eyes as if to say we were being watched. "Come back at dusk." So back we came at dusk, and there, under the counter, was a splendid parrot. The price was higher than expected because, as the seller explained, it spoke three languages: Spanish, English, and the language of the Miskito Indians on the Caribbean coast.

It wasn't until later that I realized that my visit to the market told you everything you wanted to know about the Sandinistas' revolution—the fervent pride of those who sought a new order for Nicaragua, the disappointed who saw the hypocrisy and bankruptcy of the leftist regime, and those who would carry on as they always had whether it was legal or not.

Nicaragua, like all the so-called banana republics of Central America, had been as close to being an American colony as it could be without an actual colonial administration. Central America might have remained independent, but it wasn't allowed a long leash, "not in our backyard," as it was said. Fidel Castro had badly frightened the United States and therefore was a hero to leftists throughout the continent. Ronald Reagan was not about to let Central America go the way of Cuba, and so heavy effort was put into backing the right against the left, first in El Salvador and then in Nicaragua. The so-called Contras, organized to fight the Sandinista government, were but another example of the kind of semi-clandestine forces America would organize during the Cold War from the Congo to Tibet. Some of these clandestine ops, like the Bay of Pigs, were spectacular failures.

Others, such as the CIA's organization of the Hmong that I had seen in Laos, ended in defeat. While others, such as the arming of the mujahideen in Afghanistan against the Russians, were a success, but the blowback from Islamic extremists who fought in that war on our side brought us the destruction of New York's Twin Towers in September of 2001.

The Middle East kept drawing me back again and again during my Boston years. We established a bureau in Jerusalem, and I would be back to be teargassed in various Palestinian intifadas. At one point I complained to Yitzhak Rabin, who was back in power, that the tear gas his country was using was unusually strong. "Well," he said, "we got it from you Americans."

I happened by coincidence to be in Jerusalem just after the Oslo Accords had been agreed upon. It was a workable formula for Israeli withdrawal from the occupied territories that had been made in secret negotiations between Israel and the Palestinians under Norwegian auspices. Prime Minister Rabin, the old soldier of many an Arab-Israeli conflict, was ecstatic. He told me he was determined not to let the settler movement, which was, and remains, so influential in Israeli politics, upset the deal. He spoke with real passion and loathing for the settlers as a destructive force in the way of peace. But Rabin was assassinated by a Jewish fanatic, and the great hope and optimism among Israelis and Palestinians that Oslo produced turned to dust. The forces against it on both sides proved too strong.

There was hope, again, when Ariel Sharon, hero to the settlers, changed his mind and had Israel withdraw from Gaza. But Sharon was laid low by a stroke, and Palestinian rockets proved to Israelis that withdrawing from territory did not bring peace. The Palestinians complained that Israel's blockade of Gaza proved that Israel had never really left, that Gaza had become a vast prison. The tragedy is that, once again, the Palestinians could not give up violence, and the Israelis could not give the Palestinians enough of the benefits of peace to win them away from violence. Without doubt the Palestinian rocketing of Israeli towns, even after Israel had left Gaza, proved disastrous for peace.

One of the startling things about returning to America was that the free-flowing exchanges, both pro and con, about Israeli policies that I had grown used to in Jerusalem days were, to some extent, off-limits in the United States. To some, any criticism of any Israeli policy was considered criticism of Israel itself, or even the Jewish people. To my surprise unfair charges of anti-Semitism were thrown around carelessly, which always seemed to debase the coinage. There is enough real anti-Semitism around without using it against people who are not questioning the legitimacy of the Jewish state, or the worth of the Jewish people, but abhorring this or that Israeli policy, or even expressing a little sympathy for the Palestinians. It became apparent that if a newspaper did not toe the line of right-wing Israeli politics, that newspaper was in for heavy criticism.

I fully understand the impulse. Supporters of Israel see Israel surrounded by enemies with only one true friend, the United States. Therefore any breach of the pro-Israel orthodoxy, any daylight between American foreign policy and Israeli policy, must be snuffed out, especially if it can affect American public opinion. This is not so in Israel, where political debate on what Israel should be doing is freewheeling.

There were other important lobbies; the Greeks and the Armenians come to mind, but the Greeks never accused anybody of anti-Hellenism.

Israel was born out of the ashes of empire, first the Ottoman and then the British. Worrying about, and overestimating, the power of international Jewry, the British, in the time of World War I promised a Jewish homeland in Palestine to ensure Jewish support for their war effort. The small print said that this new homeland could not interfere with the people already living there. The effects of the twice-promised land are still with us, with Arabs viewing the Jewish state as an intrusion similar to the Crusader kingdoms of the Middle Ages. Cries against Jews and Crusaders echo still from Casablanca to the Khyber—never mind that the Muslims won that one.

23

Oman: A Colony in All but Name

Twenty-five years ago the Sultanate of Oman was the closest thing you could find to a colony that was not a colony. Strategically located where the Persian Gulf spills out into the Arabian Sea through the Strait of Hormuz, Oman was never formally part of the British Empire but was very much under British influence and British protection. Once the Omanis sailed far and wide, owned Zanzibar, and claimed Sinbad the Sailor as one of their own. By the time I got there Omanis stayed closer to home, had lost Zanzibar, and had eleven thousand British expatriates serving as advisers in government ministries and the military's officer corps—one of them being my old pal from my Bangkok days Peter Simms, who was working in police intelligence. Even the chief of the defense staff was a British officer, as were the heads of the air force and the navy.

In the palace the forty-five-year-old Sultan Qaboos bin Said reigned, surrounded by British advisers. How he came to the throne was the stuff of fairy tales. For once upon a time there had lived an old and suspicious sultan, who became more suspicious the older he got. He did not believe in education or medicine, and his people were among the poorest in all Arabia. No one was allowed to ride a bicycle, or wear eyeglasses, without the sultan's permission. The gates of his capital, Muscat, would close at dusk and open only at dawn. If any of his subjects wished to be abroad at night they were required to hold a lantern to their faces. This was not one of the sultans who ruled in the days of Sinbad. He was the present sultan's father.

Sultan Qaboos had been trained at the British military academy of Sandhurst, as had King Hussein of Jordan, but when Qaboos returned to his country in the mid-1960s his father put him under virtual house arrest. Then came 1967 and the beginning of oil exporting in Oman. To make matters worse a full-scale rebellion was in progress in the south, supported by a pro-Communist regime in South Yemen. Clearly this wouldn't do.

So in 1970 the British engineered a soft coup that placed Qaboos on the throne and his father in a suite at Claridge's hotel in London, where he died a few years later. It was almost a bloodless coup. When the moment came the old sultan drew his pistol and, mistakenly, shot himself in the foot. The rebellion in the south was settled, and the new sultan threw his lot in with the West. Although oil was flowing, he had refused to join the oil cartel that was so bedeviling the Western powers. The new sultan became the only Arab leader to endorse the Egyptian-Israeli peace, and he has recently been helpful to America as it tries to reach a new understanding with Iran.

The new sultan told me that he was in no hurry to get rid of his British advisers, but that he was training Omanis to eventually take over. He said he was very happy pumping nearly three hundred fifty thousand barrels of oil a day for years, but in 1986, when I arrived, oil prices were falling and production was up. Because Omani oil could be picked up outside the Persian Gulf, shipping insurance was less costly. The sultan said his next five-year plan would be based on the price of oil being $22 a barrel.

The sultan's estimates were wrong, of course, and Oman has prospered along with the rest of the Persian Gulf states. When he took over there were only seven miles of paved roads in the country and only one small mission hospital. New buildings were springing up everywhere and a new university, Oman's first, was scheduled to open in the fall.

A new seaside hotel had just opened, named the Garden in Arabic. Although all but empty, it was staffed by trained personnel from many countries. The furnishings were what we used to call "Louis-Farouk," a kind of Middle Eastern version of the classic and gilded French furniture that you saw from

Cairo to the Gulf. JB joined me for a stay there, and when we walked into the empty bar a small Filipino orchestra started to play. Startled, we backed out the door, and the band stopped. Then, deciding not to be intimidated, we stepped over the threshold again and the band started up again as if someone had turned on a phonograph. It was the same in every public room, employees anxious to serve, even if there were only two people in the whole hotel. If there was anyone else staying there, we never saw them. When we went out for a swim in the gulf, several French beach attendants and lifeguards came offering towels, deck chairs, and rides on little boats, on a magnificent stretch of empty beach.

From time to time desert Arabs wandered into the palatial lobby dressed in traditional flowing robes, looking around with wonderment. They loved to sit on the plush benches and chairs in the lobby, eating seeds and dropping the shells on the marble floor.

In the south I spent a day riding with soldiers in British armored cars over the desert sands and even over the border into Yemen itself, although I was asked to keep quiet about that. The soldiers were from Baluchistan, a province in northern Pakistan, where Oman was allowed to recruit soldiers, much as the British and Indian armies recruit Gurkha soldiers from Nepal. They wore black and green turbans, as did their British officers, youngsters in their twenties enjoying a T. E. Lawrence–like adventurous life that any young officer would love to lead. For them the British Empire, then on its last legs, was still alive and well, as was the old colonial romance with desert kingdoms.

British power had long since drawn back from east of Suez, and America was now becoming the guardian power in the gulf, once again falling into the footsteps of other people's empires. Indeed, Oman had become the first country to sign an agreement allowing the United States to store military equipment on its soil for rapid deployment in case of a threat to the Persian Gulf oil supply. Iran was no longer America's friend, so new ones, like Oman, were being found. But in the mideighties, with the sultan's blessing, the country was being run by British expatriates.

24

Bad Days in Beirut

Lebanon, too, like Palestine and Jordan, was a colonial invention, carved out of Syria by the French to make a home for the Christians. As was the case with many countries of the former Ottoman Empire after 1919, the population of what would become Lebanon was not homogeneous when it came to religious beliefs. Therein lay the lethal gene with which Lebanon was born. The various confessions and factions tried to master the art of sharing power but ultimately failed. That has been an underlying problem for Lebanon and the Middle East ever after.

World War I was the great Middle East watershed, with much of the Levant passing from Ottoman control to either the British or the French. As the British got what are now Israel, Jordan, and Iraq, the French got Syria from the vanquished Ottomans, in a secret agreement drawn up by Mark Sykes of Britain and François Georges-Picot of France. The French began to develop Lebanon as separate from the rest of Syria, but its complete independence did not come until World War II. It was, and is, an independence to which Syria has never been completely reconciled.

In 1941 the British and the Free French drove out the Vichy French, in a brief campaign in which Moshe Dayan lost his eye. He was fighting with the British when a French bullet hit the binoculars he was looking through, and the eye patch he wore the rest of his life made him one of the most recognizable figures on the world stage.

A complicated constitutional compromise was arranged whereby the Lebanese president would always be a Maronite Christian, the prime minister a Sunni Muslim, and the speaker of the parliament a Shia. This worked for a while, and for the most part Lebanon stayed out of the convulsion that led to the birth of Israel. But the influx of thousands of Palestinian refugees brought with it additional tensions.

In the late fifties the old political balance began to break down, as Muslims demanded more power. The Christians, especially the Maronites, who were better educated and always favored by the French, refused to relinquish their privileges. The Shia, who had become the most numerous faction, were mostly rural farmers and were at the low end of the Lebanese pecking order. Their day was yet to come.

In 1958 political disorder prompted Eisenhower to send the marines, America's short-lived intervention into the Middle East. Being in the navy at the time, I was disappointed to see a whole American fleet steaming toward the Mediterranean without me. My poor old *Valley Forge* remained at its antisubmarine work in mid-Atlantic.

In the 1970s the old political balance between Christian, Sunni and Shia Muslim, and Druze began to disintegrate further into a civil war with startling brutality. Palestinians too, having been driven out of Jordan by King Hussein and his army in the so-called Black September of 1970, increased their numbers in Lebanon. And, as they had in Jordan, they were forming their own state within a state. To complicate matters, Syria sent its army in to restore a balance between the warring factions, and soon ended up being hated.

Palestinian rocket attacks had bedeviled Israel's northern border, and in March of 1978 a horrendous attack on a couple of civilian buses along the coast road provoked Israel into action. Palestinian terrorists had landed by sea in rubber boats, hijacked a couple of buses, and gone on a shooting rampage that killed thirty and injured many more. The Palestinians claimed credit and said the attackers were from the Deir Yassin Brigade, named after an Israeli atrocity carried out by Menachem Begin's men against an Arab village during Israel's independence struggle in the 1940s. Tit-for-tat vengeance and long memories are hallmarks of the Middle East.

A few days later in March of 1978, Israel's army pushed across the frontier deep into Lebanon, stopping at the Litani River. The Israelis left a path of flattened buildings and wide destruction that would be a prelude to things to come. This was the most serious to date of the ever-stronger Israeli military incursions into Lebanon that would last into the following century.

I drove up from Israel on Holy Thursday of that year. It was clear from Christians I talked to that the Christians of southern Lebanon wanted the Israelis to stay, fearing a return of Palestinians seeking vengeance. Christian militiamen had been looting what was left of the Muslim village of El Khiam, a Palestinian stronghold, having slaughtered about seventy Muslims huddled in a mosque just before Easter. Palestinian fighters had decamped northward, and Israeli soldiers were setting up roadblocks to prevent further looting and killing.

As for the Shia who dominated in the south, I saw them wave and cheer as Israeli tanks chased the Palestinians out. But it wouldn't be long before the Israelis were seen as occupiers, not liberators, and within time resistance would coalesce and form into Hezbollah, a far more formidable foe to Israel than the Palestinians had ever been. Israel's mistake, which America would later repeat, was to stay in occupation of an Arab country too long.

As I drove deeper into Lebanon with gathering rain clouds darkening the sky, there were reminders everywhere of a long history of war and conquest. Crusader castles, some of them having been refortified by the Palestinians, dominated hilltops, and in one section of the road, dug up by artillery shells and passing tanks, there was the stub of an old Roman column.

It seems odd to remember now, given that Iran is such an international pariah today, that in the shah's time Iranian troops were sent on peacekeeping missions around the world. At a bridge over the Litani River I met a contingent of Iranian soldiers looking miserable as they stretched plastic coverings over their field gear in the rising wind and rain. I hadn't seen Iranian peacekeepers since Saigon before the fall.

I wrote at the time, "Even Israelis themselves are beginning to wonder what their offensive into southern Lebanon has really gained them. The PLO (Palestinian Liberation Organization) has been bruised but not broken. The respite can only be temporary, and the prospects for real peace have seldom seemed so far away."

In 1982, Israel's defense minister, Ariel Sharon, persuaded Menachem Begin to have another go at the PLO, a move that seemed to break Begin's spirit when it all went wrong. The Israeli army this time headed straight for Beirut, investing an Arab capital for the first time in the long Arab-Israeli struggle. Sharon's bold idea was to crush the PLO once and for all, make an alliance with the Phalange Christian militia, and gain Lebanon as a strategic ally. The Phalange militia was formed as a Maronite youth movement in 1936, modeled on Franco's Falangists in Spain, Italian fascists, and Nazi Brownshirts of the thirties.

This was not Israel's first imperial overreach. I was reminded of the Suez War in 1956, when, with the help of the British and French, Israel attacked Egypt and hoped it could keep the Sinai. President Eisenhower and American pressure squelched that, and American pressure would come again on Israel to respect the territorial integrity of Lebanon.

I returned to Lebanon in 1982 and followed the seemingly endless columns of Israeli armor and trucks north up the coast road to Beirut, where I had been just four years before.

The Israelis were on the hills overlooking the capital but had not yet decided to enter. The problem for me was how to cross from Israeli lines into West Beirut, where the Palestinians were cornered. East Beirut was Christian, and pro-Israel, so I made my way there only to find Peter Arnett, my old friend from Vietnam. Arnett was with a couple of television cameramen in a big American car. Peter was on what he said was a booze run for the Commodore Hotel in West Beirut, which was running low on liquor. He said I could come along, so I jumped in the car. The trunk was already full of bottles.

We proceeded to drive down to the dock area that separated Israeli and Palestinian forces. At an Israeli checkpoint we were stopped near the water's edge amid a warren of ruined and abandoned warehouses. An English-speaking Israeli captain came up to the car and said we would have to open the trunk. We did, and the captain whistled and said: "You journalists certainly do drink a lot." He warned us that the Palestinian militiamen were just ahead around the corner, so we crept forward through a battered no-man's-land of broken cranes and sunken ships alongside a ruined pier. I thought this would be a cameraman's dream of war's devastation, but the TV men with me ignored it. This wreckage was all done in 1975 and 1976, they explained, and this was 1982 and a different war. One had to be careful describing or photographing wreckage in Lebanon to make sure it wasn't wrecked in the last war, or the war before that.

We held our breath for the next hundred yards, and then, round the corner, just as the Israeli had said, was a Palestinian checkpoint. An excited Palestinian with a Kalashnikov screamed at us, clearly wanting us to open the trunk. We did, and he said something I thought sounded threatening. I asked Arnett's driver, who was sweating with fear, "What did he say, what did he say?" And the driver told me that the gunman had observed that journalists sure do drink a lot.

Once in West Beirut, with Israeli shells raining down, I found a super-heated, almost surrealistic atmosphere that reminded me of what Hemingway had written about being in Madrid when it was under siege during the Spanish Civil War. Yasser Arafat, who had usually been hard to see, was giving press conferences almost daily, and Palestinian fighters expressed to me their delight that the Israelis were now at close quarters where they could be killed more easily than before. No more infiltrating in rubber boats. The Israelis were right over there, and, the Palestinians said, the difference was that the Israelis were afraid to die, while Palestinians were not.

There were several different militias in the streets, and one needed passes from them all. I was always nervous that I would give the wrong pass to the wrong group and be shot for it. In some neighborhoods bulldozers were clearing up rubble from the civil war in the seventies. I remarked that it seemed a bit odd, with the Israelis at the gates, to be cleaning up rubble from seven years ago. I was told that the rubble would be used to make barricades in other parts of the city. Holes were being dug for mines, and the city was being remade into a fortress.

It developed that there were really two different groups of foreign reporters in Lebanon. One group, many of them based in Israel, stayed with the besieging Israeli forces, while the reporters in West Beirut reported on the Palestinian defenders. Only a few tried to report from both sides. On one such foray from Palestinian lines over to where the Israelis were dug in—always a tricky proposition—I found an Israeli gun battery hard at work.

I felt very strange sitting up on a hill watching Israeli artillery rain down shells on neighborhoods where people I knew lived. West Beirut seemed to heave under the shelling, with dust rising as if from a beaten rug. I later made my way back to West Beirut and went to check up on the neighborhoods that had just been bombarded. Tom Friedman, then a young reporter for the *New York Times,* wrote that the Israelis were shelling Beirut indiscriminately, which they certainly were. But the *Times,* in its wisdom, took the word "indiscriminately" out of Tom's copy, much to his fury. Tom would later go on to win the Pulitzer Prize three times and become one of the most influential foreign affairs columnists in America. His book *From Beirut to Jerusalem* became a classic. I admired his energy and resourcefulness, and being short with a small mustache, he could be mistaken for a local. His *Times* colleague and my old pal Bill Farrell was a six-foot Irishman who always stuck out like a big toe in the streets of Beirut.

At PLO headquarters I found an unnatural calm. I asked an Arafat spokesman, Mahmoud Labadi, "How will this all end?" "There seems to be a question of where we might go," he said. "What to do with the Palestinians? Nobody wants them. We are like the Jews of old. No one wants us. We cannot even go home."

On a visit to the front line, Palestinian fighters talked about the "Zionist enemy" as if the Israelis were not citizens of a small country fearful for its safety but part of a huge and sinister plot to do in the Arabs with America's help. On the other side Israeli soldiers usually referred to the Palestinians as "terrorists," which helped dehumanize them but seemed to me contrived when you had to refer to terrorist kindergartens, terrorist hospitals, and terrorist research centers.

A source everyone wanted to see in those days was Saeb Salam, six-time prime minister of Lebanon and a leader of the Sunni Muslim community. He was in daily contact with the PLO and the Americans, who were, in turn, in touch with the Israelis, about where the Palestinians might be exiled. There seemed to be no question about Palestinian fighters remaining in Lebanon, but where they would go was still being negotiated, he said. Salam lived in a beautiful old mansion in an area as yet untouched by shellfire, and he answered questions as if he were an old Ottoman pasha. He felt it was time that the US talked directly to the PLO. For once my notebook from that period is legible, and I have recorded that Salam said: "Over the years the US government has given countless pledges to countries in the Middle East and in all the years all have been broken except one: Kissinger's pledge not to talk directly to the PLO. It is time for President Reagan to say, 'Let us talk, enemy to enemy if you will, but let us talk.'"

I caught a ride to the Commodore Hotel with Tom Friedman as night was falling. It wasn't good for foreigners to be out in the streets after dark. Even when the Israelis weren't shelling there was intermittent gunfire in the streets. People were nervous and jumpy and no good could come of being shot by mistake.

Because of the lack of electricity and refrigeration, animals were being slaughtered in the streets under kerosene lamps to provide meat for the next day. I found this unsettling because you could see the same sort of human gore in the ruins of apartment buildings and outside hospitals when the shelling began again.

Much has been written about the old Commodore Hotel in Beirut, where most hacks stayed. The great old hotels, like the St. Georges on the waterfront, had been shot to pieces, and although the Commodore was no gem, the telex worked and the management was friendly and helpful. There was a parrot in the lobby, which, for a while, became the most written-about bird on earth. Every new correspondent in town wrote about the parrot that could whistle a few bars of Beethoven's Fifth, and expertly imitate the sound of an incoming shell.

It was rumored that the owner, Yousef Nazzal, had worked out some deal whereby militias would leave us alone, and, as Hemingway figured out in the Hotel Florida in Madrid, some rooms were more exposed to shellfire than others. When I first arrived the hotel was completely full, but Bill Farrell said

I could bunk in with him. There was only one bed, but he cheerfully said I could have it. He said the one space reserved for the *New York Times* was under the bed.

There was something called the "Commodore Laundry"—nothing to do with socks and shirts. It meant that when all your chits were presented to you for payment, you could request that the bar bills be made to disappear. The total amount didn't change. It just meant that your expense account would not show just how much you had had to drink, which in many cases was considerable.

At one time cartoonist Garry Trudeau of *Doonesbury* fame had his TV reporter character, Roland Hedley III, staying at the Commodore in his comic strip. I wrote to Trudeau about the Laundry. Soon enough Trudeau had his cartoon character avail himself of this bar-bill-laundering service. I soon heard some of my colleagues grumbling that that SOB Trudeau was blowing their expense account dodge. Later, Tom Friedman wrote it all up for the world to see, but let the record show, it was Roland Hedley III who first broke the story.

Garry Trudeau's Doonesbury *cartoon television reporter, Roland Hedley lll, at the Commodore Hotel in Beirut, 1982.*

I was not there when the Israelis finally decided to descend into the town itself, so I missed the US-brokered arrangement to move the PLO and Arafat to Tunis, and I missed the shocking massacres at the Sabra and Shatila refugee camps in which Phalangist militiamen were allowed to enter by the Israelis, only to massacre the inhabitants after the Palestinian fighters had left. I was later told by Israeli sources that the Israeli army fired star shells so that the militiamen could see to do their work. The story earned Friedman his first Pulitzer, which he shared with Loren Jenkins of the *Washington Post.*

The United States was now tempted to intervene in the political failure that was Lebanon in the guise of peacekeepers. Having gotten the PLO safely out, the US sought to get both the Israelis and the Syrians to withdraw from Lebanon and establish a stable government. Gathering some multinational cover with token French, British, and Italian forces, the US stepped into the reactivated civil war by backing the fragile government of Amin Gemayel. The trouble was that the Muslims and Druze felt excluded, and Gemayel's government was too weak to impose its own order. And so as had happened before in Indochina, and would happen again in Iraq and Afghanistan, the US was taking sides in a civil war in a former French (or British) colony to impose its own will. One can understand America's desire to bring order to chaos and to arrange the world in a manner favorable to America's interests. But to differing degrees all these post–World War II military adventures failed.

In Lebanon, American marines kept getting killed, and, quite understandably, started firing back, getting deeper and deeper into the Lebanese imbroglio. The US Navy fired big guns from capital ships up into the hills, killing some people, achieving nothing but enmity. Then, in October of 1983, the marine barracks were destroyed in a horrendous car bombing. Two hundred and forty-one marines were killed. A French barrack was also bombed, killing fifty-eight French soldiers. Not since the sinking of the battleship *Maine* in a Havana harbor eighty-five years before had so many American servicemen died in a peacetime incident, and this time it was no accident.

No one should have been surprised. The car bomb had long since become the heavy artillery of terrorism, just as the hijacked airplane would become terrorism's ballistic missile in this century. A similar attack on the US embassy had killed seventeen Americans and thirty-two Lebanese in April. Hezbollah had just walked onstage, although no one knew who had done it at the time.

The Reagan administration said that it wasn't going to allow a bunch of cowardly terrorists to determine US foreign policy. The *Washington Post* editorialized that it was "inconceivable to hand the bombers the victory they sought by pulling the Marines out. American influence throughout the region could collapse," but pull out is what the Reagan administration did. The US tried to say it was simply a "redeployment," but cartoonists had a field day with classic redeployments in history, such as Napoleon's from Moscow.

Israel's Yitzhak Rabin got it right when he wrote that the United States and Israel had already lost the battle over the political future of Lebanon, that the US had picked the wrong arena and the wrong partner for its confrontation with Moscow. Gemayel was little more than the mayor of Beirut, and the sooner a compromise between the warring Lebanese factions and Syrian interests could be patched, the less severe the American debacle would be.

On one level the critics of withdrawal were right. Saddam Hussein began to believe that Americans would fold at the first whiff of gunpowder and was thus emboldened to take Kuwait seven years later. But then again, the Reagan administration did not throw good money after bad as Lyndon Johnson did in Vietnam. Reagan cut his losses and avoided the kind of quagmire that Vietnam had represented, and that Afghanistan would later be.

The Israeli pullout from Beirut did not make it any less dangerous for reporters. We were always worried about being kidnapped and chained to a radiator in the Bekaa Valley, as our colleague Terry Anderson had been for five years. The rule was you never went out early in the morning because kidnappers liked to grab you and put you in the trunk before traffic had built up in the city. I often would order a taxi at the Commodore and then change taxis just in case someone had overheard where I was going and arranged to have me stopped and taken.

Some reporters had hired apartments around town, and I remember one weird winter's night in a spacious apartment overlooking the Mediterranean, with flashes of gunfire in the Chouf Mountains off in the distance. There was no furniture in the room whatsoever, just a white wall-to-wall rug. We cooked steaks in a blazing fireplace, drinking excellent Lebanese wine. We were safe for the moment.

The Commodore could not forever remain untouched by the turmoil around it, and when religious fanatics took over the city alcohol was denounced as "the satanic beverage." One day a band of Islamic brothers came in and broke every bottle in the bar. A startled British reporter, coming home after a day's reporting, looked around him wide-eyed at the destruction. "No problem," a hotel employee quickly said, "there is more in the cellar. What would you like?" The Brit quietly said: "I guess I'll have a satanic and tonic."

There were occasional bombings of restaurants and cafés in Beirut, and a curious thing about the aftermath, when we arrived to inspect the damage, was the number of shoes left around. Explosives seemed to have the ability to blow people out of their shoes, even when they were laced. Of course there was always the possibility that some feet were left in the shoes.

Later, when cell phones came into common use, the thing I most remembered about a bombing in Israel was the number of cell phones left among the dead and injured, plaintively ringing and ringing with no one left to answer them.

I kept going back to Beirut on my swings through the Middle East, and my notebooks record my last day there in January of 1985. A wind was picking up the swirling dust, papers, and plastic bags from the rubbish piles. Clouds coming in from the Mediterranean brought intermittent rain. The city still bore the scars of nine years of war, and the shacks and shanties of the poor lined the road to the airport. I had found my Lebanese friends and acquaintances nervous and afraid, and the irrepressible Lebanese optimism seemed to have given in to despair. Grass was growing in the crumbling ruins of the old hotel district near the sea, and whole buildings cleft by bombs spilled their floors out toward the streets like messy bureau drawers.

People were no longer dying by the scores, as during the Israeli siege or the civil war, but they were dying in ones and twos and threes in random killings, assassinations and robberies, and even after everything that had gone before nothing had really changed. Nothing had been settled. "Bombings, kidnappings, foreign armies camped on Lebanon's soil, protection money, illegal imports, economic slumpflation and the promise of much, much worse to come," said a local newspaper in an editorial. "Lebanon is a zoo where people are fed to the animals." A restaurant I liked, the Smuggler's Inn, a favorite of what was left of Beirut's writers and artists, had been bombed the night before, killing four and wounding more than a dozen. Posters of Iran's Ayatollah Khomeini, a hero to the Shia, were being plastered on the walls of burned-out hotels where once, before the troubles, bikini-clad girls swam in clear blue pools.

A new and more frightening Middle East was emerging, Islam was turning in on itself and on others in this city that had once been the most tolerant in the Middle East. America had made the mistake of looking at Lebanon through a Cold War lens, rather than seeing the Lebanese factions for what they were; squabbling for power and riven by ethnic and religious hatreds. But the seeds of a new anti-American and anti-Western force were already sprouting.

As for the Israelis, they would bomb and invade Lebanon again from time to time, but it never did any good in the long run, and every year Hezbollah's rockets grew larger, with ever-longer range.

In my last dispatch from Lebanon I wrote, "For Americans the situation is frightening. The Islamic Holy War party says it is holding five Americans . . . All my Lebanese friends have warned me to be careful. 'If you were careful you wouldn't be here,'" said one. And so I left thinking I would be back. But as it turned out my reporting took me elsewhere, and I was never to see Beirut or Lebanon again.

I did, however, follow the PLO to Tunis to see how attitudes might be changing. It was before Arafat made his historic change to embrace a two-state solution for Palestine and Israel, and he was still shouting his defiance from exile in Tunisia. When I arrived in Tunis I was told that Arafat would be returning from abroad the next day, and that I should just take the day off and wait for my interview.

I went down from town to the beach, where there were splendid, French-style fish restaurants and Tunisian white wine. I ate a good lunch, and took a long walk on the beach afterward with the winter waves breaking on the shore. I felt a sharp pain in my leg and looked down to see a small dog writhing in the sand and biting at his own tail. Alas, he had bitten me, and with rabies in my fears, I found a taxi to take me to a doctor. He took me to a veterinarian instead, and in my atrocious French I tried to explain about "*le chien méchant avec la rage.*"

The vet said I should get to the Institut Pasteur just as quickly as possible, but I decided instead to call the American embassy, telling them I might be a distressed American. Ambassador Robert Pelletreau told me not to go to the Institut Pasteur in Tunis as they might not be changing the needles. If rabies didn't get me, AIDS might. I was advised to go straight to Paris.

I missed the Paris plane by minutes but took the next plane to Rome, only to find it was an Italian holiday with no doctors working. I called my doctor at Massachusetts General Hospital in Boston, and he said I had three days and had already wasted one of them. I should fly straight home and he would have the rabies vaccine ready. The best connection was from Rome to Zurich to Boston, which I took, only to arrive in Boston during a snowstorm with the pilot telling us we might have to fly on to another airport. I thought if I got out of my seat and bit the stewardess they might be forced to land, but being Swissair they found a hole in the clouds and we flew down through to land safely.

When I related my adventure to the Israeli consul he asked: "How do I know it wasn't Arafat who bit you?" I asked: "How do I know the dog hadn't come ashore in a rubber boat as part of an Israeli commando operation?"

25

The Soviet Empire Crumbles

In 1989 the Soviet empire began to fall apart. It had reached its high-water mark with the invasion of Afghanistan ten years before. That adventure became a Soviet nightmare similar to ours in Vietnam, and on February 16 General Boris Gromov led the last contingent of Russian forces across the Oxus River back into Soviet territory. No one could have imagined then that the United States military would one day come in the footsteps of General Gromov and stay even longer.

Later in 1989, Eastern Europe, which had been held by Soviet power since 1945, began to get seriously restless. Unlike previous Soviet leaders, Mikhail Gorbachev decided not to send in his tanks to quell the unrest. A rapid process of decolonialization began, with Poland being allowed to go its own way in June, Hungary in October, Czechoslovakia at year's end. East Germans were dying to get out to the west, and it was Hungary that loosened the floodgates by opening up the barbed-wire border to let East Germans through the once-iron curtain into Austria.

Even the Baltic States, which had been part of Russia's empire since Peter the Great, save for a couple of decades following World War I, wanted out. I visited Tallinn, the Estonian capital, in the autumn of that year with the *Boston Globe*'s Moscow correspondent Paul Quinn-Judge. We found that the blue, black, and white flag of Estonia was flying over the city's tallest tower, the medieval bastion that Estonians affectionately called "Big Hermann." The Soviet flag was nowhere to be seen in the old town. Tallinn, with its Lutheran churches and cobblestone streets, and its language akin to Finnish, already seemed like a separate country, even though Gorbachev was still hanging on to it. Moscow had granted Estonia a certain measure of autonomy, but total freedom was in the air. "We are meeting day and night," Estonia's prime minister said. "It's a hell of a fight, a crazy time." A Communist Party official in Tartu, Estonia's second city, told me that even the Communist Party was talking about becoming a "real party that will compete in elections."

President George Herbert Walker Bush was treading lightly and with great skill, making sure not to humiliate Gorbachev or give too much encouragement to countries like Estonia too quickly, lest it provoke a Russian crackdown. But independence was clearly on the way.

In Moscow, the Soviet Congress of People's Deputies was also in ferment. No longer just a rubber stamp for a succession of Soviet dictators, it was beginning to show some spunk unseen since the Duma met in the dawn of the Russian Revolution. A delegate from Latvia whom I met in the halls told me that the Baltic states no longer wanted their soldiers to serve in the Russian army, or to serve in Central Asia, something that did not please the generals. Gorbachev's "perestroika" was in full flower and would ultimately bring down the Soviet Union. Gorbachev hoped reform would save the Soviet Union, but as John le Carré put it in one of his novels, the Soviet knight was already dead inside his armor.

In November I went on to Warsaw, where I had an appointment with an old Stalinist, Jan Bisztyga, burly, red-faced, the official spokesman for the Polish Communist Party. We met in his spartan office at party headquarters. A picture of Lenin and a bust of Marx stared down at me. Communist tomes filled the bookcase. To my surprise Bisztyga went to his office safe, took out a bottle of whiskey, and said: "Do you want me to talk about this organization I represent, or tell you what I really think?" This was not what you usually heard from Communist apparatchiks, so I sat up straight in my chair.

Leaning across the table, looking me straight in the eye, he began to demolish the faith he had served for so many years. It was fifteen years too late to save Communism, he said. The modern world had simply passed it by. Technology had accelerated at an unprecedented pace. "Ninety percent of all the inventions since the dawn of civilization were invented in the last thirty-five years," he said, "and most of them were invented in the West."

Holy cow! I thought to myself, scribbling furiously in my notebook to keep up with his treasonous talk. This was shaping up to be a major scoop.

One of Communism's great weaknesses, he said, was the inability to perform economically. Another was Communism's inability to "change old-fashioned views of society"—the wasteful and destructive emphasis on the class war over the years. "You know very well that the workers are not the leaders of technology," he said. The world had become too pluralistic for that kind of black and white thinking. It had kept the eastern bloc in a straitjacket, thereby stunting growth. The end of the dictatorship of the proletariat had become a historical inevitability, he said.

"There is no future to the kind of bureaucratic socialism I am representing now," he said. "We will dissolve it in January. You have won." With that he shoved a piece of paper across the table, a letter to Willy Brandt, the West German head of the Socialist International. The letter said that the Communist party of Poland was preparing a party congress for January that would be its last. The party would be dissolved and transformed into a broad-based social democratic party. The principles of the dictatorship of the proletariat and a centralized economy would be rejected, and the new party would subscribe to political pluralism. Contacts with Western socialist parties would be sought for new ideas to assist in this transmogrification.

In the decade of the eighties, Bisztyga said, the West had adapted with tremendous speed to technological change, with high flexibility and dynamism. "You put all your energies into this and you won." He spoke about the books on his shelves, of how he had spent all his life believing in what Communism had to preach. But it was all turning to dust in failure.

He had a word of caution for the victors, however. The United States had badly neglected education, concentrating on an elite instead of on the broad base of educated people that an advanced economy needed.

He said that to remain a great country, the US would have to abandon rightist causes, such as armaments, and give some back to education and the environment, just as the eastern bloc would have to dismantle central planning and install individual initiative and free markets. This way the two sides might meet somewhere in the middle as the century came to a close. "I am optimistic about the future of socialism," he said, "just not this kind."

As I closed my notebook, Bisztyga helped himself to a very large glass of whiskey. I said to him: "You know Stalin would have had you shot for saying what I have just heard." Helping himself to another glass, he said: "You are absolutely right."

I hurried back to my hotel to write up my scoop and get it sent to Boston as quickly as possible. I was writing furiously when JB, who had come with me to Warsaw, said: "You had better come and hear what the BBC is saying." "Not now, JB," I said, but she insisted. So I went to where the television was showing pictures of East Germans climbing over the Berlin Wall into West Berlin. My scoop had been overtaken by a far bigger story—the biggest story of that decade.

I went downstairs to dinner, where the *Globe*'s Warsaw stringer, Anne Applebaum, and my *Globe* colleagues were already eating. I told Anne what I had heard. At first she thought I was kidding. But when she found out I wasn't, she left for Berlin. And shortly after, so did I. Applebaum would go on to a distinguished journalistic career, winning a Pulitzer Prize, and become a recognized expert on the horrors of Communist rule.

There aren't many truly good news stories that journalists get to write, especially foreign correspondents. The definition of "news" is most often "bad news." If a plane lands safely there is no story. But the explosion of joy as East Germans met West Germans was akin to that moment of joy in Jerusalem when Sadat came to make peace.

In Berlin crowds were going wild. East Germans were given a few West German deutsche marks by the West Germans and were trying to buy everything in sight. People simply flowed like water over and through the wall, the wall that had become our generation's most potent symbol of oppression. Easties embraced the once-feared border guards and caroused

all night with Westies in what may have been the biggest block party in European history.

Alexander Yakovlev, a politburo member and a leading theorist of reform in the Soviet Union, was comparing 1989 to the French Revolution in 1789 and the Bolshevik Revolution of 1917, only without the bloodshed. Communism, and Soviet oppression, born in bloodshed and murder, was dying peacefully before our eyes with very little violence.

Stories were everywhere to write, and many of us hacks, after our stories were filed, would unwind each night at Berlin's storied Paris Bar. History usually moves slowly and calmly until it lurches forward suddenly into a different era. We all knew we were at a historic turning point that was changing the face of Europe and virtually ending the Cold War.

Americans watching television in the US had a grandstand seat on East Germans dancing on the wall and people with sledgehammers dismantling it. But what they didn't see, and what became something of a sight for Berliners to gawk at, were the three tall wooden towers that NBC, CBS, and ABC had built in front of the Brandenburg Gate, with glaring lights and humming trucks, looking like Martian monsters from H. G. Wells's *War of the Worlds*. On top of these towers sat the three anchormen, like monarchs in an age when television was king. It had been NBC's Tom Brokaw whose interview with an East German official first breached the Berlin Wall. The official had inadvertently said the wall was open, and nobody then could hold back the flood.

The *Boston Globe*'s man in Berlin at the time, Tom Palmer, and I passed through the famous Checkpoint Charlie to visit the eastern zone. In so doing we passed from the gaudy, robust vulgarity of rich West Berlin into a shabby, down-at-the-heels Berlin unchanged since the 1940s. The old kaiser's imperial buildings were still pockmarked by bullets fired forty-four years before in the last Götterdämmerung of Hitler's hegemony in Europe.

Curiously, we found that the East Berliners were not all wishing for immediate reunification of Germany. "Everyone wants a Mercedes," a university teacher told us, but people were not so willing to give up all the benefits of free education, free health care, and guaranteed employment. At least not yet.

For a brief period, after the East German regime had collapsed, the new

East German government, filled with Lutheran pastors—the new defense minister was said to have been a draft dodger—was optimistic that some third way could be found. Something not tyrannical like the old East German regime, but not rampant capitalism either. I remember thinking at the time that the dynamic West Germans would swallow up East Germany in a couple of gulps, leaving these idealistic dreamers in the "dustbin of history," as Leon Trotsky had once said. And so it came to pass. Seventeen years later I would spend a winter in Berlin, and it was not always easy to find where the old wall had been. Checkpoint Charlie had been turned into a kind of museum curiosity of a dead age, and just inside the old East Berlin was a Bugatti show-room—the Bugatti then being the most expensive car in the world.

Gorbachev tried to hang on and keep things together, but events were moving too fast and by 1991 the Soviet Union itself was in the dustbin. I had picked up a postcard in Moscow printed in anticipation of the upcoming seventy-fifth anniversary of the Communists coming to power. But the Soviet Union died before it ever reached the age of seventy-five. The Russia that the czars had built up over centuries began rapidly falling apart, with the Muslim countries breaking away first. I wrote at the time that there might be nothing of Russia left except the Slavic republics, but I was wrong. The non-Russian Slavic republics soon broke away, too.

The new Russian Federation abandoned the red banner of the Soviet Union and took up instead the old white, blue, and red flag of the czars that dated from the time Peter the Great ordered some ships built for him in Holland. When the Dutch arrived in St. Petersburg they pulled down the Dutch flag and asked Peter for a Russian flag to pull up the halyard. Russia didn't have a flag, so Peter just told them to cut the red strip of the Dutch flag off the top and sew it on the bottom. Thus was born the flag the Russian Federation uses today.

The Caucasus would resist the new Russia's rule, just as it had in the nine-teenth century, and there would be terrible bloodshed in those mountains. But for the most part the Soviet Union split up peacefully.

There was a memorable moment when the Soviet fleet left the Mediterra-

nean. The American fleet admiral sent a signal to his old rivals saying, "Have a safe journey home." The Russians signaled back: "If only we knew where home is."

The Cold War, which I had thought would go on for a hundred years, was over.

26

Balkan Tragedy

No sooner had the Soviet Union dissolved than Yugoslavia, too, began to disintegrate. A union of South Slavs had been cobbled together following World War I under the name Yugoslavia. It included Serbia, which would become the dominant entity; Croatia; Slovenia; Macedonia; Bosnia; and Montenegro. Later, Kosovo would be wrested from Serbia as well to form a separate country with the help of an American bombing campaign.

Under the leadership of Marshal Tito, Yugoslavia emerged from World War II as a united Communist country with the monarchy abolished. But Tito would not accept Soviet domination. When it appeared that Tito was going to be his own man, and not knuckle under to Stalin, the Americans and other Western powers took a great interest in him and encouraged his independence.

Unfortunately, the various Slavic ethnicities and confessions never liked each other, and the moment Tito died the whole structure of the union of South Slavs started to come apart with a viciousness not seen since the Nazi occupation. Atrocity followed upon atrocity. It wasn't just Tito's death that brought on the deluge. Fear of the Soviets and an armed invasion, as the Czechs and Hungarians had experienced, was the glue that kept Yugoslavia together. Once the Soviet Union was gone, that glue dissolved.

For historic and sentimental reasons, Germany and Austria immediately favored Slovenians and Croatians, and were quick—too quick—to recognize Croatian independence. Both had once been part of the Austro-Hungarian empire. But civil war had begun between all the factions, and it looked as if the twentieth century was going to end, as it began, in Balkan bloodshed.

Sarajevo, the capital of Bosnia-Herzegovina, soon came to the world's attention as it endured a brutal siege by Serbian forces. It was a pretty town, best known for the assassination of the Austrian archduke and heir to the throne Franz Ferdinand in 1914—the spark that ignited the First World War.

In 1992 I made the rounds of what had been Yugoslavia, visiting Serbia, Croatia, and Muslims in Bosnia, and heard from many lips the frightful things that had occurred when neighbor turned against neighbor. It didn't come as a complete surprise. Even a superficial glance at Balkan history would reveal similar atrocities between the various factions.

United Nations sanctions had stopped all flights in and out of Belgrade, the Serbian capital, so you took the train from Budapest's Hapsburg-era railway station. And what a train it was, full of arms smugglers, spies, black marketeers, adventurers, troublemakers, and the odd newspaper hack, such as myself, reading Rebecca West's splendid but already then out-of-date *Black Lamb and Grey Falcon*. The old Orient Express had nothing on this train when it came to intrigue. Belgrade, once an important Cold War capital, seemed a forlorn town, infected with strongly held nationalist sentiments and an idea that Serbs were completely in the right. They had been the dominant entity in the old Yugoslavia they were trying to preserve, which was never coming back.

Zagreb, Croatia's capital, was still the little Austrian town it had been for so long before the First World War. I went to the opera—I think it was *Così Fan Tutte*—while outside you could hear heavy guns firing in the distance. I found that mixed couples, Serbs married to Croats, were having a very hard time indeed. They were being pressured to choose one community and renounce the other. Even the Serbo-Croatian language was being torn asunder, with Croats trying to find words of their own that were not the same in Serbia. Sigmund Freud's "narcissism of minor differences" ruled the day.

Slovenia, with its own distinct language, had been part of Austria before

Salzburg, and it wanted to be considered part of Europe proper rather than a Balkan country. Serbia was loath to let highly industrialized Slovenia go. After only minor skirmishes, however, Serbia did let Slovenia go, and Serbia turned its full attention to beating up on Croats and Bosnian Muslims.

Croats, too, tried to persuade me that Croatia was not really a Balkan country, as was Serbia with its Eastern Orthodox rites. No, they said, Catholic Croatia was European, not Balkan. I couldn't help remembering that in the previous century Prince Metternich had said that the Balkans began at the Rennweg, meaning at the outskirts of Vienna.

I visited the beautiful Dalmatian Coast, where JB and I had spent a holiday many years before, to find refugees camping out in the seaside hotels, lighting fires and cooking food on the marble floors of hotel lobbies. The Croatians had painted "U2" on many walls in bright red, and at first there was a general confusion among the Western reporters as to what it meant. To my generation, U2 could only mean the American spy plane that had been shot down over Russia in Eisenhower's time, causing an international incident. To the younger reporters, U2 was a rock band.

What it really meant was that the Ustaše had come back for a second time. The Ustaše were a fanatically Catholic and nationalist organization that had thrown its support behind the Nazis in World War II. They believed in racial purity and went out of their way to murder Jews, Serbs, and Gypsies. Hitler had given Croatia its independence under German tutelage. After the war Croatia was integrated back into Yugoslavia.

In Serb areas you saw references to "Chetniks," the mostly Serbian nationalists who fought against both the Germans and Tito's Communists in the 1940s. Whereas Tito's forces had been clean-shaven, the Chetniks of old wore beards, so many of the Serb forces in Bosnia in 1992 wore beards as well to represent Serb nationalism. The breakup of Yugoslavia was lifting the lid off a Pandora's box of Balkan horrors from the past.

It was the Serbs who had fought with the allies in World Wars I and II. But they were being cast as the villains this time around. The Serbs at first tried to hold Yugoslavia together by force, and when that failed, they introduced a new term for an old concept: "ethnic cleansing." The Croats may have done more ethnic cleansing in terms of numbers, but the Serbs went about it with greater brutality.

Bosnia was where all hell came together in the winter of 1992. I found it to be a war mainly against civilians. Armies didn't clash as much as they attacked each other's civilians. Whole populations were being scattered and turned out of their homes, some by force, and others fleeing to seek security among their coreligionists. As I drove through the countryside with my old friend Dusko Doder, formerly of the *Washington Post,* we could see smoke rising from burning towns.

Dusko was originally from Montenegro, but his family had had a house in Sarajevo, built before the First World War, when my house outside Boston had been built. Dusko told me of the many conflicts that had swirled around his family home, Austrians replacing Ottomans, Nazis fighting Yugoslavs, Communists against Chetniks. One day an uncle opened the front door and was shot dead. Who knew by whom? When Dusko was a child after the Second World War the curtains were all pulled shut one day, and he was told not to open them. He peeked, of course, and saw bodies hanging from the lampposts along his street. What different histories our two family houses had had, one being fortunate enough to be in a New England town unruffled by warfare since the eighteenth century, while the other was built in a cauldron of Balkan conflict.

As we drove toward Sarajevo through beautiful countryside reminiscent of Switzerland, we saw the once-neat villages where Serbians and Muslims had once lived peacefully beside Croats. Many were in ruins. Burned-out cars littered the streets, red-tiled roofs were open to the rain, and walls were spattered by bullets. Along the roads tinny-sounding automobiles and horse carts piled high with mattresses, bedding, and belongings were fleeing one side or another.

Bosnia was full of ammunition dumps, for it was in these hills that Tito had planned to fight the Russians, had they invaded. These cached weapons were now being dug up and used by all sides.

Everywhere there were reminders of past conflicts. On the road to Sarajevo a Serbian military convoy had stopped so that the soldiers could relieve themselves. There was a little monument that no one bothered to notice, saying that on the twentieth of September, 1914, "a fierce battle took place here between the Serbian and Austrian armies." Farther along another monument said that on the fifteenth of June, 1942, the "Sixth Proletarian Company of the East Bosnian Brigade" destroyed a Croatian position on this spot.

"This is exclusively a religious war," a Serbian army colonel, Kommen Karkovic, told me. "This has been going on for three hundred or four hundred years, always a religious conflict. The Communists," he said, meaning Tito, "didn't understand that. They forced us to live together, but there was no basis for it." Nobody, he said, neither Serbs, nor Croats, nor Muslims, wanted to live as a despised minority in a country controlled by the others. Separation and partition was the only answer, he said.

It was a local legend that in World War II the Orthodox Christian Serbs massacred Catholic Croats and Muslims and threw their bodies into the river Drina, while the Croats and Muslims slaughtered Serbs and threw their bodies in the Sava. It was said that the bodies of all three confessions were mixed together at the point where the Drina and Sava converge but had nothing to say to each other when they met. Memories were very long in Bosnia. Nothing forgotten, nothing forgiven. Whatever one thought about Tito, it was a Communist article of faith that different ethnic and religious groups could put aside their differences and unite under one ideological system, much as we Americans believe, but that dream was now in tatters in the ruins of Yugoslavia.

Despite all the horrors around them, people went about their normal lives as best they could, as they always do in war zones. I watched a man in Sarajevo running down a street in the rain holding up an open umbrella. He was running because snipers were known to sweep this street with bullets, and the open umbrella was obviously slowing him down. But he clung to that little bit of normality and would not fold up his umbrella in the rain.

I visited a Serb gun position in the hills above the battered city. It was late November, and the snow had already arrived. Soldiers were standing around small fires, stamping their feet in the cold and huddling in their parkas and greatcoats. Earthworks, revetments, spent cartridges, all the detritus of war were spread around us, yet nearby I saw a sign left over from the Olympic Games in happier times, pointing the way to the bobsled run.

Below me the city, where people were starving and freezing, lay in unnatural darkness. A power cut made the town look dead and deserted. A full moon was rising over the Igman, the mountain that overlooks the city where Europe's worst nightmares were coming true. It was said that Croatian forces had occupied the Igman. I was told I better leave now because this position was often brought under fire when night fell, and tonight there was a "sniper's moon."

An interview with a Muslim woman, Pemba Spaho, whom I encountered in a refugee camp sparked my curiosity about what drove former neighbors to turn on each other with such viciousness as I was encountering in Bosnia. She told me that one day, in a village where Serbs and Muslims had lived side by side without any trouble, "barricades began appearing. People were turned back, people trying to go to work, children to school. The barricades showed up suddenly. No one expected it." These were not strangers manning the barricades. "These were our neighbors. We knew them." After a while, her Serb neighbors came to throw her out of her home. "There was young Vukovic, and Tororvic," both miners from the same mine where her husband worked. Pemba Spaho knew their parents. They had been friends. Ethnic cleansing had arrived.

Ivo Andrić, Yugoslavia's only Nobel laureate, had written of a previous period of ethnic and religious hatred in his classic *The Bridge on the Drina*. "That wild beast, which lives in man and does not dare to show itself until the barriers of law and custom have been removed, was now set free," he wrote.

———

When back in Boston I spent many weeks talking to political psychiatrists, anthropologists, and historians about just what caused neighbors to turn on each other. What I found was that ethnic and religious conflicts march in lockstep with postcolonial independence: India–Pakistan, Algeria, Palestine–Israel, Cambodia–Vietnam, Iraq with its Sunni and Shia rivalries, Afghanistan with its many warring ethnicities. Each group wants to know how power will be redistributed, who will own the land, the resources. Relatively homogeneous Vietnam was different because the fight there was over ideology and national unity, not ethnicity or religion, but the end of French Indochina exposed the fear and hatred Cambodians had of the Vietnamese, who had been, like the Serbs in Yugoslavia, the dominant tribe in Indochina. Cambodians feared cultural extinction at the hands of the Vietnamese.

Empires tended to freeze ethnic and religious differences like woolly mammoths in ice. But once imperial power starts to decline, ethnic conflicts are reborn. The civil war in Afghanistan between Tajiks, Uzbeks, and other minorities against the Pashtuns that began when the Soviets left has never really ended, but promises to burst forth with renewed vigor once the Americans are gone. In Iraq, Sunni and Shia Muslims have been at each other's throats ever since the end of Saddam Hussein.

Vamik Volkan, a professor at the University of Virginia who saw the breakdown of law and custom between Greeks and Turks in Cyprus after the British left, wrote that there is a more primitive factor buried in the human psyche that comes to the fore when worlds fall apart. "The psychoanalytical view indicates that ethnicity or nationality originates much as other emotional phenomena do in clans or tribes. The sense of self is intertwined at a primitive level with the identity of the group." It used to be unfashionable to say this, but it may be genetic. We may have inherited this trait from the apelike species from whom we developed as human beings.

Xenophobia maintains the integrity of the social group, both among monkeys and human beings, anthropologists and primatologists told me. Being comparatively weak animals as individuals, both found it better to band together. And among human beings, the stress and fear of losing something, whether it be social position, livelihood, sometimes racial dominance, or one's very life, brings forth xenophobia. As political scientist Roger Masters put it: cooperation with other individuals who share your genes is more likely to perpetuate your own genes. He called it "kin selection."

In times of stress, or when a threat is perceived, people tend to define themselves more narrowly, sharply distinguishing friends from enemies, retreating into what might be called their "survival group." What I was seeing in Bosnia was similar to what I had seen in Beirut; in Belfast; in Phnom Penh, when I saw the bloated bodies of Vietnamese men, women, and children floating down the Mekong after the Cambodians had massacred them. Only when the group feels less threatened does a broader definition of national purpose become possible again.

The declaration of independence by Bosnia-Herzegovina meant that a new order filled with uncertainties was on the way. This provided the stress that dismantled all that being a multiethnic Yugoslav had once meant, and it brought people streaming back to their tribal origins. It is no coincidence that Pemba Spaho's ordeal started on the day that Bosnian independence was declared.

A political scientist named Andrei Markovits put it well when he said: "The smell of your neighbor's curry is enticing and wonderful if you are OK. If you are not OK, if you feel threatened, you may think it's smelly and disgusting and you want to beat the guy up." There had been a recent case in Cambodia when a Cambodian was murdered by his Cambodian neighbors for singing a Vietnamese song.

Economic difficulties play a big role in provoking hostility toward ethnic minorities. Turkish workers were welcomed in Germany when Germans were getting 5 percent pay raises every year. But when there was economic pullback and unemployment, Turks were no longer as welcome and attacks upon them by "skinhead" German youths became more common.

Another common phenomenon that became apparent in the breakup of Yugoslavia was what the late John Mack called "the egoism of victimization." So caught up does each group get in its own sense of hurt that it cannot conceive of the hurt it could be doing to others. This, I found, was particularly true of the Arab-Palestinian conflict. Each side was convinced that it was the aggrieved party. While you could get Israelis and Palestinians to talk about possible solutions, it was much, much harder to get them to admit any fault in how the conflict came about in the first place. "I am willing to discuss the possibility of a Palestinian state," one Israeli friend told me, "but I am not going to say we started any of this, or that it's our fault."

I always found many Israelis and Palestinians not only sensitive to any criticism of their own position, but resentful should anything be said in favor of the other. To the victim, George Orwell once said, "any implied praise of a rival organization fills him with uneasiness." I was reminded of the criticism that pro-Israeli readers had leveled at the *Boston Globe* about photographs of good-looking Palestinians appearing in the paper. Critics of a German film about Hitler's last days, called *Downfall,* said that the film made Hitler look too human. Alas, Hitler was human, representing the worst side of humanity.

Another oddity of ethnic stress is that one group will shun any contamination by the other. I was told Muslims in Sarajevo refused emergency clothing, no matter how desperately needed, if the clothing had been made in Serbia. Armenians, following an earthquake, refused to accept blood from neighboring rival Azerbaijan. Ethicist Sissela Bok called this the "pathology of partisanship," a community repeatedly engaging in behavior that is ultimately self-defeating and self-destructive. "People become obsessive and heedless of their group's long-range self-interest."

Each side in ethnic conflicts has its own "chosen trauma," Volkan said. I found Serbs wanted only to dwell on historic wrongs committed by Turks in Ottoman times. Deeds committed centuries ago were spoken of as if they happened only the day before yesterday. Turkish Cypriots wanted to dwell on the massacres committed by Greek Cypriots in the 1960s, while Greeks wanted everyone to concentrate on the Turkish invasion of Cyprus in the seventies. Muslims and Hindus in India and Pakistan all had their chosen traumas that they wanted to dwell on, and of course Israelis and Palestinians each have their own trauma that never leaves their consciousness. For Israelis the holocaust is paramount in memory, while for the Palestinians it is their loss and displacement in what Israelis call their war for independence and what the Arabs call "the Catastrophe."

A common characteristic of ethnic or religious conflict is competition between a dominant group wanting to hold power—in the case of Yugoslavia, the Serbs—and a subordinate group or groups wanting to achieve power. I had seen this in Northern Ireland, in South Africa, in the struggle between Palestinians and Israelis. I would later see it in Iraq, where the American invasion empowered the Shia and disempowered the traditional rulers, the Sunni Muslims. We did it again in Afghanistan when we removed the Pashtuns from power and empowered the Tajiks.

One key element to conflict resolution is a recognition and discussion of historical wrongs, but that isn't easy when there is disagreement about the wrongs. Perhaps the best example is South Africa's Truth and Reconciliation Commission, but in South Africa's case one side simply handed the reins of power over to the other side, which is unusual. In Northern Ireland, Protestants and Catholics agreed to postpone the final decisions about the distribution of power between communities and leave it to a political process. In Yugoslavia neither of those things happened, and resolution came only after the warring sides wore themselves out fighting and agreed to arbitration.

The Bosnian War ended during the Clinton administration when Richard Holbrooke banged some heads together in Dayton, Ohio. He deserves much credit, but it wouldn't have happened if the combatants hadn't decided that there had to be some compromises.

There were many in the United States who said we should intervene militarily to stop the horrors of Bosnia, just as there are those who said the same thing about Syria twenty years later. But I thought then, and I believe now, that it is dangerous to get mixed up in other people's civil wars until they themselves are ready to end them. At that point diplomatic intervention can help to find ways out of the impasse in which the warring parties find themselves. Military interventions tend to make things worse.

"Each side viewed the other with distrust . . . No guarantee could be given that could be trusted, no oath sworn that people would fear to break, everyone had come to the conclusion that it was hopeless to expect a permanent settlement, and so, instead of being able to feel confident in others, they devoted their energies to providing against being injured themselves . . . Cruelties that people once considered unthinkable became commonplace."

This was the verdict of Thucydides on the conflict between Athens and Sparta, but his words are equally applicable to Europe during the long struggle between Protestants and Catholics—the echoes of which linger in Northern Ireland—and in the Balkans and the Middle East today.

27

Saddam Hussein Goes to War

It seems hard to believe now, when Iran and Israel are such mortal enemies, that before the shah fell it was possible to fly directly from Tel Aviv to Tehran on El Al, the Israeli national airline. It was all a part of Israel's strategy of forging an alliance with a non-Arab power in the region to counterbalance the hostile forces allied against the Jewish state. Israel had tried, and ultimately failed, to make a deal in Lebanon with the Christians, who were Arabs but feared Muslims more than they disliked Israel. Later Turkey would fill that role, until a more Islamic government came to power, and until Israel heavy-handedly killed Turkish citizens on a Turkish boat trying to bring relief to Gaza in defiance of the Israeli blockade.

In the seventies Israel's friend was Iran, Muslim, but Persian not Arab, with a proud and ancient culture. Nixon and Kissinger had put great faith in the shah as a protector of American interests in the Middle East and supplied him with a cornucopia of arms. The shah even started looking into the possibility of nuclear weapons.

When I arrived in Tehran from Israel in 1976, Richard Helms, former director of Central Intelligence, was our ambassador. I asked Helms how the shah felt about a CIA man as America's envoy, and he told me that the Russian ambassador had asked the shah the same question. According to

Helms, the shah fixed the Russian with a hard stare and replied: "At least I know the Americans have sent me their top spy."

Protests against the shah were gathering force, but we had no idea then that the entire monarchy was on the verge of collapse. It seemed then that the Iranian state had enough force to repress dissent. When Iranian militants later took over our embassy, keeping our diplomats hostage for 444 days, I wondered if Helms's having been a previous ambassador hadn't added to Iranian suspicions that the embassy was nothing but a nest of spies. My cousin Moorhead Kennedy was one of the hostages, and his wife, Louisa, became a sort of spokeswoman for the anxious families.

During that trip to Iran I received one of the strangest invitations of my career. Savak, the dreaded Iranian secret police, invited me in for a chat to brush up their image, they said. Savak had a fearful reputation for torture, and I went with some trepidation to Savak headquarters lest I hear screams from the cellars. But it was all very civilized and polite. I listened while Savak big shots told me that they were really nice guys and that the West had gotten it all wrong about them. They flatly denied that there had ever been any torture and said that Savak was only there to uphold order and prevent Communists from taking power. Defending the country against the Communists was sure, they thought, to win American sympathies. However, theirs was not a story that checked out.

The shah was then our man, and Saddam Hussein in neighboring Iraq had thrown his lot in with the Russians; that was the basis of American foreign policy at the time. Things got a lot less black and white when the shah fled and Ayatollah Khomeini returned from exile. The takeover of our embassy resulted in Iran becoming our enemy and Iraq our friend. President Carter's failed mission to rescue the embassy hostages, with burned helicopters and dead Americans in the desert, was the final coffin nail in his presidency. The breach with Iran has lasted thirty years, the hostages being our "chosen trauma," and our support for the shah being theirs. Iranians remember, too, that the CIA and the British engineered a coup against an elected Iranian leader, Mohammad Mossadegh, in the 1950s.

In 1980 Iraq's Saddam Hussein, ever the opportunist, decided to invade

Iran in hopes of annexing Iran's oil-rich western province, in which a large Arab minority lived. It was a brutal war with hundreds of thousands dead that went on for eight years with minimal coverage in the West. We didn't have a dog in that fight, and many Westerners rather hoped that the two would fight on for years and exhaust themselves.

Nonetheless, so great had been our humiliation at the hands of Khomeini, and so great the fear that his brand of extreme Islam would sweep the Middle East, that we tilted toward the Iraqis, giving them important intelligence data. Fear of Islamic extremism began to vie with Communism in our national nightmares. This was popular with our Sunni allies Saudi Arabia and the gulf states, who feared an appeal to their Shia minorities.

I arrived in Baghdad to cover the Iran–Iraq War in the spring of 1986. Consumer goods were plentiful in the shops, couples strolled in the cool of the evening on the banks of the Tigris, and the little riverside restaurants were open. War seemed far away until the occasional Scud missile came thundering in from Iran to take out half a city block. I could hear these explosions in my hotel room at night, but they were infrequent enough not to disrupt the life of the city. You began to feel that you would have to be very unlucky to be hit by a Scud, a little like being hit by lightning.

The cult of personality was in bloom, and pictures of Saddam Hussein were plastered on walls wherever I went. The Iraqi foreign office gave me reams of propaganda material showing why western Iran really should be eastern Iraq.

Perhaps most disconcerting were the small yellow-and-white taxis with coffins on their roofs coming up from the front on the Basra road. It was the Iraqi Army's custom to simply order a taxi to come to the morgue. There the driver would be given some money and an address, and a flag-draped coffin would be strapped to the roof. This would be the only death notice that mothers and widows would get. No telegram, no consoling officers at the front door. Just a taxi with a coffin and a driver demanding a signed receipt.

There was a story going around Baghdad in those days of one taxi that came down a quiet neighborhood street with two coffins on the roof, the driver obviously looking for an address. Sighs of relief were breathed when the taxi passed door after door, but all of a sudden the taxi stopped, backed up, and stopped again in front of a woman's house to deliver the corpses of both her husband and her son. She collapsed, but the driver waited until she could sign his receipt.

Much was being made of a man who had been personally decorated by Saddam Hussein. His story was being extolled throughout the country. It seemed that the man had killed his own son for being a deserter, and was thus being held up as an example of Iraqi patriotism.

Given Saddam Hussein's strict control, I found people afraid to talk to foreigners. I had read Foreign Minister Tariq Aziz's description of the Ba'ath Party as "not a conventional political organization, but one composed of cells of valiant revolutionaries." For "valiant revolutionaries," read "brutal thugs." The government's pitch to visiting Western reporters was that Iraq was secular, while Iran was run by anti-American religious fanatics. The pitch wasn't wrong, but it didn't make Iraqis the good guys either.

I went down to Basra, Iraq's oil port in the Shia-dominated south, to attend a press conference. General Adnan Khairallah, minister of defense, deputy commander of the armed forces, first cousin and brother-in-law to Saddam Hussein, was briefing the press. He, like so many Iraqis, sported the same trimmed mustache as, and bore a striking resemblance to, Saddam Hussein. The Iraqis were then trying to recapture the Faw Peninsula, where the Shatt al-Arab waterway meets the Persian Gulf, and were encountering stiff resistance. In fact the Iraqis had been trying for two months to oust the Iranians with little success. The general wanted to assure the world that, although it might take a long time, there was every opportunity to turn the Faw into a mass grave of Iranians. Some foreign military attachés told me that Iraq had air superiority and more and better armor. But the pilots were afraid to fly low, and the ground troops were reluctant to close with the Iranians. Therefore it was Iraqi artillery that thundered day and night, and could be heard all the way to Kuwait fifty miles away.

The Iraqis were better equipped than the Iranians, but Iraq had only fifteen million people against Iran's fifty million, and the Iranians were willing to take horrendous losses, fighting with a degree of religious and patriotic martyrdom that the Iraqi soldiers lacked. While the Iraqis used Soviet equipment, Iran was heavily dependent on American arms, and that pipeline had been cut when Khomeini came to power. The Iranians were buying Soviet arms now, helped by Libya and Syria, whereas the deeper-pocketed Saudis and the Gulf Arabs were helping Iraq.

Both sides were growing weary and it was becoming a matter of which side could keep this up the longest. In the end it would be Khomeini who sued for peace, a bitter pill to swallow because he had promised to fight on until Saddam Hussein's regime was toppled. That proved beyond his reach, and after eight years of bloodshed, the lines returned to where they had been before the war began.

During my visit the titanic struggle was in its sixth year and still going strong. Estimates of deaths on both sides were reaching up to one million men. I joined a small group of reporters, I being the only Westerner, for a tour of the front. We were taken to the ruins of a mud village on a scarce bit of high ground amid soggy swamps of reeds and date palms, half of them blackened trunks, topless and shattered by shellfire. Artillery was banging away to the rear, but up where we were there was only an occasional crump of mortars and desultory machine-gun fire from the Iranian lines. We saw yellow-green camouflaged tanks of Soviet manufacture dug into revetments—not the best use of armor, and a mistake the Iraqis made again when facing the Americans the next time around.

On ground recently captured from the Iranians there were abandoned hypodermic needles littering the ground. The Iranians had been issued antidotes to the poison gas that the Iraqis occasionally used, a practice that had earned the Iraqis condemnation from the United Nations Security Council. Saddam Hussein later used gas against his Kurdish minority in the north when they got out of line.

The battle, as happened often in the Iran–Iraq War, had become a war of hydraulics, with the ebb and flow of water greatly influencing the fighting. Iraqi engineers were trying to pump water out of the marshland so as to deploy their armor, while the Iranians were trying just as hard to keep the area flooded. An unusually heavy rainy season was helping the Iranians.

Oddly, oil prices were actually falling at that time when one might have thought they would be rising due to disruptions in supply. Both Iran and Iraq were pumping oil overtime in order to pay for the war effort. OPEC, the Organization of the Petroleum Exporting Countries, was unable to hold production down, and so prices fell.

One of our press party at the front, an intrepid Turkish reporter in a white jacket and designer jeans, kept agitating to get closer to the Iranian positions. Our Iraqi escorts thought we should move farther back. The Turk jumped up on a sandbagged berm to get a better look, and brought down incoming Iranian mortars on our position. The Turk then loudly demanded to be taken to the rear immediately, so our tour of the front was a little shorter than it might have been.

Having been thwarted in his invasion of Iran, Saddam Hussein turned his gaze toward neighboring Kuwait, and in the summer of 1990 he struck, taking the world by surprise. The first president Bush drew a line in the sand, saying, "This will not stand, this aggression against Kuwait," and he started to build an international coalition against Saddam Hussein.

I felt at the time, and I feel now, that the senior Bush did the right thing. Saddam Hussein had gone into Kuwait like a gangster knocking over a gas station. Unlike our leaders during the Vietnam War, who had gone in trying to back, and then replace, a French colonial enterprise, George Herbert Walker Bush had no desire to stay in Iraq, no desire to bend the region to his will. It was get the Iraqis out of Kuwait and withdraw, without any of the neoconservative nonsense to which his son fell prey: that the US could change the Middle East by force.

I went back to Baghdad while American and coalition forces were building in Saudi Arabia in January of 1991. It was a time when Middle East airports were jammed with people trying to get away. Like coastal residents warned of an oncoming hurricane, people were fleeing to higher ground. I was astonished to find thousands of Vietnamese leaving for home. I had no idea Vietnamese were being employed in Iraq.

Baghdad, in the eye of the storm, was an apprehensive city. Saddam Hussein was hanging tough, having persuaded himself that the Americans were paper tigers, afraid to take casualties, who would fold at the first whiff of gunpowder. I remembered, however, it was the Iraqis who had been afraid of casualties in the face of the more numerous and more motivated Iranians just a few years before.

I made the usual rounds of Iraqi officials, and in every office there was a flickering television set turned to CNN, which had recently changed the way everyone got their breaking news. Yet no one, certainly not the Iraqis, felt they were keeping up with what was really happening. "Tell me truthfully and frankly," whispered a Ministry of Information official responsible for shepherding the foreign press. "Is the news positive or negative?" The guardians of information had become the inquirers as a sense of helplessness fell over the city.

Foreign embassies were drawing down their staffs and destroying their papers, just as I had seen them do in Saigon and Phnom Penh fifteen years before. At the American embassy, all the files had been burned in August, and a "read and burn" policy was now in effect. Nobody wanted to repeat the Tehran experience, when Iranians were able to put together shredded papers laid out in an airplane hangar. Ambassador April Glaspie, who had tried, and failed, to warn Saddam Hussein that the United States would not stand for an invasion of Kuwait, had long since left.

Joseph Wilson, who later gained fame as the husband of outed CIA operative Valerie Plame in the lead-up to our next war against Iraq, was serving as chargé d'affaires. From time to time he would hold briefings for the press, and reporters from many countries would crowd into his office. Unlike my first visit to Baghdad, there was no lack of reporters on hand this time around.

Wilson would come out from behind his desk and lean against it, facing the world's press. He had a little black box at his fingertips on his desk, and if a reporter asked a rude question, as some were wont to do, he would press a button on the box. "Fuck you, fuck you," came a tinny little voice from the box. Wilson had made his point, but no one could quote him as having used impolite language. The box spoke for him.

Saddam Hussein kept spitting his defiance, saying that the "mother of all battles" to come would be the fiery Armageddon out of which good would emerge over evil. "Victory is close," he told his people. "Palestine will be liberated, Jerusalem will be liberated, as will the Kaaba and the Prophet's burial place." Saddam was threatening Saudi Arabia, guardian of the Muslim holy places, and, although staunchly secular himself, Saddam was wrapping himself in the green flag of Islam. Genealogists were found to pronounce that the Iraqi dictator was a direct descendant of Muhammad.

A hastily convened Islamic conference was organized, and well attended by Middle Eastern clerics hostile to the United States. The American Black Muslim leader Louis Farrakhan showed up, presumably to polish his reputation as a firebrand. He left the conference early and, cornering him in the lobby of his hotel before he left, I asked him his impression of the conference. "They're all crazy," he said, "all they want is war." But he did allow that Arabs felt crushed and humiliated by the West.

I saw none of the popular enthusiasm in the streets that I had seen when Egypt's Nasser defied the West and seized the Suez Canal in 1956. The people of Baghdad, weary of eight years of war against Iran, were sullen and resigned. The authorities tried to organize demonstrations, but they were lackluster. One day schoolgirls were dismissed from school and brought to the American embassy, where they held up little signs saying: WHAT SADDAM SAYS IS WHAT THE COUNTRY WANTS.

Iraq seemed to be playing a Scheherazade game of keeping on talking for a thousand and one nights. "Dialogue for a year is better than war for one day," said Information Minister Latif Nassif Jassem, but time was running out. Secretary of State James Baker agreed to meet Tariq Aziz, still Iraq's foreign minister, in Geneva for a last-minute diplomatic effort to avoid war. Baghdad seemed to fall silent when the two met, with everyone who had a radio or a television glued to the news. It was useless, of course, but well worth the effort on the part of the Bush administration. The gathering coalition needed to see that America was making every last diplomatic effort to avoid war.

Reporters, many staying in the Rasheed Hotel, were beginning to wonder how we were going to get out when war came. Would we be held hostage? British reporters were planning to drive across the desert to Jordan in Land Rovers with extra gasoline. I filed my story early one day and went down to the market to see if I could catch the mood. There I found a beautiful Aladdin's lamp made of silver. I bought it, and back at the bar of the Rasheed that evening I produced my Aladdin's lamp and said: "Look at this, guys. I have found my way out of Baghdad. All I have to do is rub this magic lamp and I will be transported." A laconic Texan caught me up short by saying: "David, I got the same arrangement with my dick."

As it was, the American embassy planned an orderly evacuation, and as my main job would soon be to oversee the war coverage back in Boston, I decided to head home. At dawn on evacuation day, Wilson had the American flag lowered from the roof of the brown embassy building near the Tigris. Technically, diplomatic relations were not being severed. The embassy remained open with its Iraqi staff. "We took the flag down because we didn't want it desecrated in any way," Wilson said.

Wilson had arranged a charter flight with Iraqi Airways to Frankfurt, Germany. Diplomats from Canada, the Netherlands, Belgium, Norway, Switzerland, Austria, and Finland had been invited by Wilson to join us in a chartered 727. There was a sense of finality as we gathered at the airport.

The Iraqi staff processing our departure were unfailingly polite, showing none of the hostility one might expect on the eve of an American invasion. When we got to Frankfurt, however, I saw that the baggage handlers in Baghdad had not shown the same restraint. When my garment bag, which I had checked, came off the baggage carousel it was immediately apparent that it was soaked with urine.

The *Boston Globe* put all its efforts into its war coverage, but before the war was over I flew to Tel Aviv to see how Israel was managing. Showing superhuman restraint, Prime Minister Yitzhak Shamir went along with Bush's request not to enter the war even though Iraqi Scuds were being fired at Tel Aviv. Saddam Hussein hoped to break up the coalition arranged against him by dragging Israel in on America's side. He failed, but Tel Aviv felt a little like Baghdad had during the war with Iran. Scuds were coming down, but the life of the city went on.

Everyone was given a gas mask in case some of Saddam's Scuds should include nerve gas. I was given mine the minute I stepped off the El Al flight.

We were also given hypodermic needles that you could jab in your leg if nerve gas got you before you could put on your mask. Saddam Hussein never did use poison gas against Israel, as he had against the Iranians, but who could be sure he wouldn't? Tragically, there were several suffocations caused by people putting on their gas masks improperly, and a few deaths from panicked people having jabbed themselves when there was no gas and dying of heart attacks.

By coincidence, I had a scheduled interview with Shamir the morning the war ended, and the Israeli prime minister's first words were that he wished we would have removed Saddam Hussein from power. I left Israel to drive overland to Cairo, where I had a scheduled interview with Egypt's president, Hosni Mubarak, who essentially expressed the same wish. His forces had been part of Bush's coalition.

I could see their point, but I came to see President Bush's point better in a memoir he wrote with Brent Scowcroft: "Trying to eliminate Saddam, extending the ground war into an occupation of Iraq, would have violated our guideline about not changing objectives in midstream, engaging in 'mission creep,' and would have incurred incalculable human and political costs . . . The coalition would instantly have collapsed, the Arabs deserting it in anger and other allies pulling out as well. Under those circumstances, there was no viable 'exit strategy' we could see, violating another of our principles. Furthermore, we had been self-consciously trying to set a pattern for handling aggression in the post–Cold War world.

"Going in and occupying Iraq, thus unilaterally exceeding the United Nations' mandate, would have destroyed the precedent of international response to aggression that we hoped to establish," Bush wrote. "Had we gone the invasion route, the United States could conceivably still be an occupying power in a bitterly hostile land. It would have been a dramatically different— and perhaps barren—outcome."

I could have wished that more had been done to save the Iraqi Shia in the south at war's end. The Shia rose up against Saddam Hussein with Bush's encouragement, and were crushed by Saddam Hussein. But George H. W. Bush was absolutely right about the dangers of becoming an occupying power. Would that his son had listened to his father the next time around.

With the war over, I flew to Saudi Arabia hoping to get into newly liberated Kuwait. On a military flight to Kuwait City my plane had to turn back the first try; the smoke from the Kuwaiti oil fields that Saddam Hussein had set alight had turned day into oily night. When the wind changed, however, I flew in and was taken to see the burning wells up close. Nothing I had seen on television prepared me for actually being there. The fire raced out of the earth as if the doors to hell had been opened. The sound, like a great roar, was deafening. American experts were already there preparing to snuff out the fires, which wasn't going to be easy.

I went into town to one of the glitzy high-rise hotels on Kuwait's waterfront. The lobby had been looted by departing Iraqis, and expensive Parisian dresses and handbags were strewn about on the floor. There was no hotel staff and no power. You simply went upstairs and helped yourself to a room. The best rooms were at the top, but it was a long walk. I picked a room about a quarter of the way up. There was no one to make up your room in the morning, so if you wanted the bed made you simply moved to another room. The water supply was intermittent. So you filled your bathtub when the water was on.

Staying in the same hotel was my gallant colleague Elizabeth Neuffer, who had been doing a wonderful job reporting for the *Boston Globe*. Her best story was about the Mutla Ridge where American planes had caught a convoy of Iraqi armor and stolen cars and buses carrying loot from Kuwait City. The Iraqis were trying to retreat back into Iraq when the Americans swooped down, strafing and bombing. I had been out to see the damage. A long column of burnt-out vehicles and tanks stretched for miles along a main highway. Charred corpses could be seen still in their stolen cars. Still other decomposing bodies could be seen in the surrounding desert where they had tried to escape. Elizabeth was later killed in the next war against Iraq, her car having crashed on the way back to Baghdad from an appointment in Samarra.

But in Kuwait City Elizabeth was doing her best to carve out a bit of domestic sanity amid chaos. She cooked a delicious meal of lamb stew in a helmet on a Bunsen burner she had found somewhere in the city. Outside, as night fell, newly liberated Kuwaitis roamed around the waterfront firing off guns in the air.

The next morning I got up early and went out in the dawn's light. The crowds firing guns in the air had gone home, and the smoke from the oil wells was blowing in another direction. I thought I might take a walk, but immediately a jeep with soldiers screeched to a stop. I showed them my credentials, but I was frog-marched into the backseat. I tried to explain I was a reporter, one of the few words of Arabic we all knew, but the soldiers kept saying, *"La, la,"* which I knew meant no.

They told me what I really was with great vehemence, but I didn't understand them as they drove at high speed through the dawn light. Finally the jeep came to a stop, and I was told to get out and squat on a little stool they produced on the sidewalk. I was at what appeared to be a checkpoint of some kind. It was clear they wanted me to wait, and as they were heavily armed I thought it useless to try to run.

Finally an English-speaking officer was produced, and I asked him what the charges were, and what was the trouble? He explained that the soldiers were saying I was not a journalist, but a friend of the nation. "George Booosh number one," he said, and all the soldiers, waving their weapons, joined in: "George Booosh number one, George Booosh number one." At that a hearty Arab breakfast was produced for me, and it was clear that I was to finish it up to the last crumb and date while the soldiers stood smiling around me. I was in the right place at the right time to be appreciated as an American abroad.

28

Baghdad Nights

The new century brought the disquiet in the Muslim world to the American homeland, and no one is likely to forget that beautiful September day when hijacked airliners hit New York's Twin Towers. If I wanted an example of American resilience, however, I found it in New York at a coffee shop near Ground Zero. A sign in the window said: INFIDELS WELCOME.

In one of the greatest over-reactions in history, however, President George W. Bush decided to overthrow Saddam Hussein even though, for all his horrible faults, he had had nothing to do with the destruction of the Twin Towers, which killed more people than had been killed at Pearl Harbor.

I returned once more to Baghdad in the autumn of 2005 when America's war with and occupation of Iraq was going horribly wrong. My plane from Amman, Jordan, spiraled down in the same sickening way that my last flight into Phnom Penh had done, and for the same reason—to avoid ground fire from insurgents. I was met by several Iraqis who immediately took my hand luggage and a Scot who introduced himself to me by saying: "My name's Mackenzie, I'm a mercenary." This was part of the *New York Times* security apparatus, which John Burns, the *New York Times* bureau chief, had arranged. The *Times* now owned the *Boston Globe,* and although I had retired from the *Globe* in 2000, I was still writing a column for the *Globe* and the *International Herald Tribune* in Paris, both *New York Times* properties.

America had conquered Iraq in record time, but there was no plan for what to do next. Saddam Hussein's army had faded away, but instead of trying to reassemble it to keep order, the US dismissed the soldiers, without pay, and a full-scale insurgency was in progress. Westerners were being kidnapped and beheaded on videos, begging for their lives. The arrangement was that the *Times* would take me into Baghdad, and back to the airport when I left. In the meantime the *Globe's* somewhat less imposing security would look after me.

The Iraqis opened the trunk of an armored Mercedes limo to reveal half a dozen machine guns, which my Iraqi bodyguards took out to make room for my suitcase. The Mercedes was black with bulletproof windows as thick as my thumb. With two Iraqis in the front seat and a chase car full of armed men behind us, Mackenzie and I settled into the backseat for the ride into town. Many people had been ambushed and killed on the airport road, and I couldn't help thinking Saigon was never this bad. One of the exit signs said JIHADI EXIT. It was only referring to a section of town, but I gulped when Mackenzie instructed the driver to take it.

I was delivered to the Hamra Hotel, where the *Boston Globe* office was. The Hamra was one of two or three hotels with blast walls and bodyguards where journalists were staying. The *Globe's* resident correspondent, Anne Barnard, welcomed me and I was booked into a room. As night fell we heard a tremendous explosion not too far away. It was a cement mixer, filled with explosives, trying to blow up the nearby Palestine Hotel. I later saw film, caught on a security camera, of the truck going backward and forward, trying to get through the rubble of a blast wall. Luckily for the hotel, the truck failed to get in close, but the driver blew up his truck anyway without doing too much damage to anyone but himself.

Anne said: "You better call your wife and tell her that you are okay. Tell her that it wasn't this hotel." Anne explained that communications were so fast with a twenty-four-hour news cycle that someone was bound to call JB about the bombing even if she herself was not watching or listening to the news. It was a concept I hadn't considered, and I realized I was in a new century and a new era of news reporting. In Laos, in the sixties for example, when I first began reporting from there, there was no possibility of calling the United

States. It was trouble enough calling across town. Anne handed me her cell phone and I called JB. And sure enough, not ten minutes after the blast, someone had called JB to tell her a hotel had been hit in Baghdad.

The next morning I went around to the *New York Times* office, in the *Globe*'s unarmored car with Anne's security team and a chase car too. Chase cars were used to foil ambushers when and if they stopped the lead car. I trusted Anne to have chosen good guards and translators, and she was guided by her invaluable assistant Sa'ad al-Izzy. But how would we ever know if one of our guards could be bribed to hand us over to jihadis for decapitation? I never could make up my mind whether it was safer to be in the *Times*'s armored car that could withstand a major attack, or whether an armored Mercedes was a statement that someone important sat inside and that it was therefore worthy of attacking. Maybe the *Globe*'s nondescript and battered old cars were safer for being less conspicuous.

I found John Burns to thank him for the airport run, and he showed me the suicide truck's radiator, which had risen into the night sky and landed in the *New York Times*'s garden. I noticed there was a mess of feathers stuck to the twisted metal. The radiator had hit a bird on either the way up or the way down, and I thought not even a bird on the wing is safe in this city. I soon realized that this was a far more dangerous Baghdad than the one I had known when the only real threat was an occasional Scud missile. The kidnapping threat was far worse than in Beirut in its worst days, and here I was, at the age of seventy, in the most dangerous environment I had ever known.

Baghdad was not the town I had remembered from nearly twenty years before. There was no more strolling down by the Tigris in the cool of the evening. No going out to restaurants. You feared for your life when you went outside, and any socializing was done in hotel rooms. Anne had a few of her colleagues in for dinner, and even then cell phones would ring from editors overseas. Guest after guest would go away from the table either for privacy or to get slightly better reception. Gone, too, were the days when reporters could file their stories and then relax, have a good meal, and maybe have a little too much to drink. Reporters now had to constantly file for their newspaper's website, updating endlessly. I wondered how they ever had enough time to report if they were always updating for the website and twenty-four-hour news cycles.

Iraqi politicians lived in guarded compounds to protect themselves, not only from insurgents, but from each other. The assassin's hand was never far, and death squads from one faction or another roamed the city. Sometimes they came disguised as police. At other times they were the police. One day a few of us went to interview the then–vice president, Adil Abdul-Mahdi. He spoke optimistically about a future of accommodation and compromise leading to a cessation of violence. But in midsentence he was called away. He returned to end the interview early, saying: "Excuse me, please. They have just assassinated my brother."

Baghdad was full of uncollected trash and rubble. A civil war between Sunnis and Shia was reorganizing Baghdad's neighborhoods, and murdered bodies could be found on the streets every morning. Just about the only safe place in town was the famed walled and fortified Green Zone, where the Americans and their allies huddled. Even there you could get an occasional mortar round. I met General Martin Dempsey, who later became chairman of the joint chiefs. In 2005 he was in charge of training an Iraqi army to take charge of the country. It was easy, he said, to train men to fight. Harder to teach them about logistics, how to keep an army in the field. But beyond our control were Iraq's political leaders, who could use the army to fight for this or that faction instead of the nation as a whole. It was clear to me that Americans might have their ideas about what the new Iraq should become, but there was no consensus among the Iraqis. Today there is still no national consensus in Iraq. Sunnis and Shia are still bitter rivals and the Kurds have drifted off into an independent state in all but name.

Someone had briefed General Dempsey about me, because he immediately asked me about Vietnam. It was a shock to realize that none of the soldiers here had been in a position of responsibility during the Vietnam War. I was a relic of the past. What I did not say to General Dempsey was this thought: Here we go again. Whereas in Vietnam we were falling into the footsteps of the French, here we were trying our hand where the British had failed, going down the old colonial roads, trying to force yet another people to be more like us and adopt our values.

Even that old champion of empire Winston Churchill had written to Lloyd George in 1920 saying: "There is something very sinister to my mind in this Mesopotamian entanglement," Mesopotamia being what the British called Iraq. "Week after week and month after month for a long time we shall have a continuance of this miserable, wasteful, sporadic warfare . . . Why are we compelled to go on pouring armies and treasures into these thankless deserts?"

Why indeed?

With the events of September 11, 2001, all the rage and resentment of the Islamic fundamentalist revival I had been tracking for almost twenty years seemed to come together. The specter of terrorists being able to pull off such a spectacular event was something entirely new. America was about to spend almost a decade fighting in a country that had nothing whatsoever to do with 9/11.

I wish I could say that I had been as resolutely against invading Iraq as I later became. I had been impressed after the first Gulf War with how close Saddam Hussein had been to having a nuclear weapon, and I had believed, to my great regret, Secretary of State Colin Powell when he addressed the UN on Iraq's nuclear program. It was all nonsense of course. There wasn't any Iraqi nuclear program. But I did write at the time that we had Saddam Hussein in a box, and that it would be better to concentrate on the unfinished business in Afghanistan and allow the nuclear inspectors more time to do their work in Iraq.

President George W. Bush brought to the White House none of the experience and measured judgment of his father. The second President Bush projected bravado but was essentially a weak president who turned over far too much power to his vice president, Dick Cheney, and let him play a role no other vice president had ever played in the history of the republic, or hopefully will ever play again.

The neoconservatives had a plan ready after the events of September 11, and George W. Bush bought into it. The plan was that America should use its power, and the opportunity that 9/11 presented, to spread democracy by force. Iraq would be the showcase. An American-inspired democracy would transform the Middle East, undermining autocratic states, ensuring an oil supply outside the oil cartel's grip. The new Iraq would recognize Israel, too. "The way to Jerusalem is through Baghdad," some said. This last fantasy was encouraged by the slippery Iraqi exile Ahmed Chalabi, who sold the Bush administration a Middle East equivalent of the Brooklyn Bridge.

I tried to see Chalabi in Baghdad, but someone in his entourage had Googled what I had written about al-Qaeda and the planners of 9/11 having been in Afghanistan, not Iraq. So I was told that Chalabi would not waste his time seeing someone who "thought those Saudi summer camps in Afghanistan more important than our mission in Iraq."

In the end, our conquest and occupation of Iraq did not transform the Middle East. All we achieved was to empower Iran and the downtrodden Shia at the expense of the Sunnis, who had always held power in Iraq. Iraq is still sorting out that transformation. Yes, Saddam Hussein is gone. And who can regret that? But our greater ambition for Iraq—I would say fantasy—has been thwarted. Reality was harder to change than the neoconservatives ever imagined.

For a long time I had trouble believing that my country would get into another Vietnam-style mess less than thirty years after the fall of Saigon.

The Sunni Awakening that turned against al-Qaeda in Mesopotamia, and a troop surge, saved Iraq from total catastrophe. Life in Baghdad is certainly better now than it was in 2005. But nothing has been resolved. Sunni and Shia have not learned to share power. The Kurds in the north still want their independence and their oil, and the level of violence in Iraq would be unacceptable in any other country. The neoconservative dream of transforming the Middle East to our liking by invading and occupying Iraq proved to be a chimera.

Anne Barnard had to leave town on an assignment, but before leaving she warned me that there had been intelligence reports that our hotel would be attacked as the Palestine Hotel had been when I first arrived. I can remember one night standing on the balcony of the *Globe*'s office looking down at the blast walls and wondering just where the attack on my hotel would come. And sure enough, another suicide bomber in a truck filled with explosives did visit the Hamra, doing more damage than had been inflicted on the Palestine. But by that time I was gone.

The basic flaw in the Bush administration's contention that the US could go it alone, scorning old alliances and transforming the Middle East by force, was that after the Cold War the US was more in need of allies, not less. During the Cold War many countries, fearing Soviet expansion and Communism, had had to shelter under America's wing. But once that threat was lifted, we were less, not more, able to dictate to the world.

My old friend and former colleague Fred Kaplan put this very well in his book *Daydream Believers,* subtitled *How a Few Grand Ideas Wrecked American Power.* To "preserve American influence in this geopolitical setting," Kaplan wrote, we could either "don the mantle of explicit empire," or the United States could "revitalize alliances, renovating the old ones, cultivating new ones." For the end of the Cold War had not repealed the old political laws of power balance, just made them more difficult to achieve.

George W. Bush chose to don the mantle of empire, whereas his father believed in alliances. But Americans were never good colonizers. Whereas the British had men, and women, too, who knew and spoke all the languages of Britain's far-flung dependencies and had steeped themselves in their culture and mores, Americans tended to think none of that mattered. Foreigners needed to be more like Americans. And so we stumbled down the corridors of empire thinking that the world would have to learn our ways. Perhaps the essence of George W. Bush–era arrogance came in remarks made to writer Ron Suskind in 2002 by an anonymous White House aide. He scorned the "reality-based community . . . people who believe that solutions emerge from your judicious study of discernible reality . . . That's not the way the world really works anymore," the aide said. "We are an empire now, and when we act we create our own reality . . . We are history's actors."

And what bad actors, full of sound and fury, they proved to be.

My exit from Baghdad gave me a glimpse that the new, American-liberated

Baghdad was not going to be so very different than the centuries-old Baghdad of before. Sa'ad al-Izzy took me around to procure an exit visa which I would need before I left the country. The building was a warren of tiny offices with people shuffling about with their papers from one office to another. It was a time-consuming business, but Izzy carried it off with just the right mixture of polite deference and insistence.

I can't remember now how many offices on different floors we had to go to in order to get yet another form stamped. And in each office there was a functionary, sometimes male, sometimes female, who would look you and the papers over before stamping them with official looking rubber stamps. The key to the whole process was the wads of money—never too much but just enough—that Izzy would slip into the pile of papers or into a furtive palm. In the end, the green exit visa from Iraq was stamped into my passport. No visa has ever meant so much to me in my life, and I looked forward to the short flight to Jordan and safety.

Not so safe after all, as it turned out. A hotel in Amman, the capital of Jordan, was bombed shortly after I arrived, but again it was not my hotel.

29

To the Khyber Pass

The Soviet invasion of Afghanistan in December of 1979 was yet another shock to the beleaguered administration of President Jimmy Carter. Unwritten rules had been broken. Never before had the Soviets sent troops outside their sphere of influence in Eastern Europe. Afghanistan had been for centuries a buffer state between Russia and British India, now Pakistan. The British–Russian rivalry caused by Russia's expansion into Central Asia had been dubbed "the Great Game." By attacking and occupying Afghanistan the Soviets had taken the game beyond a point where czars had dared to tread.

In the days of the nineteenth-century Raj, the British had sent army after army up through the Khyber Pass to subdue unruly Afghans. None of these invasions was ever completely successful or decisive, and some ended in absolute disaster. On India's northwest frontier the British fought seemingly endless punitive campaigns in their own territory to subdue rebellious tribesmen who, again and again, raised the cry of jihad, or holy war, against the infidel, just as they do today. These campaigns were immortalized by Rudyard Kipling in stories on which I grew up. I have on my bookshelf Kipling's *Tales of India,* the cover of which shows a turbaned and bearded Pathan at full gallop being pursued by a mounted and equally hard-riding British officer with pistol drawn.

The "Durand Line," drawn by a British cartographer at the end of the nineteenth century to establish a border between British India and Afghanistan, remains today the international border between Pakistan and Afghanistan. The British were more interested in geography and controlling mountain passes than they were in the tribes. The result was, and is, that the Pathans, or Pashtuns as they are now called, live on both sides of the border. The Afghans never really recognized the Durand Line because they thought the frontier lands on the British side should be theirs, as they once were before the British came.

To make matters more complicated, the lands just on the British side of the border were never fully incorporated into the Raj. They were designated as "tribal territories" with a semiautonomous status, a situation Pakistan inherited. These tribal territories were perfect hiding places for the Taliban when they were driven out of Afghanistan after the American invasion.

JB and I made a quick visit to Afghanistan in 1971 to see the giant Buddhas of Bamiyan, which the Taliban later destroyed. We stayed in a yurt near the towering carvings hewed out of solid rock and watched the shadows play over their faces in the changing light of passing clouds. The Taliban destroyed these glorious monuments, built as a new religion was spreading from India to China, because the Muslim faith condemns the portraying of human faces. Blowing up the Buddhas was a crime against civilization, but even in pre-Taliban days the Buddhas' faces were pockmarked by bullets fired by outraged Afghans. It is only because these earlier desecrators lacked dynamite that the Buddhas weren't destroyed sooner.

I didn't know it at the time, but those were the twilight years of a golden Afghan age under King Zahir Shah, before a coup that deposed him, before the coming of a Communist government, before the Russians, the mujahideen, the Taliban, and before the Americans. I wish I had stayed longer, because Afghanistan was never to be the same again.

In 1984, and again in 1987, I spent some weeks on the North-West Frontier, in Peshawar, Pakistan, which had become the center of clandestine CIA and Pakistani intelligence operations to support the Afghan resistance against the Russians. Peshawar had once been the winter capital of Afghanistan. Hundreds of thousands of Afghans were fleeing into Pakistan, filling hastily erected refugee camps along the frontier. Nearly five million Afghans, almost one-third of the prewar population, set up shop in Pakistan or Iran during the Soviet occupation. Some would never leave, altering Pakistan forever.

After suffering humiliation in Vietnam, the CIA saw its chance to really stick a thumb in the Soviet eye, and so money and matériel started to flow into Peshawar to aid the Afghan resistance. Americans and Saudis may have been the paymasters, but it was the Pakistani intelligence agency, Inter-Services Intelligence, or ISI, that really ran the show.

One of the tragedies of Afghanistan is that no outside power has ever really cared about the Afghans for the Afghans' sake. Interventions have always been because of fear of some other power's intervention. The British involved themselves in Afghanistan for fear that the Russians might be trying to do the same. The Russians invaded a century later because they were afraid that even a Soviet-friendly Afghan government would be overthrown by the forces of Muslim reaction, or that the United States would gain undue influence. And so, in 1980, the United States stepped right into a replay of the nineteenth-century imperial struggle against the Russians who now ruled Kabul. A new Great Game was afoot.

I thought at the time, and I still think today, that it was right for Washington to oppose Russia's grab for Afghanistan. But the "blowback" has troubled us ever since. "Blowback" is the fireman's term for a fire that pushes back and harms those fighting the fire. The CIA uses it to describe an operation that does the same thing. Some say the US should have backed less radical Muslims in our effort to undermine Russian rule. But we backed the extremists because they were the most effective at fighting the Russians. It was probably the most successful CIA operation in history, but those religious zealots who honed their skills fighting the Russians eventually turned on us.

The Russians spent the better part of a decade rampaging up and down the country trying to stamp out the mujahideen, as the holy warriors were called. But from their safe bases in Pakistan the mujahideen could never be really defeated, and in the end Russia had to leave. It also must be said that the Muslim fighters showed an indomitable will. I often think of that now that America is fighting some of these men who were our allies in the Soviet days, as well as their sons and grandsons.

Today, after having stayed even longer than the Russians, the US and its allies are preparing to leave. Like the Russians, we were always frustrated because our enemies found safe havens in Pakistan, and like the Russians and the British before, we were never able to break the Pashtun spirit.

The author examining the "Landi Kotal Local" that ran between Peshawar and the top of the Khyber Pass in northwestern Pakistan in 1981.

In the eighties Peshawar was an exciting place, full of intrigue, with the Islamic fighters who back then were on our side. My home was Dean's Hotel, a sprawling compound of little cottages and a spacious garden in the heart of Peshawar. In those days you could take a train called the Khyber Mail up from Rawalpindi and hire a "tonka," a little horse cart, to take you into town to Dean's. Another train, the Landi Kotal Local, would take you up from Peshawar to the top of the Khyber Pass in a little steam engine dating from the 1920s. The train traveled through the tribal territories, where I began to see men getting on and off at different stops without buying a ticket. Most of them were armed, as most men in the tribal territories were. I asked one of them why he had not bought a ticket, and, slapping his rifle, he said: "This is my ticket."

It was my first indication that the law did not really extend west of Peshawar. Alas, the Landi Kotal Local no longer exists and its tracks today lie abandoned.

There are certain places in uncertain times that become centers of intrigue and mystery, and Peshawar in the 1980s was one of them. The *New Yorker* writer Richard Reeves wrote that if Dean's Hotel didn't exist "Graham Greene would have invented it. Men with submachine guns came there, springing from Datsuns, and walking quickly across the facing gardens to step into the midday darkness of the rooms of Americans who said their business was export-import or investment." People could be seen conversing intensely in the garden because everyone assumed that Pakistani intelligence had bugged the rooms.

I saw familiar faces of aid workers I had known from previous conflicts, and, of course, journalist friends from other wars. One time I was having dinner at Green's, another Peshawar hotel, when I saw a man I knew I had seen before but couldn't place. I couldn't resist going up to him and asking him where we had met. "Were you on the border commission in the Kashmir in '47?" he asked.

"No," I said, and he rattled off other disputed barricades where he had been. At last I remembered. This was General Ted Mataxis, one of the first Americans sent to advise Lon Nol's army after his coup against Sihanouk in Cambodia.

We reminisced about Cambodia for a while, and then I asked: "So what are you doing in Peshawar?"

"Oh, I'm retired now," he said.

"Yes, but you are not living in a bungalow in Florida. What brings you to the North-West Frontier?" He said he was helping to supply prosthetic devices for wounded Afghan refugees.

"General?" I said with obvious disbelief.

"No one here but us humanitarians," he said with a smile, his eyes rising to the ceiling.

There were intelligence agents all over Peshawar in those days, even from the dreaded KHAD, the Kabul equivalent of Russia's KGB. They were often blamed for mysterious bombings and killings, but there was enough friction between rival mujahideen groups to explain most of the violence in town.

One spent one's days interviewing various mujahideen factions, often back from "going inside," meaning over the border to battle the Soviets. Osama bin Laden was then known as an Arab with some money to help the cause but not taken seriously as a fighter. As I had missed him in Saudi Arabia, I never looked him up in Peshawar either.

The refugee crisis was always a story, and one time, when I had invited JB to join me on the frontier, we hatched a scheme to conduct interviews together in the refugee camps. The zealots among the mujahideen were reluctant to allow a man to interview their womenfolk, so JB was to take an interpreter to interview women while I interviewed the men.

On one memorable occasion I was interviewing a tall and bearded "muj," as we called the mujahideen. Kalashnikov in hand, belts of bullets draped over his shoulders, he cut an impressive figure as only Afghans can. He was telling me in vivid detail his adventures inside Afghanistan. "I kill Russians," he said. "I go jihad."

The woman JB happened to be interviewing inside a tent asked her, "Is that your husband talking to my husband?"

"Yes," said JB.

"Well, my husband is telling your husband how he goes on jihad and kills Russians," she said. "He says that to all the foreigners. But I can tell you he never goes on jihad. He's never seen a Russian. And will he fetch water? No! Will he get firewood? No! Will he help with anything around camp? No he will not. He just tells people like your husband he's going on jihad."

It was a lesson that we reporters can skate only on the thin ice of reality, often falling through into the cold waters of lies and misrepresentations.

There were other reporters who made their reputations "going inside," taking long and dangerous journeys with the mujahideen deep within Soviet-occupied Afghanistan. I only visited one mujahideen camp in a kind of no-man's-land, just over the border, but so close to Pakistan that the Soviets never came. I felt silly dressing up in Afghan robes and hat. But the purpose was not to fool anybody. It was to allow the Pakistani border guards to simply look the other way when we crossed the frontier.

No one had to instruct Pathans on the use of terrain, an instructor, whom I took to be Pakistani, told me. On that they were masters. They throw their robes over themselves and simply melt into any fold in the earth so you could pass right by them and never see them. They knew not to expose their hands when Russian planes and helicopters were near. Their brown hands might blend in with the earth and rocks, but their fingernails might reflect the light. They were born guerrilla fighters who had never really succumbed to foreign rule when the British were here, and now they were slowly driving out the Russians. But they were not used to modern weapons.

"Any fool can fire a mortar," said the instructor. "But if you don't hit somebody with it on the third round he is going to be on top of you." There were targets painted on the hillsides for the Afghans to practice their skills with light machine guns, grenade launchers, and recoilless rifles. I was told it wasn't wise to give them heavier guns or tanks. The Russians would have liked nothing better than to have our muj come out and fight a conventional battle. "No, we will play to our strengths," the instructor told me. "Lightning-fast hit-and-run raids, ambushes, land mines, that sort of thing."

All their weapons were Soviet models or Chinese, to be used interchangeably with whatever the mujahideen managed to capture from the Russians. Between two peaks I saw a wire strung, with a model airplane for them to practice firing at. The model would slide down the wire, and the hardest thing for the muj was to learn to lead the plane like you would lead a bird with a shotgun. In another part of the base they were practicing sabotage. I was asked if I would like to try my hand. With a push on a plunger and a roar of explosives, a plume of dirt and rocks went skyward and a model of an electric pylon sank to the ground. A crowd of gleeful Afghans cheered and laughed.

In another part of the base pipe bombs were being made. Bits of ordinary-looking plumbing, stuffed with explosives, were being prepared to smuggle into Jalalabad and Kabul. The idea was that one innocent-looking pipe would be smuggled in by one man, another bit of pipe by another, and the explosives by yet another. Then the parts would be put together once inside the enemy-held city. That way if they were searched on the way in they were less likely to be discovered. It was much safer than trying to smuggle in hand grenades, the instructor said.

Bottles filled with gasoline, the famous Molotov cocktails, were being prepared. "When you mix some soap and egg white in with the petrol," said the instructor, "it sticks to the target exactly like napalm." The trick with a Molotov cocktail was to stuff a rag into the bottle filled with gasoline and light it just before you threw the bottle. Your timing had to be just right so that the bottle would burst into flames just when it hit and broke.

The instructor told me that one of the mujahideen's problems was that excited young men would want to take the gasoline-filled bottle by the neck and fling it end over end. Often the gasoline spilled down their wrists and arms and set them on fire before they could throw. It was better to throw a Molotov cocktail like a football, not tumbling end over end.

The CIA had helped them solve the problem, the instructor said. He had some white powder you could put in a bottle with the gasoline that would ignite when exposed to air. With this the muj could toss the bottle any way they wanted and it would burst into flame on impact.

I thought of all this many times when I visited Kabul more than twenty years later when we Americans, like the Russians before us, were the ones trying to suppress an Islamic insurgency in the countryside, and the insurgent training camps were just on the other side of the Pakistani border. Years later, when America had replaced the Russians as the dominant power in Kabul, I often looked at a passing Afghan in the streets wondering whether he might be concealing the smuggled pipe bomb that might blow me up.

In 1987, however, the new "Stingers," American handheld antiaircraft weapons, were coming into use, to deadly effect. The thing the mujahideen feared most was the Hind armored helicopter gunships that the Russians deployed against them. But with the Stingers everything changed. Estimates were that the guerrillas were shooting down at least one Soviet aircraft a day. But more important than shooting Soviet planes and helicopters down, the Stingers were keeping them up. The Soviet pilots no longer dared to come down low for fear of being hit, which gave the mujahideen a great advantage.

I reported that the Russians had been having trouble with their Muslim troops, many of whom were deserting, a foretaste of the breaking up of the Soviet Union that was only a few years away.

Mikhail Gorbachev knew that his country was becoming weary of the war, and, as President Obama would later do, he told his generals he could give them a couple of years to turn things around, and if that didn't work, the Russians would withdraw. And withdraw they did, in 1989, over the Oxus River back into Russian territory.

As President Nixon had wished for Vietnam, Gorbachev hoped he could build up an Afghan force that could survive a Russian troop withdrawal. And to everybody's surprise the Afghans under Najibullah did survive for almost three years, keeping the major cities and towns and his lines of communication open for as long as the Soviets kept pouring in money, weapons, and ammunition. In fact, Najibullah's regime fell to the mujahideen only when the Soviet Union itself fell apart, in 1991, and the ammunition stopped coming.

"And our man lasted twice as long as your man in Saigon after you left," said Russia's ambassador to Kabul, Andrey Avetisyan, who had done his time in Afghanistan as a young diplomat during the Russian occupation. He said the Soviet Union, like the Americans later, did not really think about the difficulties the British and other invaders had had in Afghanistan. After all, this was the Soviet Union, Soviet exceptionalism. He explained how the Russians really thought they were coming to help the Afghans, but he said they found out over the years that Afghans really didn't like foreigners coming into their country to help them and the Russians, as did the Americans later, thought Afghans should be more like them.

One wonders now, in hindsight, if Gorbachev's plea to the United States to help him get out of Afghanistan, keeping some sort of compromise government in power in Kabul, might have been a better solution than what ensued. But Washington was still too intent on punishing the Russians to really consider it.

And so Kabul fell. The mujahideen started fighting among themselves for Kabul as dogs fight over a discarded bone. The Tajiks, Uzbeks, and other minorities finally took charge of Kabul, much of which now lay in ruins, until the Taliban, who were almost all Pashtuns, took back Kabul with the help of Pakistan. The Tajiks and Uzbeks were pushed into small pockets of resistance near what had now become Uzbekistan and Tajikistan. They called themselves the Northern Alliance.

At first Afghans, and the United States, too, welcomed the Taliban. Anything to restore order out of the chaos that followed the infighting between mujahideen factions. Pakistan had helped the Taliban in their conquest, backing the Pashtuns, who straddled the border and were Afghanistan's largest ethnic group. The Pashtuns were Afghanistan's traditional rulers as well. The severity of the Taliban's primitive brand of Islam soon became evident. The Taliban represented the most backward of Pashtun rural society, blended with Wahhabi intolerance imported from Saudi Arabia. Afghans have always been strict in their religion, but Taliban rule went against the grain of Afghan tradition as much as Communism had done, only in the opposite direction.

The extreme version of Islam that the Taliban imposed reminded me somewhat of the Khmer Rouge. Both wanted a simple, agrarian society, uninfluenced and uncorrupted by the West, one under the heel of a radical form of Communism, and the other under a radical and uncompromising form of Islam. Both wanted to push their countries into a purer, simpler past. The Khmer Rouge forced people from the cities into the countryside. The Taliban didn't go that far, but Mullah Omar, the Taliban leader, refused to rule from Kabul as all previous leaders had done for centuries. He preferred to rule from Kandahar, his Pashtun base, and not from Kabul, which he considered akin to Sodom and Gomorrah.

Osama bin Laden's terrorist act against New York and Washington, and the subsequent American invasion, simply brought the Tajiks, and other minorities, back into power in Kabul, driving the Taliban Pashtuns into their redoubts along, and across, the border with Pakistan. We came to get Osama bin Laden but we let him get away into Pakistan, where he would find sanctuary until the Americans finally found him and killed him years later.

The Taliban had begun as a reaction to mujahideen corruption and high-handedness. A mujahideen commander had kidnapped a girl and taken her to his base. An outraged Mullah Omar got a band together, freed the girl, and hanged the mujahideen commander from the barrel of his own tank. The Taliban was born, and with Pakistan's help, they fanned out in pickup trucks across the country, capturing city after city and town after town, except for the Northern Alliance enclave in the far north.

I learned that Mullah Omar wanted to get rid of Osama bin Laden when it became clear that al-Qaeda was going to draw down the wrath of the West, but he dared not go against the iron rule of hospitality demanded by a Pashtun custom called Pashtunwali. Mullah Omar hoped that bin Laden might leave of his own accord and go to Chechnya where a Chechen leader had offered him sanctuary. Mullah Omar was not certain where Chechnya was, but in any event Osama bin Laden remained in Afghanistan until he made his escape to Pakistan after the American invasion.

When I visited Kabul in 2003, under the auspices of New York's Council on Foreign Relations, along with two former American ambassadors, Nicholas Platt and Frank Wisner, there were hopeful signs that something could be done. Afghanistan had been so devastated by so many years of invasion, occupation, civil war, and then the radical Islam of the Taliban that I thought the country might accept foreigners trying to help them recover, despite their traditional resistance to foreigners. Also, the Afghans did not consider themselves an occupied people. The Northern Alliance had liberated Kabul from the Taliban, not American forces, although we gave them plenty of help. Music was playing again. Girls were being educated. The horrors of Taliban rule were over.

So much of traditional society had been crushed by the Soviets and the Taliban that turning a new leaf seemed possible. But the Americans and their European allies imposed a highly centralized government, which went against the grain of Afghanistan's more decentralized political traditions. It was also clear that American assets and attention were shifting away toward Iraq. The moment when Afghanistan might have been molded into something different was quickly passing.

Perhaps the most haunting moment of that visit was a trip to the old Soviet officers' club on the outskirts of town. The club was in ruins, but one could see it had once had a lovely view. It was concrete, and not marble, but its ruin had the same finality as the relics of ancient Rome that dot the Mediterranean littoral. Or as Kipling would have put it, the Russian presence in Afghanistan, like the British before it, had become one with Nineveh and Tyre.

Another portent of things to come was a visit to Pakistan that our council group made on the way home. Platt had been ambassador to Pakistan, and Wisner to India, and the Pakistani foreign office had filled an auditorium with foreign-office personnel. In a free-ranging discussion, it quickly became apparent that suspicion and mistrust of the United States was at a fever pitch, and these foreign-office types belonged to Pakistan's educated classes, whom one might expect to be more understanding and pro-American. This was a forewarning of just how bad America's relations with Pakistan would later become.

When I returned to Peshawar in 2010 I found a city nervous and frightened. Islamic militants were bombing police stations and Sufi shrines almost weekly. The Sufi tradition, with its long history of mysticism and Muslim saints, was as much an anathema to the Pakistani Taliban as the softer Catholic traditions had been to Oliver Cromwell's seventeenth-century avenging Protestant zealots in England. Pakistanis may have helped put the Taliban in power in Kabul, but like the Americans, they were now experiencing the blowback as the Pakistani Taliban turned on them.

In 2010 Dean's was no more; the hotel—the cottages, lawns, gardens, and gray and black crows in the trees—had all been swallowed up by a giant shopping mall on the site.

The Pakistani military took me over the storied Malakand Pass into the tribal territories where Winston Churchill had been when he was a young officer just beginning his military and literary career. We were in three Japanese pickup trucks painted military green. The first and the last were filled with Pakistani soldiers and had a machine gun mounted to the truck bed. I was in the middle. My escort officer assured me that there was no danger from mines planted in the road. The road had been swept for mines, so the only danger was from "suicidals." There was always the possibility of a suicide bomber stepping forward to blow himself and us up as we passed through villages only recently captured back from Muslim extremists.

I was to spend the better part of two days and a night with the Bajour Scouts in the Bajour tribal agency, who were trying their best to keep the militants at bay in their sector of the North-West Frontier. In the officer's mess one might have thought the British Raj had never ended. The regimental silver gleamed, and silent servants served us tiffin. Many of the Pakistani officers at the table wore a red patch that signified having been wounded. I thought to myself that this was a higher proportion of wounded than I would have seen in an American officers' mess in Afghanistan. Across the frontier was Afghanistan, where the Americans were having their own troubles with the Taliban.

I had come with ears full of American complaints that the Taliban was enjoying safe sanctuary in Pakistan, which the Pakistanis wouldn't or couldn't do anything about. In Bajour I heard a different story. The Taliban, when pressed by the Pakistani military, could simply slip over the border into Afghanistan, where the Americans were thinly stretched, and find sanctuary there. The Americans were unable to stop them. The truth was that Pashtuns had always slipped back and forth across the Durand Line. It was supposed to mark the frontier between Pakistan and Afghanistan, but the locals never paid any attention to it, unless they knew that whoever was chasing them might stop at the border. The realities of nineteenth-century frontier warfare were still in force, to the frustration of both the Americans and the Pakistanis.

Not that the Pakistanis weren't purposely harboring some of the enemies of the United States. Pakistan was, and is, obsessed with India—something the Americans never seemed to appreciate. Pakistan knew that America would someday leave, and Pakistan would be stuck with whatever mess we left behind. So Pakistan wanted to hedge its bets with some of the militants who might one day rule in Kabul to prevent it from falling under Indian influence.

Just as America had made many mistakes in its Cold War zeal against the Soviets, so was Pakistan similarly obsessed with the perceived threat from India. Some of these fears might seem ridiculous to Americans, but our failure to recognize how deep Pakistan's Cold War feelings against India ran always meant that Pakistan and the US were talking at cross-purposes. The difference in agendas was similar to what Henry Kissinger had commented on years before.

Pakistan always hoped for a strategic relationship with the United States. But what America wanted was a transactional relationship. In effect we were saying to Pakistan: We give you a lot of money, so do what we say and do it right now.

I found on my return to Kabul that same year that whatever chance America might have had to transform Afghanistan was long gone. Security had deteriorated all over the country, and you dared not even drive out into the hills for a picnic, as had been possible before. Whole sections of Kabul that had been destroyed during the civil war were now being rebuilt with fancy mansions, many of them with drug money.

America's special representative to Afghanistan and Pakistan, Richard Holbrooke, told me just before he died that our ticket out was to train the Afghan army to take over its own security. It sounded just like the old Vietnamization program that both Holbrooke and I had known from that previous war. I asked General William Caldwell, the man in charge of training the Afghan army, what had happened in the seven years since I had been there. I had seen Afghan soldiers being trained then. Why were things in such bad shape now? The general said that real and proper training of the Afghan army had not really begun until 2009. Why? Because the US had underestimated how the Taliban would reorganize and come back to fight us. Caldwell was convinced that training was now on the right track, but Afghan soldiers stole from the locals and were almost as hated and feared as the Taliban. An Afghan officer explained to a photographer friend that he stole from the locals because he had paid a bribe for his commission, and that stealing from villagers was his only way to get back his investment.

I met another officer involved in training Afghans, a British officer named Dickey Winchester. He had on his office wall a famous painting of the last stand of the Forty-Fourth Regiment of Foot, standing back-to-back at a place called Gandamak as Afghan tribesmen closed in for the kill in that terrible retreat from Kabul in the winter of 1842. Britain lost an entire army in the passes between Kabul and Jalalabad. Only one man managed to stagger out alive and uncaptured.

"Do you know why that happened?" asked Winchester, looking at the print. "Because we didn't pay off the tribesmen," he said. And indeed I would agree that if there is to be any good coming out of America's longest war it would be better to keep money and ammunition coming even when our soldiers are gone. But he was aware that the NATO presence in the country had become a problem itself. He quoted Lord Roberts of Kandahar, a nineteenth-century British general, who said one hundred years ago that the less the Afghans see of us the more they will like us.

General David Petraeus, the hero of the Iraq War, was installed in Kabul, bringing new theories of counterinsurgency that would protect the population. It sounded to me like a reinvention of the wheel, for the same tactics had been tried in Vietnam with "strategic hamlets." I felt that the real lesson was that it is very hard, if not impossible, for foreigners to pull off counterinsurgency in a foreign land. It had not worked in Indochina, nor Algeria under the French, and was not working in Afghanistan.

I had previously met Petraeus during one of his trips back to America and had asked him what books he was reading. He said he was reading General Grant's memoirs of the Civil War. I said to myself, hmmm, the general to whom a president turns when all others have failed? Petraeus always said that Afghanistan was not like Iraq, but you wouldn't know that from the talk around his headquarters, where it was fully expected that success in Iraq could be replicated in Afghanistan.

When I reached Kabul, General Petraeus didn't have time to see me, but I e-mailed a request to know what the general was reading about Afghanistan. The reply was Thomas Barfield's excellent book *Afghanistan;* the now largely discredited *Three Cups of Tea;* a book by a mujahideen commander about tactics used against the Soviets; and Winston Churchill's *The Story of the Malakand Field Force,* about fighting Pashtuns on the frontier a century ago. Churchill wrote that Britain's "Forward" policy, roughly equivalent to America's invading Muslim countries a century later, was the correct policy but was doomed to failure. It would fail, Churchill wrote, because Britain had "neither the troops nor the money to carry it out." I always wondered if Petraeus had read Churchill's book all the way to the end.

Journalists in Kabul often chose to stay in nondescript guesthouses, with no sign on the street, in the hopes that they would be overlooked by Taliban looking for Westerners to kill. Mine was called the Gandamak, gallows humor in the extreme. You had to knock at an unmarked iron door on the street before armed guards would let you in. Then you had to pass through an iron room with the door closed behind you and the door in front locked, until you were eyeballed through a gun port. Only then were you buzzed in through the second door into the courtyard of the Gandamak. The arrangement was common in restaurants frequented by Westerners.

In the Street of the Chickens, where I went to buy JB a Christmas present, I was approached by an Afghan man with his face wrapped against the November cold. He came up to me and took my hand. I had a moment of apprehension because the year before a woman in a burka had come up to take the hand of a Western woman in this same street. The Afghan woman had then blown herself and the Western woman up, wounding several others in the street. My apprehension was not lifted when he asked me, in heavily accented English: "Are you Christian?" I replied that I was a "person of the book." But he didn't want to blow me up. He wanted to tell me that when the Russians were in Kabul they were not afraid to walk the streets, because many were Muslims. Americans, on the other hand, were rarely seen on the streets of Kabul. They rode around in big armored automobiles dressed in flak jackets, afraid to be with the people. The lesson was that Americans would do much better if they were Muslims, because Muslims were less fearful.

I left feeling that a deeply corrupt society was not going to be able to produce the necessary loyalty to the state that a good army needs. As in Saigon, so many years before, Afghan soldiers were deserting in high numbers. But even more sinister, Afghan soldiers were increasingly turning their guns on their American and European trainers, something that never to my knowledge happened in Vietnam.

The feline and soft-spoken president, Hamid Karzai, became more and more embittered and embattled, and by 2010 our man in Kabul had become a burr under America's saddle. Americans always put so much faith in elections. But Karzai knew that Afghan rulers ruled by giving favors here and suborning loyalties there. It is fatal to show weakness because, as Karzai well knew, for exactly one hundred years, from the peaceful death of the "Iron Emir," Abdur Rahman, in 1901, until Karzai himself was put in power in 2001, every single emir, king, or president of Afghanistan has been either murdered or driven from office, and often both. Karzai needed to distance himself from the Americans so as not to seem the puppet of the Americans that he, in fact, was.

Ambassadors Platt and Wisner and I had met Karzai in his palace in 2003. His bodyguards were American, rather than Afghan. Perhaps he did not trust his warlord allies, many of whom were in the palace room where we met. Karzai sat on a thronelike chair, and as he conversed with us I saw his attention wandering to something on the rug in front of him. It was a peanut. No, don't pick it up, please, I said silently to myself as Karzai leaned forward in his chair. Those tough guys with the hard faces around you in this room will not understand. Leaders of Afghanistan do not pick up peanuts off the floor. Leave that to someone else. To my relief he leaned back and resumed the conversation.

Seven years later, in 2010, corruption was mounting to the degree I had once seen in Saigon and Phnom Penh. Afghan big shots were taking suitcases of American taxpayers' money out to Dubai. Just as in Indochina our money had been taken out to Bangkok, or as Iraqis had invested the American taxpayers' money in Jordanian real estate. America had poured in more money than the Afghanistan economy could ever absorb, and had thereby unwittingly, and carelessly, contributed to its corruption.

I do not think the Taliban will be able to impose the same regime over the country as it did before, once the Americans leave. Afghanistan is not the prostrate country it was when the Taliban first came, and the other minorities, the Tajiks, Uzbeks, and the rest, are too well armed and organized. Also, the old balance between urban and rural has shifted radically to the urban. Afghan city dwellers had always been more open to education and women's rights than the more conservative countryside, and the wars have brought a great deal more people into the cities. The civil war into which we stepped in 2001 will continue and gain in ferocity when we leave. If there ever is to be a settlement, the more conservative rural Pashtuns are going to have to be accommodated politically, and this will mean some accommodations will have to be made to include their religious views. I don't think this means a return to Mullah Omar's rule, however.

Of course not all Pashtuns are Taliban, but enough of them are to make it seem that America's longest war had transmogrified into a war against the Pashtuns, absolutely the last people you would ever want to go to war against on their own turf. The writer John Masters, who served in the British Army on the frontier in the 1930s, recalled how when one of the many campaigns against the Pashtun tribesmen was over, and the British were giving out campaign medals, the Pashtuns asked for their medals. But you were the enemy, the British said. Yes, but you could not have had a Waziristan campaign without us, came the reply. Throughout the ages, Pashtuns have fought against foreigners, and when no foreigners are around they fight among themselves. The Taliban knew enough to brand themselves as anti-foreign holy warriors, hoping to wrap themselves in a nationalist cause just as they had done against the Russians.

The American game plan in 2010 was to keep killing Talibs, inflicting such pain that they would one day come to the negotiating table. It was the same philosophy Lyndon Johnson had espoused in his bombings of North Vietnam. But neither the North Vietnamese nor the Taliban were susceptible to American ways of thinking.

Afterword

I left Afghanistan on a cold November morning with a dusting of snow on the hills above Kabul. Winter was coming. The mountain passes would soon be snowed in and the so-called fighting season would be coming to a close, at least until the following spring. My last interviews at NATO headquarters and at the American embassy had all been full of optimism. Once again, as I had been in Vietnam and Iraq, I was invited to join the conspiracy of wishful thinking. General Petraeus's plans for counterinsurgency were going nowhere. Nation building was out of style, and everybody around Petraeus was talking about "Afghanistan good enough." What "good enough" actually meant was never defined, but it seemed to me to be akin to what was being said in Nixon's time: a "decent interval" for Vietnam—meaning that America would leave behind a government and an army that could hang on for a few years after we left. After that, well, it would no longer be our affair.

How could my country have once again gotten itself into a quicksand situation of long, protracted warfare in a foreign country in a culture about which we knew very little? As we had followed the French into Indochina, here we were following in the footsteps of the British and the Russians, attempting to impose our will on Afghanistan. This was a country that had defied foreigners trying to tell them how to run their lives for centuries. At first I thought it remarkable that the lessons of Vietnam could be so quickly forgotten. But then I happened to see a picture of Dick Cheney and Don-ald Rumsfeld sitting in President Ford's office as Saigon was falling, and it occurred to me that maybe they hadn't forgotten. Maybe they thought: This time we will get it right.

So it was that America invaded Afghanistan and Iraq, not just to remove al-Qaeda and Saddam Hussein, but to rebuild both countries in our image. No doubt the United States needed to confront al-Qaeda in Afghanistan after being so grievously struck in 2001. But to stay a decade in a war against the Pashtuns—none of whom were in the planes that struck the Twin Towers—represents the kind of mission creep that the first President Bush so feared. As for the Iraq War, the hope that an Americanized Iraq could somehow transform the region was an unrealistic fantasy on the part of those who mis-understood the nature of both American power and the Middle East.

————

Today Muslim extremism has replaced Communism as our primary secu-rity threat, but even at its most malign it cannot compare with the dangers implicit in the Cold War—two heavily armed nuclear powers threatening each other with mutually assured destruction. Schoolchildren are no longer routinely taught what to do in a nuclear attack, as we were in the late 1940s.

The twin passions of fascism and Communism that enthralled and threat-ened so many in the twentieth century have long since dissipated, and I am sure that, in time, the rage that now sweeps through the Muslim world will also lose its fire.

There are among my countrymen those who would still have us intervene in other people's civil wars and be more aggressive in international affairs. Every country wants to shape the world around it to its liking, and America replacing Britain in the role of world policeman was seamless in that Britain and America shared the same basic values of liberal democracy. The US Navy, in which I served, long ago took over from Britain the role of keeping the world's sea lanes and world commerce open and free.

I have always believed that, on balance, American leadership has been a force for good in the world. But the fifty-year process in which colonialized peoples sought to free themselves from foreign rule following World War II was less understood than the rise of Soviet hegemonic intentions. Too often we failed to realize when nationalism trumped other ideologies, and that Communism was never monolithic. Later, in our Muslim wars, we seldom could sort out tribal and ethnic differences in the countries we invaded.

There was always a strong missionary urge in colonialism that carried over into our efforts to install democracies in Indochina, Iraq, and Afghanistan. The Portuguese and the Spanish, who first went forth to conquer other lands, wrapped their greed for gold and spices in clothes of militant Christianity. They persuaded themselves they were going forth to save souls. The declared aim of many expeditions was to convert the heathen. "*Conquista espiritual*" was what the Spanish called it. The French had their "*civilisatrice*." The British, too, cloaked their commercial interests with a mission to bring civilization to benighted races. Rudyard Kipling, on America's acquisition of the Philippines in 1898, urged Americans to "take up the White Man's burden" and bring enlightenment to our "new caught sullen peoples, half devil and half child."

One of my favorite advertisements from that period shows Admiral Dewey, presumably after his victory over the Spanish fleet in Manila Bay, washing his hands in a shipboard sink with the caption "The first step towards lightening The White Man's Burden is through teaching the virtues of cleanliness. Pears' Soap is a potent factor in brightening the dark corners of the earth as civilization advances."

The Krag-Jorgensen repeating rifle was the standard battle weapon of the American forces during the Philippine Insurrection in the late nineteenth century, and the saying was: "Underneath the starry flag, civilize them with a Krag."

The Soviet Union, too, saw it as its mission to project and protect Communism in other countries. When General Boris Gromov led the last column of Russian armor across the Oxus following the failure of Russia's Afghan war in 1989, he said: "In spite of our sacrifices, we have totally fulfilled our internationalist duty."

In this century promoting democracy by force became our version of internationalist duty and *conquista espiritual*. Never were both more in evidence than when Americans flocked to Baghdad full of zeal to impose an American-style constitution upon that prostrate country, maybe even a flat tax, and turn Iraq into a beacon unto the entire Arab world. We learned to our sorrow that democracy is best exported by example, not military force. In Afghanistan, Americans began to think that purple ink on an Afghan finger, showing that the individual had voted, was the end-all and the be-all of tribal rivalries and ethnic tensions in that tragic land.

The first step towards lightening

The White Man's Burden

is through teaching the virtues of cleanliness.

Pears' Soap

is a potent factor in brightening the dark corners of the earth as civilization advances, while amongst the cultured of all nations it holds the highest place—it is the ideal toilet soap.

A Pears' Soap advertisement from the 1890s invoking "The White Man's Burden."

Even when military intervention has been necessary, and in my view this would include Korea and Afghanistan, mission creep took over. General MacArthur's drive across the Thirty-Eighth Parallel, attempting to unite Korea, instead simply beating back Communist aggression, brought China into the war and got a lot of people unnecessarily killed, achieving nothing other than the status quo ante.

I spent too many years covering the tragic, and in the end inarticulate, struggles in Indochina, with the United States trying to prop up an ancient regime bequeathed to us by the French in order to "keep the past upon the throne."

America needs to keep engaged in the world, and isolationism is not the answer. But I am ever haunted by Graham Greene's lines rebutting the "quiet American" who thought bombs could further democracy in Indochina. What people want is "enough rice. They don't want to be shot at. They want one day to be much the same as another. They don't want our white skins around telling them what they want."

It seems that throughout my entire life in the news trade, America has been intervening and fighting against people whose fathers, grandfathers, and great-grandfathers fought against Europeans telling them what to do or what they want. Few Americans want to think of themselves as colonialists or fighting for empire, but time after time we have sent our soldiers to die in foreign lands so that we might impose our will where others have gone before and failed. It would be one thing if we had been successful, but so many armed interventions in the last half century have ended in disappointment or outright failure in other people's empires.

———

What of that couple that sailed on the *Queen Mary* for a life of adventure more than a half century ago? For my part I loved the news trade, and I always thought my old boss, Henry Luce, got it right when he capsulized what it was like to be a foreign correspondent in his prospectus of *Life* magazine, a new publication he was starting the year after I was born:

Afterword

"To see life; to see the world, to eyewitness great events: to watch the faces of the poor and the gestures of the proud: to see strange things—machines, armies, multitudes, shadows in the jungle and on the moon . . . to see things thousands of miles away, and things hidden behind walls and within rooms; things dangerous to come to . . . to see and be amazed; to see and be instructed."

I was always amazed that people would be willing to pay me to travel in strange places and write about what I saw.

I wouldn't diminish the excitement of covering Washington or city hall, or the tumultuous world of sport. But seeing the world, and witnessing great events thousands of miles away as well as things dangerous to come to is the provenance of the foreign correspondent.

And what a tradition it is: William Russell reporting from the Crimea and the battlegrounds of our Civil War. G. W. Steevens, whose book *With Kitchener to Khartoum* is here in my library. David Halberstam in Vietnam, Dexter Filkins in Falluja, Sebastian Junger in Afghanistan, and on and on. None can say the news trade isn't important.

Here stands America, still the greatest power on earth. How can a democracy make intelligent decisions if it is not informed about what's going on beyond its borders? Without reporters in the field the giant is blind, barging into rooms and breaking the furniture.

We journalists sometimes get it wrong, of course, and there are stories and columns that I wish I could take back. But Philip Graham of the *Washington Post* got it right when he called journalism "the first rough draft of history."

But what of JB? What was it like for her to live in unsettled places with a husband so often away, to receive phone calls telling her that I had been shot, to be taken to hotels where there were bombs in the bathroom? How did it all look from her perspective?

"Well, I guess I was young and very much in love," she says, "and thrilled with having a family and young children, and thrilled with Asia. I was a real Sinophile. I had studied Chinese, and China was going through the Cultural Revolution at the time. I had worked at Johns Hopkins School of Advanced International Studies, and was fascinated by everything that was going on. Southeast Asia was an extension of this, adventurous, fun, wildly romantic.

Our children got to see Tin Hao festivals in Hong Kong, water festivals in Bangkok, and elaborate Hindu cremations in Bali.

"As for you being away so much, Sadie said it all at a young age when your stepmother called and asked to speak to us. 'Pops is in Cairo and Mums is in the bath,' came her reply."

Would it have been better, JB, if you had had your own career instead of having to move every few years?

"You will remember that before we were married," she said, "I had a job interview with Richard Bissell, head of the CIA's clandestine operations. Who knows, maybe I would have ended up trying to recruit you, and run you, as an agent in the field?"

But all that moving. Did you feel you were being dragged around the world?

"If I was going to live with you I was going to have to move, and who else but me could put up with someone like you?" she said. "How many times have I told you when reading your columns that you didn't need that last sentence, that it was time to wrap it up? You need to end this now."

And that was that.

Acknowledgments

I would like to thank my agent, John "Ike" Williams, of the Kneerim, Williams & Bloom Agency, who first encouraged me to write this book nearly fourteen years ago, and his two assistants, Kate Flynn and Hope Denekamp, who were ever helpful. Thanks go to my friends Ward Just who made many helpful suggestions along the way, to Jonathan Randal whose knowledge of Lebanon was so useful, to Jim Sterba for helping me with today's Ho Chi Minh City, to Vinton Lawrence for advice on Laos, to J. Christopher Porterfield who helped me with matters concerning *Time* magazine, and to Tim Page who supplied me with invaluable photographs.

To the staff of Federal Express/Kinko's in Needham, Massachusetts, who helped numerous times, goes my appreciation.

Special thanks go to Assistant Editor Jonathan Cox, for whom no request for help was too difficult, and to my team at Simon & Schuster, Julia Prosser, Elizabeth Gay, Gypsy da Silva, Marilyn Doof, Robert Ettlin, Jackie Seow, Elisa Rivlin, Stephen Bedford, and to my publisher Jonathan Karp. My copy editor, Aja Pollock, saved me from countless errors, and if there are mistakes or errors remaining they are not hers. And lastly, my thanks and gratitude go to Alice Mayhew, my revered editor who took a chance on me and brought this book into existence.

H. D. S. Greenway
Needham, Massachusetts
January 1st, 2014

Photo Credits

Index

Index

Index

Index

Index

Index

Index

Index

Index

Schanberg, Sidney, 143–44, 146, 149
Scheherazade, 81, 248
Schuster, Al, 55
Scoop (Waugh), 28
Scott, Thomas, 5
Scowcroft, Brent, 250
Scroll and Key, 9
Scully, Vincent, 9
Sea Dragon, 48–49
SEATO (Southeast Asia Treaty
    Organization), 109
Sein Win, 117–18
self, sense of, and group identity, 237
self-determination, unequal application of, 3
Sephardic Jews, 185
Sepik River, 165
September 11, 2001, terrorist attacks, 202,
    253, 257–58, 270, 280
Serbia, Serbs, 231, 232, 233, 234, 235, 239
Serbo-Croatian language, 232
Shadow over Angkor (film), 136
Shamir, Yitzhak, 186, 249, 250
Shanghai, China, 49, 50
Shan State Army, 118–19
Shan States, Burma, 110, 118–19
Sharon, Ariel, 193–94, 203, 212
Shatt al-Arab waterway, 244
Shaver, Mike, 129
Shawn, William, 84
Shepheard's Hotel, 197
Shia Muslims, 196, 210, 211, 236, 239–40,
    243, 250, 256, 258
Shovell, Cloudesley, 54
Sider, Don, 62
Siem Reap, Cambodia, 151, 152
Sihanouk, king of Cambodia:
    abdication of, 136
    accession of, 135
    Khmer Rouge backed by, 135
    Lon Nol's deposition of, 138, 142, 265
    restoration of, 150, 152*n*
    Vietnam War and, 137–38
Sihanoukville, Cambodia, 138
Silberstein, Reuben, 189–90
Simms, Peter, 110–11, 131
Simms, Sanda, 110, 118
Simons, Howard, 161
Simpson, Wallis, 21
Sinai, 181, 195–96
Singapore, British colonial legacy in, 112
Six-Day War (1967), 181, 182, 198
Skull and Bones, 5, 9

Slovenia, 231–33
Smith, Red, 167
Smith, Terry, 167, 180, 183, 188
Somoza, Anastasio, 200–201
SOSUS (Sound Surveillance System), 13
Souphanouvong, prince, 124–25
South Africa, 239, 240
South China Morning Post, 51
Southeast Asia:
    colonial legacy in, 112–16
    ethnic conflict in, 112, 127, 142
    fall of Saigon as end of colonialism in, 97
South Vietnam, 33
    Catholics in, 57, 122
    departure of US troops from, 77–78
    see also Saigon
South Vietnamese Army (ARVN), 41, 106
    collapse of, 87–88
    Easter Offensive and, 71–72
    morale of, 44, 53
    secondary role given to, 53
South Yemen, 206
Souvanna Phouma, prince, 124–25
Soviet Congress of People's Deputies, 224
Soviet Union, xii, 2
    Afghanistan invaded by, xiii, 200, 202,
        223, 261, 262–63, 264, 265–69, 279,
        281
    Egypt and, 191
    fall of, 223–29
    India's relations with, 170
    see also Cold War
Spaho, Pemba, 236, 238
Spanish Civil War, 41, 61, 213
Spanish empire, 281
Sports Illustrated, 17
Sri Savang Vatthana, king of Laos, 125, 133
Steevens, G. W., 284
Sterba, Jim, 114
Stern Gang, 186
Stevenson, Charles, 121
St. Georges Hotel, 215
Stinger antiaircraft weapons, 268
Stone, Dana, 70, 140
Story of the Malakand Field Force, The
    (Churchill), 275–76
"straggler bag" missions, 113–14
Straker, J. T., 14–15
stress, and ethnic and religious conflict,
    237–39
Stroheim, Erich von, 197
submarine warfare, 12–13

Index

About the Author

H. D. S. (David) Greenway has been in the news trade as a reporter and editor for more than half a century, reporting from more than eighty countries and colonies on six continents. He has covered conflicts around the globe for *Time* and *Life* magazines, *The Washington Post*, *The Boston Globe*, and *Global Post*. His work has appeared in *The New York Times Magazine*, *The New York Review of Books*, *The New Yorker*, *The Atlantic*, *World Policy Journal*, and the *International Herald Tribune*. He lives in Needham, Massachusetts, with his wife of fifty-four years, JB.